Warwick University Cari

Explanation in Caribbean Migration

Perception and the Image:
Jamaica, Barbados, St Vincent

Elizabeth M. Thomas-Hope

MACMILLAN
CARIBBEAN

© Copyright text E.M. Thomas-Hope 1992
© Copyright illustrations E.M. Thomas-Hope 1992

All rights reserved. No reproduction, copy or transmission of
this publication may be made without written permission.

No paragraph of this publication may be reproduced, copied or
transmitted save with written permission or in accordance with
the provisions of the Copyright, Designs and Patents Act 1988,
or under the terms of any licence permitting limited copying
issued by the Copyright Licensing Agency, 90 Tottenham Court Road,
London W1P 9HE.

Any person who does any unauthorised act in relation to this
publication may be liable to criminal prosecution and civil
claims for damages.

First published 1992

Published by THE MACMILLAN PRESS LTD
London and Basingstoke
*Associated companies and representatives in Accra,
Auckland, Delhi, Dublin, Gaborone, Hamburg, Harare,
Hong Kong, Kuala Lumpur, Lagos, Manzini, Melbourne,
Mexico City, Nairobi, New York, Singapore, Tokyo.*

ISBN 0–333–53503–0

Printed in Hong Kong

A catalogue record for this book is available from
the British Library.

Series Preface

The Centre for Caribbean Studies at the University of Warwick was founded in 1984 in order to stimulate interest and research in a region which is now receiving academic recognition in its own right. In addition to the publication of the papers from annual symposia which reflect the Centre's comparative and inter-disciplinary approach, other volumes in the series will be published in disciplines within the arts and social sciences.

Of all the world's societies, those of the Caribbean have been among the most mobile. Migration has been a leitmotif of the region throughout history, whether forced migration of African slaves, semi-forced migration of indentured servants, free migration of Europeans or the migrations, largely for economic reasons, of the post-colonial period. Migration whether within the Caribbean itself, or to Central and North America, or to Europe, has become a *rite de passage* for Caribbean peoples. Many studies have been made of this phenomenon using push-pull approaches or more recent sophisticated labour-supply analysis. Globalist studies in the context of the international division of labour have analyzed the economic and social structure of the migrants' own country; the labour demands of the host society, as well as the political beliefs and socio-economic circumstances of the migrants themselves.

Migration affects not only the individuals involved but the society they leave and those to which they migrate. Our understanding of this complex phenomenon, therefore, requires analysis at a variety of levels. It has been a common assumption that migration is a consequence of rational decision. This study attempts to shift the emphasis by examining the role of individual perception and image, and to further existing interpretations by examining migration behaviour from the perspective of Caribbean people themselves. This is a novel and provocative approach, bringing a new dimension to the study of Caribbean migration. It should serve to stimulate discussion at a time when the processes and function of migration are being challenged and re-evaluated under the impact of a rapidly changing international environment.

Alistair Hennessy

For Trevor

Contents

	Series Preface	iii
	Acknowledgements	vi
	Introduction	1
CHAPTER 1	Theoretical perspectives on Caribbean migration: Perception and the image.	15
CHAPTER 2	Three islands: Jamaica, Barbados and St Vincent	37
CHAPTER 3	The micro-environments of migration	63
CHAPTER 4	Migration and the propensity for migration	84
CHAPTER 5	Evaluations of work, education and modernization in migration behaviour	108
CHAPTER 6	Accessibility and information in migration behaviour	126
CHAPTER 7	Integration and mental images	144
	Conclusion	159
	Appendix	168
	References	169
	Index	181

Acknowledgements

A study which incorporates so many aspects of Caribbean national and international experiences could not have been accomplished without the assistance of a wide range of people and institutions. My debt of gratitude, therefore, is a large one.

Without financial support this study would never have been possible either in the major periods of data collection or, later, as follow-up work was carried out. In this regard, I would especially wish to acknowledge the Ford Foundation (USA) for two awards on which the early field work and part of the later work was conducted. The Overseas Development Institute (United Kingdom) and the International Development Research Centre (Canada) funded other aspects of my research which enabled me to spend extended periods in the region. This gave me the opportunity to build upon my earlier interests and bring a greater longitudinal perspective to the work than otherwise would have been possible.

In the periods of data collection the staff of the following institutions were particularly helpful: the libraries of the University of the West Indies at Mona, Cave Hill and St Augustine; the Institute of Jamaica; the Rhodes House collections of the Bodleian Library, University of Oxford; the British Library, London; the libraries of the American Geographical Society and the Research Institute for the Study of Man, New York; the libraries of the Institute of Commonwealth Studies and the Institute of Latin American Studies, University of London; and the Sidney Jones Library of the University of Liverpool.

Similarly, I am deeply indebted to the representatives of the Census Division of the Statistical Institute, the former National Planning Agency (now the Institute of Planning) and the Town Planning Department (Physical Planning Unit) in Jamaica; the Census Division and the Department of Health in Barbados; the Census Office and Extra-Mural Department of the University of the West Indies in St Vincent; and the United Nations Planning Project teams which at the time were located in Jamaica, Barbados and Antigua.

During my periods of work in the field, I was affiliated in the first instance to the Department of Geography at the University of the West Indies, Mona, and later to the Institute of Social and Economic

Research. On each occasion, the attachments provided me with an academic base which proved invaluable. For that and all the help given I thank the staffs concerned.

I have a particular obligation to three individuals who, at different stages and in different ways, have been especially supportive and helpful in the formulation of my ideas. The teaching and works of Professor David Lowenthal (University College, London) and Professor Peter Gould (Pennsylvania State University) – from very different perspectives – inspired the development of my own views on the importance of perception in the analysis of society. Dr Colin Clarke (Jesus College, Oxford) and David Lowenthal together have given consistent encouragement to my work in Caribbean migration, which sustained the effort over many years. To all three I express my warmest thanks.

I am also most grateful to Professor Alistair Hennessy (University of Warwick) for his encouragement as editor of the Warwick series; Professor Robin Cohen (University of Warwick) for his constructive criticisms of an earlier draft of this work; and Professor J. Edward Greene (University of the West Indies) for his support of my research as Director of the Institute for Social and Economic Studies at Mona. I am likewise grateful to Professor R. Mansell Prothero and the staff at the Department of Geography, University of Liverpool, for facilitating my periods of research leave which enabled me to complete the work on which this study is based.

My final debt of gratitude is to those Jamaicans, Barbadians and Vincentians from all walks of life, who alone were able to provide me with the information which could make an empirical study of this type possible. Despite their occasional perplexity at my questions about the migration which had occurred from their households, they nevertheless discussed candidly all the points put to them. For their openness and generosity I am extremely grateful. I can only hope that my analysis and interpretation of the information with which I was entrusted will contribute to a greater understanding of this important component of the Caribbean experience. Yet for all the things omitted and any errors unwittingly committed, I alone am responsible.

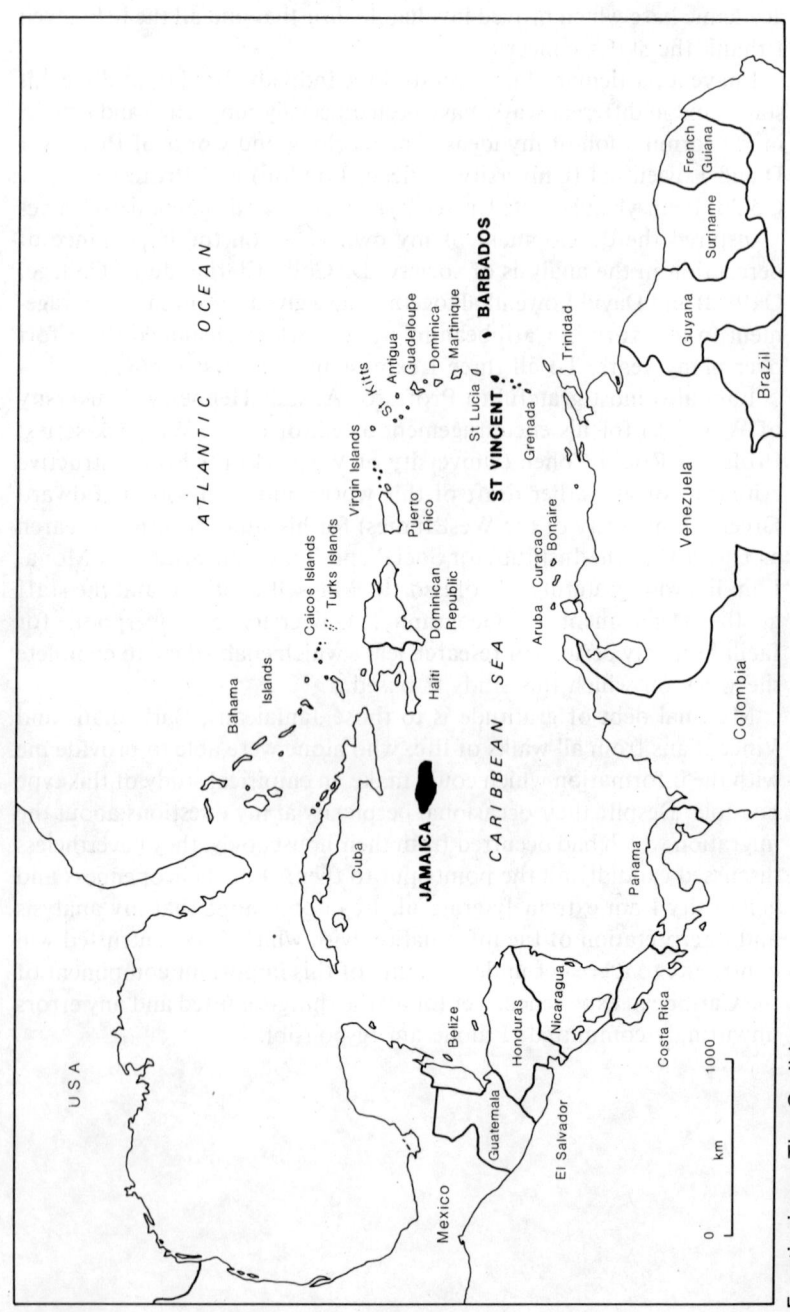

Frontispiece: The Caribbean

Introduction

The latent consciousness which embraces migration has not been adequately taken into consideration in explanations of Caribbean migration nor the dialectic between migrant and non-migrant fully appreciated. 'The emigrants and islanders', Brathwaite (1986: 7) observed, 'are the two main types that make up the present West Indian sensibility'. At the heart of this sensibility lies 'the desire (even the need) to migrate'. In this light, the migrant cannot be portrayed as a mere product of materialism derived from the location in the global political-economic periphery. The migrant reflects as much, if not in many cases more, the social and cultural implications of that specific location occupied in the periphery. It is from the particular temporal, spatial and social position in which people are located that mental images are formed and migration has meaning.[1]

Migration 'opportunities' to Caribbean people are themselves a mirror reflection of the migration 'requirements' of countries outside the region seeking to augment their labour force. The extent to which the Caribbean is perceived to be a potential source of labour for metropolitan capital development determines the evaluation of the Caribbean, or specific parts of the region from the outside. On this is based the nature of legislation controlling the volume and characteristics of immigration at any particular time. This has produced a self-perpetuating process whereby the reputation of Caribbean migration propensity has kept alive the very opportunities for migration on which each Caribbean society's main image of the world is based. The view of Caribbean migration as the movement of labour has dominated perceptions:

> So you have seen them
> with their cardboard grips,
> felt hats, rain-
> cloaks, the women
> with their plain
> or purple-tinted
> coats hiding their fatten-
> ed hips.

> These are the Emigrants.
> On sea-port quays
> at air-ports
> anywhere where there is ship
> or train, swift
> motor car, or jet
> to travel faster than the breeze
> you see them gathered:
> passports stamped
> their travel papers wrapped
> in old disused news-
> papers: lining their patient queues.
>
> (Brathwaite, 1967: 50).

At times working class, skilled or unskilled labour movements have predominated, at other times middle class and high level occupational groups have been in the majority. For each social class the movement has been characterized by different patterns, different purposes and different meaning.

The intention in this study is to further advance existing interpretations of migration behaviour from the perspective of Caribbean people themselves. This does not make assumptions of rational decision-making based on knowledge of alternatives but, on the contrary, is based on the role of perception and the image in migration behaviour, with all its inaccuracies and inconsistencies in relation to the so-called objective world. The image is influenced by factors not readily understood, for not all behaviour is the result of rational decisions or even conscious thought. The point is that the dimensions of the environment which directly or indirectly affect the individual is the environment of reality, whether or not it is fully understood. Detailed or correct information about the migration destination and the precise purpose for going was frequently not known and certainly of little or no consequence in the behavioural process which led to and ended in migration taking place. Referring to the Caribbean labour migrations through the twentieth century up to the peak of the movement to Britain in the early 1960s, Brathwaite cogently expressed this situation:

> Where to?
> They do not know.
> Canada, the Panama
> Canal, the Miss-
> issippi painfields, Florida?

Or on to dock
at hissing smoke-locked
Glasgow?

Why do they go?
They do not know.
Seeking a job
they settle for the very best
the agent has to offer:
jabbing a neighbour
out of work for four bob
less a week.

What do they hope for
what find there
these New World mariners
Columbus coursing kaffirs?

What Cathay shores
for them are gleaming golden
what magic keys they carry to unlock
what gold endragoned doors?

(Brathwaite, 1967: 51).

Migration in Caribbean social institutions

The institutions of Caribbean society have evolved to accommodate and perpetuate migration. At the same time, migration and the behaviour associated with the process have helped shape and continued to reinforce the structures and practices of the society itself.

Class is no less significant in migration behaviour than in any other form of institutionalized behaviour. Yet analysis, or even recognition of this, has been noticeably absent from the literature. Migrants have been regarded as a socially homogeneous group, or else it has been assumed that only one social class migrates. In either case, the differences in the migration pattern and behaviour have been subsumed or not recognized at all.

The upper classes moved to metropolitan centres, with which they had close cultural affinity, when their social or professional interests seemed better served there than in the Caribbean. Thus the migration among the upper class groups has been characterized by the permanent departure of the family unit (with the exception of students), and the return of few, if any, remittances; that of the lower classes by the movement of individuals leaving with the intention of returning. These patterns differentiated by class are reflected in other institutional aspects of the migration process.

The relative proportion of men and women in any particular migration phase can be explained partly by the selectivity of the available work at the destination. At times a male labour force has been required for construction, heavy industry, transport or agriculture; at other times, nurses or household domestic workers have been in demand and the migration of females sponsored.

In addition to the deliberate selection of migrants by sex, also important are gender roles within the wider institutional structure which facilitate, even encourage, the high potential for the migration of both sexes. The pattern of male and female migration reflects the wider institutional structures of each class.

There has evolved a much greater mutual sense of social and economic independence of men and women in the lower classes as compared to the upper classes. This has allowed increased opportunities for individual migration as opposed to migration of the family unit. The lower-class family and household accommodates the periodic absence of either male or female household head as an acceptable practice.

Female-headed households account for between 25 and 46 per cent of the total households in any Caribbean country according to the population censuses for the Caribbean. Whether recognized as head of household or not, the lower-class woman frequently assumes a large share, if not the sole responsibility for the welfare and economic support of the household. From the point of view of reliance on wage labour, the lower-class woman, just as much as males of the same social status, has a high migration potential because of her equally high level of motivation for securing employment and ultimately some measure of upward mobility. Thus the Caribbean lower-class woman seeks migration opportunities and migrates in her own right and not simply as a dependant of the male migrant. Indeed, it is invariably the woman who spearheads the subsequent migration of other family members.

Kinship networks of the lower-class family are well adapted to migration by means of a reciprocal system of obligations (Olwig, 1977, 1987; Midgett, 1975; Pessar, 1982b). Members both of the household and wider family traditionally help facilitate the migration of a member through financial assistance or undertaking the responsibilities of the migrant. Economic support or gifts, depending on the level of obligation deemed appropriate, are expected of the migrant in return. Children are absorbed into other households on an unofficial, but effective, arrangement of reciprocal support from the migrant (Davison, 1962).

Lower-class strategies for making a living depend on flexibility in the type of work the individual is willing and able to undertake. This system of multiple occupation, common among men and women, not only enables people to engage in whatever work opportunities exist in their home locality at any particular time, but it also permits the combination of work of various kinds abroad while still maintaining a basic livelihood at home (Dirks, 1972: Philpott, 1973; Midgett, 1975).

Land tenure practices among the rural populations of most Caribbean countries further accommodate the sequential or long-term absence of household and family members, giving a sense of security of tenure to those who stay, as well as to those who migrate. This system of inheritance is based on an ideology of cognatic descent whereby children of either sex inherit rights to land from both parents. (Besson, 1984; 1987). Closely interconnected with the entire institutional structure which evolved, land tenure practices of this type provided the newly formed peasantries – the future small-farming populations of the Caribbean – with a measure of security in the event of migration. This is a security hardly measurable in economic terms, but highly significant in symbolic and psychological terms.

The continuities in the pattern and process of Caribbean migration, despite dramatic changes in both international and national contexts, reflect the deeply-rooted significance of migration to the society. The value of migration to the expansion of capital is in the labour it provides as an economic commodity; the value of migration to Caribbean peoples themselves is in the adjustments which it has facilitated in the face of constitutional, economic and social change. So successful were these strategies of adjustment that they became institutionalized to form an integral part of Caribbean culture.

Migration in Caribbean consciousness

To Caribbean people, as to most others, places abroad are significant in a number of contexts. Mental images are nurtured to some extent by national influences based on economic and political linkages, but also by the sense of cultural exile and the search for a meaningful past. The image of the ancestral homeland of different racial sectors of the population, reinforces antecedent traditions and helps create and legitimize an acceptable cultural identity. Africa and India most recently assumed significance in Caribbean views of the outside world. These places compete with, and among some other groups even replace, the importance of the European country of former colonization. But neither Africa, India nor any other ancestral homeland of Caribbean people actually dominates the commonly held image of the outside world. Overall, the countries to which Caribbean people have migrated and the metropolises of Europe and North America with which ties have been strongest and upon which dependency has been greatest, are those countries to which people look in the pursuit of realizing personal objectives and goals. Thus they form the clearest components of the image of the world external to their own particular island or country.

Caribbean people order their external universe in direct relation to these opportunities for migration. At the simplest level of interpretation, 'foreign' or simply 'out' denotes all overseas countries known to be past or present migration destinations. Some people speak of their own island versus 'foreign' reflecting how, to them, their world is comprised of only these two entities. For a large number of people, such places are differentiated only by name; to the better informed, they are distinguished by known or imagined characteristics.

Stereotypes have developed and strengthened about countries abroad as Caribbean populations have been incorporated into their labour markets. Once created, each stereotype becomes fixed and finally altered only when a forceful new set of information contradicts the earlier view. Chapter 1 highlights the fact that new information neither obscures former impressions immediately nor totally changes the old image.

Mental images of places outside the home island incorporate as 'true' or 'real' not only what people have known, or thought they knew, about the external world, but also what they believe. Belief is an important foundation upon which perceptions are based; for it is not simply that people believe what they see, but they see what they believe. Furthermore, memory of the past is as important as contemporary fact in determining mental images.

It is common knowledge in the former British colonies of the Caribbean that the United Kingdom no longer offers the opportunities for migration that it did in the 1950s and 1960s, nor does it any longer play the once vaunted role of 'mother country'. This myth, assiduously fostered by colonial administrators, had gone a long way to determine the relationship of British West Indians to Britain and thus the position of Britain in the images held by those people. Despite the unfavourable information received, views are still tempered by impressions of the past and there is a lingering sense that conditions could not be as bad as they are reported to be. The former positive image of Britain is neither easily nor totally changed by new information.

The reverse situation also holds true, whereby negative stereotypes from the past persist even when new positive information is received. Earlier perceptions of Africa are not readily erased from the images currently held. Even the greater prominence given to Africa through education, the news media and new cultural trends in the Caribbean, has not altered completely the prejudices of the past. Nor have modern day changes in Africa blotted out Caribbean images of an Africa which existed in colonial times.

An invisible topological surface may be imagined of places varying in the extent to which they are most prominent, closest and clearest to the islands' inhabitants at any one time. The perceptual fields or points of reference to which Buttimer (1972: 286) refers as, 'Geodesic space', is 'expanded and contracted by the ties of kinship, language, and special interests'. In the Caribbean those special interests invariably include or are dominated by migration. In any particular context, specific countries and cities stand out as foci in the mental images of the people involved. These surfaces change with time. Different countries come into focus from the overall blur of the perceived outside world according to the intensity and type of information which is transmitted from them.

The spheres of contact established historically and maintained by Caribbean countries through political and economic linkages determine the overall framework of the national information field. Colonial and former colonial territories in the Caribbean have usually been in closer contact with their metropolises than with any other parts of the world or even with other Caribbean territories. Elite groups in the Caribbean have moved with ease between their Caribbean homeland and their metropolitan centre for education, work and pleasure.

Formal metropolitan linkages alone have not dominated information flows. The migrants themselves and the interest they generated as minority groups were the initial factors in determining the sources and diffusion patterns of information to most of the populations of Jamaica, Barbados and St Vincent. As a result, the information field of each Caribbean territory depends, in large measure, upon the location, size and age of its migrant communities.

The more recent the emigration, the greater and more frequent the information flows. As Caribbean communities overseas have become increasingly dominated in number by second and third generations born in the host country, so interest concerning them back home has diminished proportionately. Unless migrant communities are replenished continually with new arrivals, as for instance in the case of the USA, there is a gradual decline in coverage by Caribbean press agents, which eventually ceases altogether and, simultaneously, personal networks are reduced.

In the last stages of this process, reports are dominated by obituaries of deceased immigrant settlers. This has been true of items in the Jamaican press about Costa Rica and Panama – migration destinations of the early decades of this century, in Barbados about Cuba and Panama, and in St Vincent with regard to migrants to Aruba. Earlier destinations and those where the migrants formed only small groups were largely ignored by the media, and among the current generation of islanders such places were virtually unknown. Nicaragua, Guatemala and Honduras fell into this category of forgotten former Caribbean migration destinations. Information transmitted from abroad feeds the collective impression of foreign places, forming a heterogeneous landscape – the information surfaces.

The information from migrant communities and potential opportunities both through the media and through personal networks of communication conditions the views and expectations generated of migration itself. Each generation of Caribbean people since the emancipation of slaves has witnessed a 'demonstration effect' based on the migration of the preceding generation (Thomas-Hope, 1978).

The strong disposition towards migration has led to, or has been associated with, an optimism that has brought about the favourable translation of information almost irrespective of the nature of that information. Those who themselves are not keen on migrating or have a low propensity for, or poor image of migration are also those who see the risk and other negative aspects of the process. This is reflective of the perceptions held, not of objective circumstances. The questions which this raises relate to the need for explanation of the factors which condition the image. Secondly, it raises the question pursued in Chapter 4, of the implications of the image of migration for migration decisions and behaviour and thus the configuration of the migration landscape.

Migration behaviour

Some explanations of Caribbean migration have gone as far as evaluations of the characteristics and inequalities of the global system, and the position of Caribbean people in the context of the international division of labour. Other studies have probed the economic and social structure of the countries from which migrants have left; some have included political issues. The more functional approach has focused upon the socio-economic circumstances of the migrants themselves. However, interpretation at the level of societal meaning and personal consciousness has scarcely been touched upon.

Between the dynamics of global market forces and the specifics of the event of individual spatial displacement, are the class relations and internal dynamics of societies, as well as the experiences, evaluations and behaviour of people themselves. Whether ultimately migrants or forever non-migrants, they are all active agents in the process.

The implications of migration, its meaning and the beliefs which surround it, relate to all Caribbean peoples, movers and stayers. It affects them not just as individuals, but as a society. Making the decision to move, therefore, is neither unique nor isolated. But neither is the pattern of movement random, though elements of chance are always involved in the process. At the macro-level of explanation, migration is a reflection of specific historical circumstances and the directions of movement biased towards the places of colonial linkages together with new destinations where labour is required. At the micro-level, migration is highly selective of people according to their position in the total national system or national space. Furthermore, the process of selectivity of migrants does not have a mechanical effect as in the movement of objects under the force of centrifugal 'pushes' and gravitational 'pulls'. Nor are they instinctive, to be explained by models or environmental gradients.

There is a complexity in migration on account of the complexity of human behaviour where the particular disposition, attitude or mental conditioning promotes a positive orientation towards particular action. The circumstances responsible for such conditioning are themselves brought about by the structural factors inherent in international political economies, the needs of capital formation and other means of production and, in the last analysis, the nature of migration legislation or incentives. Where the individual potential for migration coincides with the appropriate domestic and material circumstances, access to information about the opportunities and regulations of moving, then active migration takes place. Thus, migration behaviour is the product not only of international and national political economies, but of the particular location of the individual within that historical-structural framework. Explanation of migration behaviour must not refer solely to the characteristics of the structural framework but to the dynamics of the connections between these factors and the behaviour of the social group and individual.

Empirical and theoretical approaches have sought explanation of migration from different perspectives and by applying different scales of analysis. Each has contributed to explanation of the process, some with emphasis on the structural framework within which migration occurs, others on the specifics of particular flows. There remains the need for explanation of the tendency or potential for migration within the historical-structural framework and the connection between the tendency and actual movement.

It is possible to gain some understanding of the process at the behavioural level, and thus advance existing interpretations of migration behaviour, by examining the components of the migration process – the potential and actual move – and attempting to understand the relationship between the two. In seeking explanation of migration at the level of decision-making it is essential that the potential migrant is taken into account. Such an approach has been proposed in connection with internal migrations between different parts of the same country (Mabogunje, 1970). In studies of international migration attention has been confined to those persons who actually make the move, yet potential migrants are of major significance as decision-makers, whether or not conditions lead to their actual move.

People may be regarded as potential migrants when the latent consciousness that ascribes a positive view of migration leads to the intention, the desire, or even the sense of the need to migrate. Who actually goes and when, where, and for how long, are factors controlled by conditions both inside and outside the country of residence. These factors fashion the nature of the controls and agents of final selectivity in the migration process.

'To conceptualize the situation is one thing', wrote Brookfield (1969: 76), 'to find ways of incorporating the perceived environment into empirical method is quite another.' In order to operationalize the concepts outlined, the actual world was taken as a starting point. In the first instance it was the place where migration occurred. But as an influence in migration behaviour the perceived, rather than the actual, world is taken to be the more significant. This is not to suggest that these two aspects of reality are necessarily contradictory. As Lowenthal (1967: 249) remarked, '... though the perceived world in some respects falls short of and in others transcends the more objective consensual reality, yet they at least partly resemble it'. The perceived environments of the various populations are discussed in Chapter 5 and the extent to which they have contributed to explanation of the patterns of the migration behaviour is assessed.

The perception of opportunities within a particular locality is determined by an interaction between the individual's value system and the image of the real world. As discussed in other contexts, the meaning of the environment is then incorporated into the image (Downs, 1970). This adjustment, which is expressed as a decision, can occur without overt action. It is followed in some cases by search for more information and the attention to practical matters involved in making a move. Such behaviour occurs in and affects the real world. Furthermore, it becomes part of the real environment which in turn is perceived variously by other individuals, either within a short period of time or even a generation or more later.

The environment or actual world was further taken as a source of information. Accessibility increased the interaction with others and the information received. The environment of an individual is not circumscribed solely by the immediate physical surroundings. The extent to which the environment is extended outwards from the individual's home location may be measured by the type and amount of information received from outside, a reflection of the accessibility of the individual within the national and international space. Accessibility as a meaningful surrogate for location, in all its socio-spatial aspects, is dealt with in Chapter 6. This in turn is followed (Chapter 7) by a discussion on that critical relational dimension of the image which reflects the individual's sense of position or level of integration within the total experiential environment or life space.

Individuals are located within the networks of economic opportunity and political influence as well as of social position and power relationships. Location in these networks is critical to the individual's mental image and influences all migrants – from the transient to the refugee.

Thus the location of a place and the people at that place are both cause and consequence of the information received and images generated. How the location factor affects migration behaviour has never been hitherto examined.

Location and the image

Location is a critical factor in the behaviour of people, including their migration behaviour. For location is not a simple concept of designation in physical space, but one involving position in social space as well – that is, position in society and networks of societal interaction.

Location is integral to the very nature and characteristics of any given locality, and to the perspective from which the inhabitants of that locality view themselves and the world. Thus it matters that the decision-maker belongs to a country in the global periphery, influenced by the political and economic forces which determine and control the pattern of the international division of labour. But this is not the sole locational factor which matters in determining the nature of the migration process. The location of the country within the global periphery to which the decision-maker belongs is significant; as is the extent of the country's contact with the channels of information from the places most relevant in the context of migration. These information linkages are, in turn, affected by historical-structural factors which in part reflect the size, economic importance and strategic position of the place both in the past and currently. Location within the country of residence is also important in determining the position of individuals within the total system and, therefore, the nature of their overall environment. The extent to which the location is urban or rural, industrial or agricultural, central or remote, modernized or containing only basic amenities, are all of major significance in determining the nature of the environment.

Location is not solely confined to the dimension of space and its manifestation in place; location in time is just as real. At any place, the environment or actual world varies by the year, the decade, the generation. Besides, the decision-makers evaluate the environment from a particular point in the experience of the society to which they belong. They act on the basis of the corporate memory of what has past. The practical circumstances of the national and international environments also change with time, and are variable in the impact upon the configuration of the global division of labour. Labour demands of the metropolises, attitudes towards migrants of various categories, together with policies and legislation to enforce them, greatly affect the controls in the system. Furthermore, policies influence the nature of the information which is generated and transmitted to the countries and localities of the potential migrants.

Finally, the individual's location in society affects the image of the real world. Social space, like physical and temporal space, has several hierarchical levels. Citizenship of a country on the periphery determines, at the most general level, the individual's location in the international social space. Membership of a particular social class within the country on the periphery provides a further level of specificity of location in the national social space. Role within the local community and position in the family and household indicate, at the detailed level, location in social space. Each of these levels in the social hierarchy is associated with constraints and opportunities in terms of access not only to information but also to capital and other resources, access to political power and to social status. Further, location in the social space hierarchy determines position in the network of social relationships, the nature of institutionalized patterns of behaviour, and of the obligations, responsibilities and privileges expected. All these alter the perspective from which the individual sees the world and thus it affects the nature and tenacity of the image.

Three Caribbean islands

Most interpretations of Caribbean migrations have been founded on generalizations made at the regional or island level. It is true that in any global sense a single Caribbean territory represents a detailed unit for investigation, but the island level of scrutiny is too large or inappropriate, except for establishing broad explanatory frameworks.

At the other extreme of scale are those studies which have concentrated upon a single village community, or highly restricted sample. These microcosmic views of society, like those of very large scale, offer many valuable insights into the migration process, but have failed to create the kind of framework within which many of the major factors governing the process may be explored. No one country will be at the same stage of development at any one period of time. Different communities in different places are variously integrated into the national life.

Three islands are included in this study – Jamaica, Barbados and St Vincent. The structural characteristics of the three islands are outlined in Chapter 2, and the spatial and social variation in each discussed. Not only do places differ in their characteristics, but the class composition, as also class relations, vary from one place to another. To avoid the type of generalization which occurs when treating an entire country as a single unit, and to study the dynamics of the migration process as it relates to people in different locations, a range of types of locality in each of the islands was examined comparatively. Chapter 3 outlines the range of micro-environments of the three islands and shows how the detail of the community, household and individual has been incorporated into the island-wide comparison.

The time dimension also is important and frequently subsumed in migration studies. In numerous ways, the specific period in which migration takes place is highly significant in terms of the opportunities available for migration through immigration legislation abroad, and the political mood of society at home. These factors influence the nature of the migration fields, as well as the volume and the selectivity of the migrant populations. Even more fundamental is the fact that in the long run migration influences corporate memory, the nature and locations of family migration networks and migration status of the household.

The period upon which this study concentrates is from the mid-1970s to the beginning of the 1990s. But information pertaining to past migration from households refers back to the late-1950s, thus providing information spanning some thirty years. In many respects this era was highly significant with regard to Caribbean population movements, for it includes the massive migrations to Britain in the post-World War II years. New migration systems were emerging based on the introduction of legal constraints on movement to the United Kingdom after 1952, the beginning of extensive Caribbean migration to Canada and the expansion of migration to the United States throughout the 1960s. The mid-1970s were a significant threshold in the pattern of migration with a major peak in middle-class migration to the United States and Canada. This was followed later by the re-introduction of farming contracts also to the United States and Canada, and the spontaneous development of short-term migrations both within the Caribbean region itself and also to other locations nearby.

Summary

A conceptual framework for Caribbean migration must incorporate the three major components of the overall system within which the migration process occurs: the international, national and household dimensions.

The international factors have produced structures inherent in the unequal development of countries on the periphery, versus those at the centre. These have had implications for dependency, the international division of labour and the resulting transfer of labour as value for the expansion of capital. Internal political, economic and social structures are manifest and articulated in the pattern of social stratification and class relations. At the final stage are the micro-environments of localities and communities which directly and indirectly influence the households and individuals of which they are comprised.

These three sets of factors implicitly constitute a nested hierarchy of explanatory levels in the total process. But the perceptions or images of the world which individuals carry in their mind represent the way in which the combined international, national and household circumstances – including constraints, expectations and opportunities – impact upon the individual. To examine the nature of these cognitions brings us closer to understanding the role of the totality of environmental influences in human spatial behaviour.

Notes

1 To avoid repetition of the term 'international migration', for the purpose of this study the term 'migration' will be used to imply all movement across national boundaries, whether within the Caribbean region or outside. Further, the term will be used to include such movement for any purpose other than a tourist visit. Where reference is intended to be made to internal migration this will be specifically indicated.

CHAPTER 1

Theoretical perspectives on Caribbean migration: Perception and the image.

The extent to which Caribbean migration has evolved its own dynamic, rooted in social institutions and consciousness, has been omitted from the concept of migration in most of the academic literature. The paradigms which have dominated thinking in relation to international migration, present a conceptualization of a movement at all times responding to negative conditions. As a result, analyses frequently have confused explanation of migration in general with causation of one movement or type of movement in particular. To take the analysis beyond the particular to the general, a conceptualization is needed that can incorporate all aspects of migration including its apparent inconsistencies, varying characteristics and return flows.

Explanations of Caribbean migration have included a number of approaches, principally from an economic or materialist perspective and with major contributions from a societal perspective. The political standpoint has been explored to a much more limited extent. To extend and, at the same time, deepen existing explanation of the migration process, the level of consciousness and the behaviour of the participants must be further understood. To attempt this, it is essential that the tendency for migration, and not solely the volume and timing, be explained. One must in the first place move away from the conceptualization of the process based on episodes or incidences of negative conditions in the objective environment, and seek explanation of migration in the context of the ongoing aspects of Caribbean life and livelihood.

Economic approaches

Within an economic framework, reductionist or materialist interpretations have been the most prominent theoretical perspectives applied to the subject of migration. Grounded in the ideas of equilibrium theory (Rostow, 1960; Todaro, 1976), human migration has been conceptualized as an economic resource responding to the gradient of labour supply and demand within a macro-economic framework. The reductionist approach has also taken the form of functionalist, microanalytic models of voluntary individual movement in response to unevenly distributed opportunities. No fundamental distinction has been made between domestic and international movements.

Functionalist interpretations

The functionalist approach, grounded in the neo-classical economic intellectual tradition, has been the basis for most empirical studies of Caribbean international migration. Though most of these studies have not developed a theoretical argument, a number of them have come within the general framework of the functionalist, microanalytic approach.

An underlying premise of the functionalist approach is a behavioural perspective. However, the behavioural viewpoint interprets migration as the cumulative result of individual decisions based on the rational evaluation of the costs and benefits of moving from points of negative to positive attraction under forces articulated as 'pushes and pulls'. Assumptions of the push-pull model of maximization of profit or advantage in migrating have been accepted all too often without serious question, some interpretations simply broadening the concept of the 'economic environment' to include political and social aspects as well.

Criticisms of empirical studies based on the functionalist approach have focused upon the fallacy of the idea that a phenomenon as complex as migration could have a single cause (Koot, 1974). Furthermore, that conclusions about individual rational choice could be based on the 'evidence' of aggregate data of migration streams was unscientific. This approach was further operationalized in empirical work so that the global circumstances surrounding the movement were subsumed or ignored, and conditions at source and destination examined in isolation or put in opposition to each other (Davison, 1962; Peach, 1968).

At the same time, many of the factors which have been referred to as causal factors of migration have been manifestations of wider systemic structural inequalities. These factors have usually referred to some aspect of overpopulation, chiefly interpreted in terms of unemployment rates (Roberts, 1955; Tidrick, G. 1966; Glass, 1960; Davison, 1962), or labour demand versus labour surplus (Peach, 1968; Girling, 1974; Palmer, 1974, 1983). Contrary evidence comes from the fact that workers migrated even when their labour was in great demand in the home country (Thomas-Hope, 1977, 1978). Later, in the massive out-migration to the United Kingdom in the late-1950s and early-1960s, the loss of the skilled worker was noted (Senior and Manley, 1955; Roberts and Mills, 1958). Losses of trained personnel from Jamaica in the 1970s resulted in such competition between government ministries for staff that a general climate of instability was created. Furthermore, professional jobs, especially in medicine, had to be filled by immigrants, mostly coming from India and Sri Lanka (Hope, 1985). A similar situation occurred in the fields of banking and finance resulting in a chain of events whereby, it was reported, personnel were no sooner trained by a company than they migrated or 're-located' to engage in similar work in North America (Dixon, 1980). Labour demand and surplus, like other indices of overpopulation, are too complex to provide a simple explanation for migration.

Further criticisms of the application of the classical economic theoretical approach to decision-making in relation to migration, have pointed out the futility of examining human behaviour in relation to optimization based on decisions of single-minded, economically rational people, who had perfect knowledge of the alternatives and their consequences.

The notion of the 'satisficer' was introduced, intending this to be added to the economic factor in explaining behaviour so as to modify explanations based on economic maximization (Simon, 1957). The concept of 'utility' (a measure of 'value') was introduced by Wolpert (1965) to account for the fact that although intendedly rational people are limited in their ability to perceive, calculate and predict, they still differentiate between alternative courses of action. Place utility, Wolpert suggested, is the individual's subjective measure of the degree to which the opportunities at a particular place permit the perceived or actual achievement. In a further attempt to replace the theory predicated upon the concept of optimizing behaviour, the idea was introduced that decision and choice are controlled by sub-optimal behaviour, described by Golledge, Brown and Williamson (1972) as 'bounded rationality'. This was based on the premise that decisions are tied to a number of different objectives, giving rise to the conflict of goals and uncertainty about roles.

It can hardly be disputed that aspirations, values, measures of prestige and satisfaction are not based solely on economic criteria. In the first place, Caribbean migration could sometimes be regarded as more *obsessional* than *rational*. Certainly, behaviour may be regarded as optimal in relation to the information available, and in relation to the individual's goals. But both an information filter and a goal filter separate the objective world from the perceived world. This is to recognize that persons of widely differing experiences in a decision-making situation are not likely to act in a homogeneous manner. This replaces the deterministic notions of migration occurring as a result of a set of objectively identified criteria. People do not evaluate the environment and its opportunities or constraints simply on the basis of their impressions of the 'here and now'. The evaluations are largely tempered and conditioned by corporate memory, past experience and future hopes. It is only by probing the evaluations of the entire society of migrants as well as non-migrants that the migration process can be explained and, in the light of this, both the general pattern and the apparent anomalies in the migration behaviour can be understood.

Historical-structural interpretations

From an historical-structural perspective, studies have chiefly applied models of the centre-periphery relationship in the global division of labour (Sassen-Koob, 1981; McLean-Petras, 1981a and 1981b; Cohen, 1987) and the transfer of value (Watson, 1982). Labour, which has been regarded as the workers' only commodity, is seen to enter the migration system as part of the international exchange and transfer of value. Yet all migrants do not sell their labour and some are themselves petty capitalists, using their own migration to further their objective of capital formation. Furthermore, there are other migrants who, though taking their labour power abroad, are not part of the exploited proletarian class in the Caribbean in the first place but part of the upper middle class.

Movement is not always aligned to need. In times of direct labour recruitment there is virtually total alignment; however, when greater freedom is permitted this is not the case. The greater the freedom, that is, the fewer the restrictions on the selectivity of entry, the less aligned the migrations of a workforce to the demands of labour have proved to be. This was reflected in the occurrence of migration far in excess of the British demands for labour in the period of post-war reconstruction. The migration to Central America in the late-nineteenth and early-twentieth centuries likewise exceeded the demand for labour.

The materialist models provided no explanation for the contradictions in the system. It is these very contradictions in the movement of labour as a servant of capital which draws attention to the fact that yet another process or set of processes must be occurring within the overarching dynamic of the transfer of value for the advancement of capital.

Essentially, both the functionalist equilibrium approach and the historical-structural approach treat migration as a uni-dimensional process of economic exchange or transfer of value. Further, they assume migration to be a constant in a qualitative sense, and an independent variable in a regressive sense. They subsume the potential migrant who never becomes part of the migration stream even when the conditions are conducive to the transfer of his labour. Besides, global inequalities are not solely economic nor necessarily manifest in materialist terms.

Political approach

Although political systems theory has not been considered seriously in the context of Caribbean migration, some studies have recognized the importance of political factors. Lowenthal and Comitas (1962) drew attention to the relevance of territorial size in migration, suggesting that the smaller the unit the more likely it was to lose population. A decade later, Lowenthal (1972) discussed emigration within the context of the wider socio-political perspectives of neo-colonialism. McLean-Petras (1978) examined the role of national boundaries in international migration and Cohen (1987) refers to the state as filter and regulator of labour supply.

From the perspective of political systems, explanation of international migration is derived from 'a fundamental tension between the interests of individuals and the interests of societies' (Zolberg, 1981: 7). While this is plausible in the context of refugee and other politically motivated movements, it is questionable whether it could be a major factor in other types of movement in which general social, rather than political tensions are paramount.

A further assumption of this approach is that migrants cease to be part of the political system of the countries they leave and take on new citizenship status in their country of destination. This is fundamentally contradicted in the Caribbean case, where people characteristically maintain their political involvement with their country of origin (Basch, 1987), with the notable exception of most refugees. Nor, in the Caribbean context, can international migration generally be regarded as deviant behaviour as suggested by political systems theory. This departure from the territorial organization of world societies is underlined, Zolberg maintained, by the fact that all states legitimately exercise the right to restrict the entry of citizens from other states. To presume that this demonstrates that international migration is fundamentally 'at odds with the world' is to suggest that any societal processes which are not 'natural' (in the sense of requiring no organizational controls) are deviant. On the contrary, it may well be that the international movement of people is the normative response to the concept of a global community and that states impose artificial controls and, at times, barriers, to the freedom of such movement.

One of the notable features of Caribbean migration has been its development of spatial fields which provide habitual, even institutionalized means of extending the limits of 'small-island' opportunities to incorporate a wider world. Caribbean migrants assume the permeability of national boundaries, the technique is to keep abreast of the policies which guard the perforations and the loop-holes in those policies. In this vein, Carnegie (1982) suggests that the circulation and flexibility of migration is an indication that migrants are questioning the notions of the bounded nation state.

Whichever situation one regards as the more natural in the long term, it is true that there is significant tension between the countries at each end of the migration trajectory. These tensions help determine the nature of the migration constraints imposed by states. This is borne out by the fact that Caribbean countries and metropolitan countries have always had their own priorities concerning migration and these priorities are not always or necessarily complementary. Nevertheless, in that the world is divided into 'exclusive and legally sovereign territorial states which delineate the specificity of international migration' (Zolberg, 1981: 4), it is clear that the role of the state cannot be ignored in explaining the process.

A societal systems approach

A number of studies of Caribbean migration have fallen within the overall framework of a societal approach without actually presenting a theoretical model or indicating the connections between the microanalytical empiricism of the study itself and a wider theoretical framework. As a result, many such studies, as Chaney (1985) points out, appeared to have no theoretical foundation.

Most of the anthropological studies come into this category in which one or other aspect of the societal system has been the focus of a microanalysis. Some have demonstrated the interactive elements of different aspects of the societal system (Crane, 1971; Richardson, 1980, 1983; Foner, 1973; Hendricks, 1974; Olwig, 1979). Other works have examined socio-psychological factors in the process (Philpott, 1973; Bryce-Laporte, 1976; Thomas-Hope, 1978, 1980; Rubenstein, 1982, 1983). The concept of a societal system, integrating social, political and economic structures has been the focus of other work. Thomas-Hope (1977) developed the concept of an open system to analyze Caribbean migration behaviour, and Marshall (1982b) referred to the importance to the migration pattern of small size and the fact that Caribbean islands comprise open systems. The concept of a 'social field' has provided the basis of discussion by other scholars (Cross, 1979; Frucht, 1968; Hill, 1977; Manners, 1965; Midgett, 1975; Philpott, 1973; Thomas-Hope, 1977). Some studies have concentrated on the household activities and household linkages (Pessar, 1982a and 1982b). Wood (1982: 300) makes a good case for using the household as a unit for study in order to integrate the functional aspects of migration (the 'household sustenance strategies') with the wider historical-structural factors (the 'socio-economic and political forces that affect the maintenance and reproduction of the unit'). However, he does not actually suggest how this approach could be operationalized to form the basis of explanation for the migration process.

The theory of societal systems integrates social, psychological and economic perspectives. In this framework, societal units are regarded as elements of systems and the central objects of cognition; there is an interdependent relationship envisaged between structure on the one hand and culture on the other. However, structure is here limited by its abstraction as 'a set of interrelated social positions (or units)' (Hoffman-Nowotny, 1981: 65) and structural factors derived from economic and political dimensions are subsumed or totally ignored.

A valuable contribution of this perspective is its emphasis on the role of culture, defined as the symbols of power and prestige, in determining social processes. The view is that a coincidence of power and prestige at the level of the societal unit reflects a consolidated social system, whereas the divergence (or disequilibrium) of power and prestige implies structural tensions which generate anomic tensions. In this approach migration is seen as resulting from those structural and anomic tensions and thus as a process by which tensions are reduced.

Individuals may have a more or less balanced status configuration within their own sub-system but may experience a sense of alienation because they are located at a power-deficient point in the overall system. Their location may provide only a small chance of reducing that tension. In such a case, migration may be interpreted as the attempt to give up their membership status and move to another system with a lower power deficit or a power surplus. But in Caribbean migration, people do not characteristically give up membership of the system; instead, they temporarily transfer membership. The fact that the migration may later become permanent is irrelevant at the stage of outward movement; it is the intention of temporary transfer that matters then (Thomas-Hope, 1982).

The idea that the relieving of tension through migration leads automatically towards equilibrium is not borne out by the Caribbean experience. There are wider historical-structural factors which must be taken into account which the societal systems approach alone does not include.

An image-led approach to migration

The strengths of each theoretical approach are enhanced when ideas from the other perspectives are integrated into a single, multi-dimensional theoretical framework. While each theoretical framework contributes to explanation of part of the migration process, none in isolation makes provision for conceptualizing the total environment of migration at all levels of scale and all relevant components of the system. The main lines of tension between the different theoretical perspectives, which are in the differences of macroanalytic and microanalytic approaches and in materialist versus non-materialist explanations, would be resolved if migration was conceptualized as central to the model.

The theoretical framework for migration must be able to incorporate the combination of all environmental influences, including those from global, national and local dimensions of the environment, even at the micro-level of the household. Furthermore, for active migration to take place, potential migration energy must be converted into active energy and, in the last analysis, this can only occur at the level of the individual. Therefore, whatever the wider causal factors in migration, the theoretical framework must be able to take into account the element of potential as well as action. The factors which contribute to the decision or disposition for mobility are one issue, a separate issue concerns those which determine whether or not the decision is followed by active migration and, if so, the characteristics of the move. They include the range of controls, from legislation and immigration requirements to private agents, personal financial circumstances and overseas contacts.

The argument here advanced is that environments at all levels of scale reflect historical-structural factors manifest in global inequalities, societal tensions between and within societies and political tensions between individuals and the state, as well as between source and destination countries. These structural factors are significant in the decision-making processes relating to migration through their impact on the nature of the images which are formed in the minds of the potential migrants.

From the structural tensions and inequalities of the international and national environment are sifted those elements which are relevant to the migration process from the perspective of the people involved. These all contribute to the formation and nature of the images held. Thus the image integrates the macroanalytic and microanalytic dimensions of the system rather than placing them in opposition to one another. Further, the image translates the relevant environmental factors – of both a material and non-material nature – into messages or perceptions which are meaningful to the people involved and in the particular context of migration at a particular period in time. The image is thus central to understanding the migration process.

Depending on the time and place, political tensions may be paramount in the image or societal tensions may predominate. Anomic tension may be interpreted as part of the qualitative aspect of the image. The actual migration will only take place if the migration supra-structure permits. This is determined by the requirements of capital and/or other national interests, which are articulated in migration legislation. On occasion, these needs, which though part of the environmental stimuli, are not consciously part of the image, are directly applied in order to induce migration of a particular type. Invariably, this is the case with migrant contract labour, where the needs of capital and other interests of the state are directly carried out in a particular policy followed by the recruitment of the migrants required. In these cases, the transition from potential to active migration occurs in a very specific direction and selectivity is prescribed and rigidly adhered to.

Other than the specific intervention of states on behalf of the need of capitalist expansion, at most times, the role of historical-structural international inequalities is in determining the location of people within their various communities, social classes within the national system and societies within the national frame of reference. In turn this influences the relations at the various levels of scale which give rise to the tensions with and between states as well as within and between societies.

Conceptualized within this theoretical framework, the long-run implications of migration are that a tendency towards equilibrium is unlikely. Although a number of tensions are relieved through the migration process, new ones develop through the location of foreign communities forming ethnic minorities. Furthermore, the removal of tension, whether societal or political between individual and state, individual and wider society, or between classes in the national class relations system, makes no difference to the structural arrangements and institutions which gave rise to the images influencing migration.

It is not simply the relieving of tension that matters. There would also have to be the fundamental alteration in structures which removed the forces generating images of tension or perceived deprivation.

Furthermore, it would be essential in the Caribbean case for a totally new image of migration to emerge. Given the tenacity of the image and the only slight structural changes which have occurred, the image of migration which has developed throughout modern Caribbean history is unlikely to be significantly altered.

A classic systems framework as a conceptual approach to the explanation in migration makes no allowance for the perceived environment as distinct from the actual environment. Yet both these dimensions of the environment are intrinsic to migration. This means that the model appropriate for analysis of the migration process must include the existence of the two separate, but closely connected, planes of reality – that of the actual or objective reality and that of the perceived reality or the image. The decision-maker lies at the interface of these two planes.

The image which conditions migration behaviour involves both real and imagined worlds, phenomena which are experienced as well as those not experienced but nevertheless believed. Location in the total matrix of place, time and society determines the amount, type and meaning of the influences which emanate from the environment in different ways at the global, national and local levels of scale.

The perceived environment and migration behaviour

The distinction between the perceived world and the 'real world' is not necessarily significant; for if the image were 'unreal', or an untrue abstraction of reality, it could not survive. The truth of an image, in terms of its reflection of reality, is measured by its stability and survival from one generation to another. Further, the validity of the image is confirmed by the success of the behaviour which it promotes (Boulding, 1956). Thus the terms 'real world' and 'image' are used to distinguish not between reality and myth, but between phenomena external to the individual – that is, in his or her environment, and internal – that is, in his or her mind or 'psychological life space'. The perceived environment is taken to mean 'the whole monistic surface on which decisions are based' (Brookfield, 1969: 53). This 'surface' – the mental impression of an individual's world, the totality of knowing, or cognition – comprises the image.

The nature of the image

The image incorporates the individual's total environment, including natural and non-natural, visible and non-visible, experienced and simply heard of, near and far, past, present and future. It represents the culmination of knowledge against a background of values, beliefs, aspirations and goals which are tinted or modified by emotions and personality.

Despite the total nature of the individual's world from which the image is derived, and hence the use of the term 'surface' to describe it, one should not be misled into thinking that the perceived environment or image is a *continuous* surface. In the first place, it is not necessarily, and very rarely, a cartographic replication of the actual or objective reality in the mind's eye. Secondly, unlike an object of perception (a percept), which is sustained by the information in the environment or, literally, seeing what is before us, an image is something we maintain both as memory when the environmental stimuli have gone and also, in many instances, when the stimuli do not appear to justify it (Tuan, 1975).

An image begins as a percept, registering environmental impressions and then it undergoes further transformation when circumstances prompt its recall. In the present context, those circumstances relate to decisions concerning migration. What this indicates, and must be underlined, is that environmental circumstances convey different meanings according to the particular context within which they are recalled. A high opinion may be held of a particular place in the context of scenic beauty, but conveys no meaning in relation to migration unless it is evaluated in that context. The image of migration itself is critical in determining the image of the environments brought into focus.

The image is comprised of fact and concept. Certain aspects of the image are constructs of the mind whereas other aspects, conditioned by emotions and personality, are properties of the mind. The importance of this distinction is that the image is the culmination of fact, value and emotion, influences from outside the individual as well as conditioning factors from within.

Neither fact nor emotion is generated by the individual without being influenced by socio-cultural factors. The image expresses in various direct and indirect ways the corporate beliefs, views, experience and memory of the larger social group. These elements of the image are transmitted to each generation, permeating them to different degrees, according to their level of receptiveness.

It is generally recognized that people's behaviour results from the interaction of biological, personality, socio-cultural and environmental factors (Moore and Golledge, 1976; Walmsley, 1982). However, it seems reasonable that explanation of behaviour should be based on the premise that within any population exists a similar combination of personality types.

Though the image is personal, it is not private. Part of the image of the world possessed by an individual is the belief that this image is shared by those other people with whom one perceives oneself to have similar views (Boulding, 1956). Indeed, it is because the image is shared by others that stereotypes develop and, in turn, these inform individual images, thus reinforcing and perpetuating a general view. Of course, the precise nature of the image will vary from one person or group of persons to another and, in general, the degree of similarity in the image is consistent with the extent of similarity or shared characteristics and experiences of the group, be it a nation, social class, community, family or household. Studies have shown conformity in the image based on similarities of cultural and locational background (Gould, 1969). It is also apparent that culture influences the perceptions of individuals who are part of that culture (Goodey, 1973). Indeed, as Hall (1959, 1966, 1968) suggests, the way in which people perceive and use space is cultural, or at least an articulation of culture.

A further attribute of the image is that it enables the individual to rehearse spatial behaviour in the mind; it is a means to structure and store knowledge; to create imaginary worlds which depict attractive goals such as those that 'tempt people out of their habitual rounds' (Tuan, 1975: 210). This is particularly important with respect to migration, since it is not the differences between places or even the perception of the differences which are so important as the image of migration itself. As Tuan observed (1975: 211), 'Goal-oriented migration is characteristically human'.

The components of the image

The image is comprised of a number of dimensions each containing various elements, some tangible, others intangible. The disaggregation of the image into its component parts as outlined by Boulding (1956), demonstrates the multifaceted and wide-ranging nature of the interacting elements in the mind of the decision-maker.

The spatial and temporal dimension
The spatial aspect of the image is the view or awareness of one's position in the world at different levels of scale. The temporal image conveys

to the individual the sense of location in a dimension of time, including the sense that there is a certain time of one's life which is appropriate or best for one sort of activity or another, including migration. It should be noted that the temporal and spatial components of the image are not to be confused with the location of the individual in physical space and at a particular period of time.

Though the image has a dimension of, or is located in space and time, both places and time periods vary in their significance to different individuals. There is nothing absolute about the meaning of either place, time, events in space or time, or even information about events in space and time. Therefore, in various ways, place or space and time are relative phenomena and provide heterogeneous media within which people's cognitions are developed.

The relational dimension

The image is comprised of a field of personal relationships and an awareness of self within that network. This includes an awareness of one's social, economic and political position and role within the international framework, as well as within the home country, the social class to which one belongs, the community, the family and the household. Each aspect of this self-awareness reflects the implications of the individual's location in the total social space.

In addition to the awareness of self in social space is also the position in social space which is not consciously understood but which is important nevertheless in determining the composition of the image. In particular, it determines the type and volume of information which is received by different individuals and the framework within which that information is understood. The relational dimension of the image is affected by the reference groups against which people consciously and subconsciously evaluate their own position.

The conditional dimension

Individuals are not only aware of their position with respect to place, time and status in society, together with its constraints, roles and responsibilities, but they are also aware of themselves in a world of natural laws. Thus there is incorporated into the image a conditional element. This involves an awareness that if certain events were to occur, certain other events would be likely to follow. The logic is informed by personal or corporate experiences of the past. But the experiences of the past also convey different lessons, warnings, guidelines and encouragement, pessimism and fear or optimism and hope. The differences in these conveyed guidelines are, in turn, determined by the emotional framework with which the image is constructed and sustained.

The emotional dimension

Elements generated by the emotions are a further dimension of the image. Knowledge in the sense of information about the objective reality becomes part of the image only in so far as the screened truth is fashioned by emotions which come into play in the context of migration, notably those regarding fulfilment or frustration, satisfaction or dissatisfaction, aspiration or resignation, hopefulness or hopelessness, confidence or fearfulness, forward looking or nostalgia.

Closely allied to the emotions are attitudes. Each emotion generated with respect to migration is invariably influenced by attitudes of adventure-seeking or risk-taking. Since attitudes are deeply rooted in personality, the more cautious migrate once the chain of family and friends has been well established and the risk factor thus greatly reduced. The longer a migration phase to a particular destination continues, the more people in this category become part of the stream.

The emotional dimension of the image reflecting hope, aspiration and other such qualities of the mind, strongly indicates that the image is comprised not only of elements of fact in the way information is often regarded to exist, but also the very important element of value.

The value dimension

Value is concerned with the rating of the various aspects of the overall image in terms of some measure or concept of better or worse. Each individual possesses one or more such measures or scales in the image.

The various scales contained in the mind ensures that only like is compared with like. For example, there is a scale of economic betterment, of general betterment, of educational opportunity. There are scales against which are evaluated the avenues to upward social mobility, social recognition and prestige; those which provide the greater opportunities for returning home in an improved position.

It does not matter whether a place or a set of opportunities exist or not within the objective environment, these scales are only used to evaluate aspects of the world or environment which are known and meaningful to the individuals themselves. Hence a country which has many opportunities for work and advancement is omitted from the Caribbean person's image of the world of opportunity if he or she knows so little about it that it cannot be entered on to the value scale for measuring.

The qualitative dimension
The image has a dimension of quality with respect to uncertainty or certainty, probability or improbability, clarity or vagueness. This dimension of certainty or uncertainty of the image is important in the interpretation of the implications of the image for behaviour. Frequently belief is based on information received from places and from persons whom one has never met. Also the image may involve the future and thus a time dimension which one has never yet experienced. In all these cases, the qualitative dimension of certainty or uncertainty is critical in influencing the nature of decision-making.

Image formation and change

A fundamental question in understanding the nature and the subsequent role of the image in decision-making and behaviour concerns the formation of the image itself. The image develops and changes throughout the life of individuals and social groups through the effect of change in both the external or objective world as well as in the values and beliefs which are held. 'One thing is clear,' Boulding affirms:

> the image is built up of all the past experience of the possessor of the image ... Every time a message reaches him his image is likely to be changed in some degree by it, and as his image is changed his behavior patterns will be changed likewise. (Boulding, 1956: 6-7).

Location and the formation of the image
The perceived environment and the actual environment are separate entities, however close a similarity there may be between them. Even though aspects of the actual environment are the result of people's activities, it is only the perceived environment that is 'always and wholly a cultural artifact' and part of a separate sub-system in which the sources of information are the main energy flow (Brookfield, 1969: 64).

There is also an important distinction between the information or messages which contribute to the formation of the image and the actual image itself. The receipt and distribution of information within a population alters with changes in social and economic structure, political organization, physical infrastructure, education, advertising, the approach and extent of coverage of the mass media and the activity of other agencies devoted to the diffusion of information.

Once the information is received it must be translated into meaningful messages which in turn go towards the construction of the image. The translation of information into a message is dependent upon the mental frame of reference or values of the receivers of the information – the people themselves. But a factor not realized or articulated is that the formation of the image is also conditioned by the actual world in its entirety, not simply the world as it is perceived and accorded meaning by individuals. Hence much behaviour is not consciously understood by the actors themselves. They only have glimpses of the reasons simply because the image is only a glimpse of the real world which is influencing them in various important ways.

Structural factors are among those environmental influences which affect the image. They determine the nature of the international inequalities which form the environments of the decision-maker and influence the relativity of his or her position within the total international and national system. At the same time, structural inequalities influence the psychology of a society, and result in the dependency mentality characteristic of Caribbean society. This greatly affects the perceived advantages of migration, especially if it is directed towards the metropolises. Thus structural factors play a major role in the constitution of the mental fabric upon which the values of the society and social group are based.

Overall, the symbolism of the environment and its opportunities and the meaning of migration are socio-psychological expressions of cultural and structural aspects of reality. The environment, in the sense of objective reality, is not solely physical in a natural sense, nor is it solely cultural. Both these are a reflection of historical-structural realities and relational aspects of them. Thus the image reflects the historically derived societal structures and the particular psychology of the society and that sector of the society to which the individual belongs. 'Part of the image,' states Boulding (1965: 6), 'is the history of the image itself.'

This brings us to the question of the role of belief in the construction of the image. Belief is determined by information and experience, whether personal or received as information from others, which becomes firmly entrenched in the individual's frame of reference. There is also a certain, in some cases a very significant, element of faith which goes towards the formation of a belief.

A belief is a tenuous foundation of the image which explains resistance of the image to change except on demonstrably firm grounds: strong enough that is, to counter the strength of the basis on which the former belief was founded. The image is reinforced by all subsequent information and experience conducive to its retention and highly resistant to any message which is not.

Change in the image

The collection or stock of individual images in the society determines the general or corporate view. In order to understand the dynamics of that view it is necessary to understand the ways in which change is effected in the individual image.

Change occurs through the combined impact of the messages received by the individual from the environment and the changes which occur in the value system of the individuals themselves. Messages refer to information, circumstances or occurrences which convey meaning at the societal and individual level.

The impact of messages on the image

Firstly, messages received may bring about no change in the image at all. Secondly, messages may affect the quality of the image with the result of clarifying or making less clear, making more certain or introducing elements of uncertainty. Thirdly, as sometimes occurs, the image may change in quite a radical way. Fourthly, a message may bring about a re-evaluation of self, one's position in social space and sets of relationships, one's opportunities or constraints, obligations or aspirations. This will have the effect of altering the fundamental basis on which information from the environment is converted into messages.

The impact of messages received may have no significant influence on the image for various reasons. The image in the context of migration, is a tenacious construct. It is developed on the basis of personal experience, and from a particular cultural or social perspective; it is also supported by the evaluations of others in the same societal group. Thus, a message will have an impact on an existing image depending on: a) how firmly entrenched that previous image was; b) the nature of the message relative to the previous message held; c) the source of the information and the level of confidence placed in that source. In this regard, friends and relatives are a highly effective source of information.

A further aspect of the issue is that the messages which generate images are not entirely derived from the environment, but some of these image-forming stimuli are generated by people themselves. Information, either in the form of journalistic reports or personal communication, is really the evaluative response to occurrences or phenomena in their environment. It is, therefore, directly or indirectly reflective of the images held by the reporter. In turn, the receipt of that information brings about a further alteration in its meaning as a result of the different image to which it relates in the mind of the person receiving it. The difference in the meaning of the information communicated depends on the degree of similarity in the images possessed by the two parties involved. The greater the similarity in their images (based, of course, upon their values and reference groups in the first place), the less will be the alteration in the meaning of the information as it is conveyed.

This means that Caribbean people abroad will transmit information containing judgements or evaluations which have been made on the basis of very similar values to those of the persons receiving the information in the Caribbean. Such information is deemed by the receiver to be of great reliability. Persons abroad prefer to transmit information which demonstrates that their migration has been successful and those in the Caribbean who have not yet migrated are seeking positive information about migration as well. The image of migration itself becomes the key factor in determining the ways in which the experiences abroad are interpreted both by migrant and potential migrant from their two perspectives within the same value judgement framework. A further important implication of this is that the corporate image is usually close to the individual image of the world and the migration process.

Change in the value system

Change in the framework of values is sometimes derived from the impact of messages from the environment through the re-evaluation of self. Other changes in the value system are derived from shifts in the fundamental beliefs held by the individual.

The value scales are perhaps the most important single element determining the effect of the messages individuals receive on their images of the world. The arrangement of information according to their value scales determines the nature of the resistance to change of the image itself. Thus an aspect of the environment rated only at a low point on the value scale will be more easily changed by new information than will a component rated very highly and thus consciously or subconsciously 'held dear' by the individual.

What this means is that for any person there is no such thing as facts determining decisions and behaviour. There are only messages filtered through a value system. Therefore, the changes of significance to the image are determined not so readily by changes in the 'objective environment' or 'actual world', as by changes in the scale of values or meaning.

In most cases, the image is resistant to major change, accounting perhaps for the radical, even dramatic way in which change occurs when it occurs at all. In the context of Caribbean migration, there is very strong resistance of the image to change, especially with respect to a particular destination regarded as desirable. This explains the persistence of prevailing images of migration and the life abroad, often despite evidence to the contrary through negative feedback. Only after a consistent and long period of negative information, or a lack of information about a certain destination, does the image of that place alter radically. Even then, as demonstrated by the Caribbean experience, for many individuals the established image is bolstered by personal views, hopes and sometimes information as well. The first impulse is to reject any information which carries a message contrary to the spirit of what is already believed or held by the image.

In particular, the images of migration, of risk, of opportunity and other relevant aspects of the process, are influenced by information about legislative changes in immigration laws, in the opportunities of working or living in a country other than the present country of residence. Not all information alters the image. This is the case usually because the information is not meaningful in relation to the existing image, even though it may well be highly significant information to someone else, or in a different context.

It is only when the circumstances of the individual are altered through age and changing experiences or responsibilities, that the individual re-evaluates the image of migration in the light of the new situation. Thus, even the life cycle of the individual, which has been used to explain certain migratory behaviour (McHugh, 1984), has not been understood in terms of the change in the image at different stages of life, especially with respect to the household and family. As in the cases of other circumstantial or environmental influences, stage in the life cycle has been used not in its proper place as influences upon the image and thus the subsequent behaviour, but rather as motivational or other determining factors in the pattern of behaviour. In making this assumption, the observer makes the further incorrect assumption that the individuals are a constant whose behaviour is a reaction only to circumstances external to them.

In summation, it is suggested that the image grows or develops within an environment of circumstances, occurrences and actions, but also one of evaluations, experiences and impressions, some of which are communicated by others and some are internally generated. Both are based on cultural values which are shared with other members of the social group. But even the cultural values themselves are derived in the first instance from historically evolved structural circumstances.

The effect of the image on behaviour

The image 'determines what might be called the current behavior of any organism or organization', Boulding observed (1956: 115). While behaviour tends to be in accordance with the strongest impulses of the image, this does not mean that the consequences of behaviour necessarily follow the pattern expected by the image.

The individual's behaviour in response to, or in conformity with, the image is expressed as a decision which in some cases involves no overt action. Whether or not the decision is followed by action depends on the existence of certain practical circumstances of the actual environment which encourage or facilitate a particular form of behaviour. So the conclusion that migration is desirable in general, or is desirable to a particular place at a particular time, will only be followed by such action if circumstances permit. In the meantime, the decision to migrate may be left pending the occurrence of changes in the real world or, prior to this happening, the image may change on the basis either of new information or a change in aspirations and ideas of what is better or worse. In other words, behaviour will be affected either through changes in the real world or changes in the value base of the image.

The linkages from the image and a decision follow on from two directions at any one time. One linkage is a search process. This has been referred to as a re-cycling process because of the recurrent nature of image formation or confirmation followed by decisions of a positive nature regarding migration, but without adequate facilitating factors to lead to the final overt action or move (Downs, 1970). Thus individuals continue to 'search' the real world for more information and the actual means whereby a move would be possible or realistic in their evaluation or their terms.

Whether the decision is to move or not to move, it affects the actual environment. The decision then, as part of the real world, passes as information to others and is translated by them to become part of the image. At the same time, the individual who had made a particular decision will, through that experience, be influenced in terms of the effect it has on the image.

The cyclical nature of the process means that the real world, the image and perceived world, the decision and the overt behaviour are all interacting continuously, whether consciously or subconsciously. The influence is felt not only by the individual engaged in migration-oriented decisions, but by other persons as well.

Theoretical implications

Based on conclusions drawn from the role of the image in other types of spatial behaviour discussed by Downs (1970), the following theoretical points can be made with respect to the image in Caribbean migration.

In the first place, the individual is the ultimate decision-maker, but decisions are rational only in so far as the options, goals and consequences of decisions are incorporated into the image.

Secondly, the image is conditioned by the location of individuals in the total social system of which they are a part.

Thirdly, people constitute complex information-processing systems involving information receipt and the translation of information into meaning which is determined, in the first place, by value, reference groups, aspirations and goals. This occurs in the light of corporate memory and transfers of experience. The translation of information into meaning also bears relation to attitudes, including beliefs and the disposition towards certain action; these are not solely individual factors but shared by social groups. Attitude perhaps takes the image closer to the behavioural intention and actual behaviour. Therefore, neither information nor migration options are absolute, both are meaningful only in relation to the individual's circumstance and frame of reference.

Finally, migration behaviour is determined by the perceived environment but is carried out and affects the actual environment. Thus there is a cyclical effect whereby linkages occur and recur between the actual and perceived worlds. Decision-makers, it is proposed, 'base their decisions on the environment as they perceive it, not as it is'. The action resulting from decisions, on the other hand, are played out in a real or objective environment (Brookfield, 1969: 53).

Conclusion

Environmental influences vary widely in type and intensity. At one end of the continuum of influence are those of an historical-structural nature, affecting in a profound way the material circumstances and socio-cultural perspectives and psychological orientations of entire societies. At the other end of the continuum are the personal, material circumstances which condition the detail of the individual's life, the social relations, customs and practices at the household level, as well as personal cognitions, attitudes and beliefs, frustrations, aspirations and goals.

Each individual and community is located in a three-dimensional space comprised of place, time and societal status. The factors which influence individuals and communities are conditioned by their position in their own society as well as the position of their society in the wider national and international framework. These factors take on meaning according to the points of reference and scales of value possessed by each group and individuals within the group. These are contained in the image and, in turn, it is from this perspective that specific aspects of the environment are evaluated and take on significance in decision-making relating to migration and the emergence of migration potential.

CHAPTER 2 | Three islands: Jamaica, Barbados and St Vincent

No three countries could ever be fully representative of the range of environments that exist in the Caribbean, but Jamaica, Barbados and St Vincent come closest to reflecting the variety of differences in size and patterns of development (Frontispiece, p.viii).

Variations in the socio-economic environment at the island level of scale exist within the context of fundamental similarities at the regional level. Thus although Jamaica, Barbados and St Vincent reflect significant differences in size and patterns of socio-economic development, like most Caribbean countries they are characterized by the structural patterns which are legacies of the region's plantation history and subsequent neo-colonial developments. The democratic governments and mixed economies of these three islands are also, in broad outline, representative of Caribbean democratic pluralist political ideologies and systems. Other political regimes in the Caribbean, like those of Cuba under Castro and Haiti under the Duvaliers, are the exception (Stone, 1986).

While at the general level, size and location, historical trends and structural factors appear to be similar, the differences of detail are important at the local level. Above all, they contribute to the differentials in the respective island's resource exploitation and economic growth, extent of underdevelopment and employment opportunity, the nature of the infrastructure and accessibility, degree of urbanization and interaction with the outside world. These variables combine to produce the opportunities and constraints of the internal and international environments within which images are formed and decision-making and migration take place. Despite the variation in circumstance and characteristics of Jamaica, Barbados and St Vincent in the Caribbean context, each has a history of active migration.

Location and size

Variations in the migration fields of Jamaica, Barbados and St Vincent are in part the result of their different locations. They are situated at disparate points with respect to labour markets and thus to important migration opportunities. This is partly an indication of the physical location of the countries within the Caribbean region, especially in terms of the configuration of transportation routes.

Taking location in a physical sense, Jamaica, in the north-western Caribbean, has been involved only very marginally in intra-regional migration to or from the southern and eastern Caribbean. Instead, Jamaicans were in the vanguard of the movements to Central America and Panama in the late-nineteenth and early-twentieth centuries. St Vincent, on the other hand, was closer to the development of the oil industry in Venezuela, Aruba, Curacao and later, Trinidad, and participated actively in the labour migrations to the centres of drilling and refining. Barbadians likewise actively engaged in the movements to the oil industry located in the southern Caribbean, as well as going further afield to destinations in the northern Caribbean and circum-Caribbean countries.

A second, more significant aspect of location relates to the position of each of the three countries in the matrix of international contact. In this regard, Barbados, with its higher regional profile, is located in a real sense much closer to the labour markets and other opportunities for migration than is nearby St Vincent. This is reflected in the fact that Barbadians were heavily represented in the migrations to Panama and Cuba early in the twentieth century, despite the physical distance. Indeed, the migration fields of Jamaica and Barbados have continued to overlap and populations from these two islands still compete in the labour markets of North America.

Location combines with size to influence migration in a number of less direct ways. In the international network of interaction, small size is compensated for by physical location in terms of accessibility and thus access to labour markets and information pertaining to labour requirements abroad. At the same time, in most cases smallness of size is associated with very limited physical resources which again, in most cases, increases the dependency of countries on the periphery upon the metropolitan centres. In this respect, therefore, small size is usually associated with greater disadvantage in the international arena and a high level of dependency. At the national level, size also affects internal accessibility which greatly influences the volume and type of information received.

Jamaica, one of the seven largest Caribbean countries, contrasts in size with Barbados and St Vincent which are two of the smallest (Table 2.1). But area is only a partial indication of size, since the nature of the terrain, together with the efficiency and extensiveness of the infrastructure, determine real distances within each country. Because

Table 2.1 Comparative measures of size

	Jamaica	Barbados	St Vincent	CARICOM (Mean)
Area (sq.km)	10,991.0	429.9	384.0	21,498.0
Population (thousands)	2,008.0	241.0	91.0	392.9
Population density	175.8	560.6	237.0	181.7
Arable land (sq.km)	4,880.0	300.0	158.4	27,684.7
Arable land per capita (hectares)	0.24	0.12	0.17	1.09

CARICOM refers to the Caribbean Community and Common Market, established on 1 August 1973, comprising the former British Caribbean colonies.

infrastructure is both cause and consequence of level of economic activity, size takes on an economic perspective and becomes a measure of the cost of overcoming distance, as well as being taken as a measure of physical space. Besides, once the concept of space or distance is understood as a measure of cost, its social implications also become apparent.

The low, flat terrain of Barbados means that distances are not increased by physical barriers. Topographic space is further contracted in terms of its economic and social implications because of its extensive and efficient infrastructure, especially transport routes. These were developed early in Barbados' history, not only because of relative ease and relative low costs of road building from a physical standpoint, but also because of the greater necessity for early development of roads to bring all parts of this once valuable sugar-producing colony into easy access for sugar production and export.

St Vincent contrasts with Barbados in all these respects. Distances are effectively greater; to be remote in a physical sense in St Vincent is to be in a social sense very much more isolated than at a similar distance from the capital in the case of Barbados.

Jamaica's greater topographic complexity sets it apart from these two situations but, like St Vincent, high relief increases real distances and increases the isolation brought about by remoteness from major population centres.

The concept of size is also influenced by population numbers. Jamaica, with a population of over two million is the fifth most populous country in the Caribbean, exceeded by Cuba, Puerto Rico, Haiti and the Dominican Republic. Among the CARICOM countries it is the largest, representing approximately 44 per cent of the total for those countries. This contrasts with Barbados where the population is about a quarter of a million and St Vincent, where it was some 91,000 in 1970. (In the absence of data from the 1980 Census, an updated figure cannot be given, especially as it departs from the 100,000 which had been estimated.)

Given the small areal extent of Barbados, its population is considerable and this is evident in its density levels of over 560 per square kilometre. Even in St Vincent, with a small population in absolute terms, the average population density is around 237 persons per square kilometre (Table 2.1).

The significance of the various dimensions of size are reflected in popular perceptions. The higher economic and political profile of Barbados in the region and outside, has created a view of Barbados as being much larger than St Vincent, which has only a very low profile. From the internal perspective their places are reversed. The more extensive infrastructure and relatively higher wage structure of Barbados makes it seem a much smaller island than St Vincent, where accessibility is so much more limited.

The meaning and impact of distance and accessibility are also affected by the communications networks such as telephone systems and traffic both within and into countries. Thus, economic levels and their implications for social interaction combine to ameliorate size. What this indicates is that size, like locational differentials, is determined as much by the physical structures of the islands as by their economic history, contemporary levels of economic activity and the extent of their regional and global involvement.

In terms of both location and size, Jamaica, Barbados and St Vincent represent in a number of important ways some of the variations which exist in the Caribbean. In particular, these are some of the variations which have had a considerable bearing upon the differing nature of the migration fields of the respective countries. The question which remains concerns the effect of location and size on the migration process itself, and especially as it is influenced by and relates to the nature, volume and diffusion of information.

Economic performance

The underlying long-term formal economic goals of Caribbean countries are to increase their levels of development. Barbados, along with the Bahamas, Trinidad and Tobago and Suriname, is a high income Caribbean country with average per capita income in 1980 of (the equivalent of) US $3,040. Jamaica, like the Dominican Republic and Cuba, is a middle income country, and in 1980 the average per capita income was (the equivalent of) US $1,030. St Vincent had an average per capita income below (the equivalent of) US $1,000, which was also the case in Guyana, the other mini states of the Eastern Caribbean (exclusive of the US Virgin Islands), and Haiti (World Bank Atlas, 1981; Economic Survey of Latin America, 1978, 1979, cited in Stone, 1986: 79).

In the Caribbean, as in many parts of the Third World, levels of development are usually measured by indices of modernization or gross domestic production. Contrary to this, it is here proposed to discuss levels of development in terms of reduction in *underdevelopment*, since underdevelopment is the historical-structural starting point of the current process. The economic performance of Jamaica, Barbados and St Vincent demonstrates some of the regional variability with respect to two main components of underdevelopment – degree of external dependence and level of internal disparity.

External dependence

Dependence on the international community is reflected in the extent to which the Caribbean national economies are controlled and conditioned by imports of capital and commodities. This is partially reflected in the degree of openness of the economy, as well as the extent to which production sustains (or is tending to sustain) national economic growth.

Caribbean economies vary in their degree of openness, measured by value of imports as a percentage of GDP (Table 2.2). In Jamaica and St Vincent, as in many other Caribbean countries, high import figures are associated with severe trade imbalances. Not only are equipment and raw materials high on the list of import costs but so too are consumer goods and food. This is indicative of the degree of dependence on metropolitan tastes and lifestyles based on items which the national economy is unable to produce, and even less able to afford.

Degree of openness is, of itself, not necessarily a constraint to economic growth. This was demonstrated by an increase in Jamaica's GDP at an average of 4.4 per cent per year over the decade of the 1960s at a time when import levels were high. Likewise, in the 1970s the rate of growth in Barbados remained at an average of 2.0 per cent when Jamaica's had fallen to an average of -3.0 per cent. More important than the value of imports relative to GDP is the percentage of value added in the importing country as well as the stability in the import demands of foreign trading partners. For example, there is a high

Table 2.2 Indices of economic performance, 1974

	Jamaica	Barbados	St Vincent	CARICOM (Mean)
GDP (millions US$)	2,271.6	185.8	34.1	343.6
GDP per capita (US$)	1,131.0	777.0	375.0	613.2
Agriculture as per cent of GDP	7.8	12.4	21.4	19.0
Exports as per cent of GDP	36.8	67.5	13.2	32.8
Imports as per cent of GDP	45.7	91.0	65.9	61.9
Agricultural exports (% of total exports)	19.5	61.7	98.2	61.1
Tourism (% of total exports)	19.4	61.5	51.5	34.47

Sources: World Bank, 1978; Europa Yearbook for South America, Central America and the Caribbean, 1987.

correlation between GDP and exports, including the 'export' of goods and services through tourism. Levels of exports fluctuate for a number of reasons.

Aside from natural disaster and other internal problems resulting in production failure, sectoral performance is particularly vulnerable to external conditions. This is evident in the sectors dependent on foreign investment, for example manufacturing; those determined by the decisions of the multinational corporations, for example the bauxite-alumina industry;[1] those, like tourism, affected by social or political conditions in the countries abroad which are the major sources of visitors, chiefly the United States. Yet, whatever the advantages of concentration on agriculture, the evidence shows heavy reliance on agricultural production to be associated with high levels of dependence on protected international markets and/or low levels of economic growth.

Jamaica's economic growth in the 1960s was due to high levels of investment in the bauxite industry, the expansion of foreign tourism and a programme for attracting foreign investment in manufacturing. This was accompanied by a decline in sugar production and a particularly dramatic decline in the relative contribution of sugar to total exports.

Jamaica's failure to achieve a higher level of sustained growth in the 1970s reflects some of the elements in the complex web of interactions between external and internal factors affecting economic performance in Caribbean countries. Unfavourable international conditions, induced by recession and rising oil prices, were compounded by the negative reaction of the international community of the 'North' to Jamaica's shift in ideological orientation with the election of a democratic socialist government. Hostility from several quarters, including the North American and local press, lack of confidence by the commercial sector externally and internally, the loss of existing investment, the virtual collapse of the tourist industry, all led to mounting economic and social pressures. These were reflected, not least, in the increased rate of violent crime and the out-flow of local private capital along with the migration of a large number of professional and skilled personnel.

Paradoxically, this situation of the 1970s was itself partly the consequence of the increasing social disparities which accompanied the sectoral growth of the 1960s. Prosperity led to rising, but largely unfulfilled, expectations, partly manifest in the occurrence of high rates of urbanization far in excess of the economic capacity of the urban centres to absorb the expanded population. Furthermore, this coincided with a period of reduced opportunities for migration of unskilled workers.

The experience of the bauxite industry further demonstrated one of the problematic aspects of external dependence on an industry with an internationally integrated vertical structure. Despite the exploitation of Jamaica's valuable bauxite reserves, and the impressive impact the industry had on the growth and diversification of exports, it has had no significant multiplier effects (Girvan, 1971). Contraction of bauxite and alumina production in the 1970s and 1980s was not compensated for by any major lasting benefits.

The 1980s witnessed a revival of the tourist industry, a new emphasis on export agriculture and horticulture, and the expansion of manufacturing for purposes of import substitution as well as export. Despite improved levels of sectoral performance in the 1980s, levels of external dependence were the same as before and the economy remained as vulnerable as ever to internationally determined factors.

In the case of Barbados, sugar was replaced by tourism in the late-1960s. By 1978 the contribution of the sugar industry to GDP declined to 6.7 per cent; by 1984 sugar contributed only 2.8 per cent to GDP largely because of the low price of sugar on the world market together with the impact of disease of the sugar cane plant. The high import levels throughout the 1970s were converted, chiefly through tourism and manufacturing, into activities which were high foreign exchange earners. With the success of these two sectors, the decline in sugar profits was relatively unimportant until the early 1980s, when performance in manufacturing and tourism declined. Markets for Barbadian manufactures, chiefly garments to CARICOM countries, were depressed and there was stagnation in the tourist trade due to recession in the United States – the source of some 50 per cent of the visitors to Barbados.

Over the 1980s there was an increase in the United States 'offshore' financial sector and by the end of 1986 150 international business companies and 46 insurance companies had located themselves in Barbados. There was total dependence of these operations upon the parent companies located in the United States.

This was a situation typical of the small Caribbean states such as the Bahamas, Cayman and the US Virgin Islands, with modernized if somewhat artificial economies based on foreign investment. The development of agro-business had occurred in Barbados but this too, as shown by the Jamaican experience, had been highly dependent on immediate distribution to the United States and efficient marketing. With the sectoral developments of the mid-1980s, the Barbadian economy was revitalized, but its external dependence meant that the economy remained vulnerable to political and social conditions and could prosper only in a climate of high international confidence and direct external control.

In contrast to Barbados, St Vincent was illustrative of the small Caribbean states where the problem was seen as a lack of modernization. The traditional reliance on agriculture for export had persisted, as also agricultural production for the domestic market and for subsistence.

Territories like St Vincent, unable to compete in sugar production even in the eighteenth and nineteenth centuries, remained economic backwaters, off the main lines of international communication and with a poorly developed infrastructure. A return to sugar production in St Vincent was attempted in 1981 but it proved uneconomic and was abandoned in 1985. Arrowroot has remained the most valuable export crop, but accounted for only 2 per cent of foreign exchange earnings in 1986. The export sector survived due to the protection of trade afforded by the Lomé Convention of the European Economic Community.

In the development of a tourist industry, St Vincent, like the other similarly small, mountainous islands, away from the main lines of international air transport and with a non-modernized infrastructure was, once again, in a poor competitive position in the Caribbean. Besides, the island's igneous volcanic rocks produced black sand, rather than the white sand marketed by the agents of international holiday travel. Nevertheless, through the concerted effort of the government in inviting foreign investment, tourism was developed during the 1970s. The price of attracting investment was a high one for the terms and conditions offered by St Vincent were hardly commercial. Land was leased at negligible rates to foreign investors in anticipation of the spin-off effects. Certainly, the positive impact of tourism to the Vincentian economy could be rated high on some counts. Tourist activity has been located on a small coastal strip of white sand beach in the south and on some Grenadine islands, yet the industry accounted for 30-40 per cent of GDP in 1974. On the negative side of the balance, only about 200 people have been employed by the industry and most of these are employed seasonally (Chernick, 1978). Furthermore, far from stimulating local production, St Vincent's tourist industry has led to increases in the import of food. In St Vincent, in 1977, the trade gap had risen to $55.1 million and, despite being a food-producing country, food was the largest single import item, comprising 28 per cent of the total (Bryden and Select Committee, 1976: 156 cited in Nanton, 1983: 235). Like all other ventures in which there has been a predominance of foreign ownership and opportunities for tax-free importations as well as repatriation of profits, the real impact upon the local economy has been minimal.

There have been no extractive industries in St Vincent and, until 1978, there was only a rudimentary manufacturing sector producing basic items (including food and furniture) for local consumption. In 1978, a British consultancy firm was commissioned to attract foreign investment into the island. The resulting industries, chiefly producing concrete, flour and furniture, were for import substitution as well as export.

Internal disparities

Indices of national economic performance are one thing, how they affect the society is quite another. Economic growth has not been indicative of the increased equalization of standards of living. On the contrary, the pattern of sectoral growth which has occurred invariably led to the widening of the gaps within the society. These gaps have been due partly to changes in ownership patterns and increasing capital-intensive, rather than labour-intensive activity, and also to the disruption of traditional production without adequate employment alternatives. The impact of economic growth has varied considerably with the pre-existing socio-economic characteristics and their compatibility with the new structures. Jamaica, Barbados and St Vincent demonstrated the nature of some of these variations.

One indicator of the social distribution of resources is given by the average incomes at different levels on the range of employment. The greater equalization of incomes in the Barbadian case contrasts with the poorer record of Jamaica. Because of the paucity of reliable data for income per capita, indices of poverty based on health and welfare are more useful for comparing material levels between and within islands. In this respect, St Vincent is one of the Caribbean islands with a large proportion of the population most acutely affected. Though varying in degree, the indices of poverty in Jamaica, Barbados and St Vincent reflect highly skewed distributions of income by social class.

In addition to inequalities in income based on socio-economic status there were additional disparities based on gender. Inflated prices were accompanied by the expectation of higher wages, similar to those offered in the new industries. This soon formed the basis of a legally enforced minimum wage, which had the effect of substantially reducing the opportunities for domestic work in private households. Meanwhile the decline in agriculture further reduced the involvement of women in the work force. These two main areas of low-paid female employment were significantly reduced, especially in Jamaica and Barbados, but the new industries did not provide a substitute. An increasing proportion of women have taken up some form of work in the informal sector, especially in Jamaica. In addition to higglering, women have worked either on a full-time or part-time, casual basis in making items or preparing food for sale. Although there have been few informal activities from which high incomes could be earned, on average, earnings have been lower in the informal than in the formal sector and there has been no security or financial compensation during times of illness or other interruptions to work.

Analyses of income have usually overlooked the additional factor that inequalities in the distribution of income have been not only social but also spatial. To some extent these disparities have been determined by the extent of urbanization, or the accessibility to industrial employment. Further spatial disparities have occurred in association with enclave industries such as bauxite and luxury tourism. The impact of these industries has been in part the consequence of the extent of disruption to traditional production against the adequacy of new compensatory developments as replacement activities. It has also been due to the higher average levels of skills which are required in capital intensive activities, other than traditional plantation agriculture. The fact that they are spatially fixed by the location of the relevant natural resources creates the close juxtaposition of industrial and agricultural wage levels, thus the spatial disequilibrium with which enclave industries tend to be associated.

Barbados was one of those small states already dominated by commercial agriculture in the form of the plantation and with no significant food producing or subsistence sector. Imports, including food, were traditionally high. Barbados was able to take advantage of the investment in two modern industries, tourism and manufacturing, and the recent off-shore financial sector with minimum disruption since, structurally, they were little different from the traditional plantation. Both traditional plantation and modern industrial sectors necessitated high levels of imports, a total orientation towards export markets, and a proletarianized work force. Further, there was no need, given the high degree of accessibility in Barbados, for any massive migration to the capital as occurred in Jamaica. Paradoxically, decline in the size of the labour force willing to cut cane in the sugar industry was compensated for by the impact of seasonal labour from St Vincent.

The situation was different in Jamaica, and different again in St Vincent. In Jamaica, spatial discrepancies in wage levels were intensified by the development of modern industries in or near Kingston and tourism in the vicinity of Montego Bay and Ocho Rios. Migration to these urban centres, especially Kingston, rose dramatically during the 1960s, and so did levels of poor housing, unemployment, social stress and crime. In the bauxite areas, the mood of euphoria which accompanied the initial period of construction of plant and harbour installations, in which large numbers of local casual labourers were employed, later gave way to disappointment and frustration. Once the companies were ready to commence production, the demand was for skilled technical workers who moved, with their families, into the bauxite areas from the cities. Others commuted on a daily or weekly basis.

Land formerly used to grow food for the domestic market as well as for subsistence was taken out of production through the sale to the bauxite companies of large properties as well as small-holdings. Tourism provided an alternative rather than a complementary sector to agriculture. Even worse, attitudes became more negative towards small-farming as the young people of the 1950s and 1960s put their sights on industry and modern economic activity, turning away from traditional agriculture. Besides, this coincided with the period of unconditional entry to Britain, and Jamaica witnessed massive out-migration from rural and urban areas alike.

It may seem paradoxical that the volume of migrants from Jamaica increased during the decade of improved levels of economic growth. The high migration rate from bauxite areas, as from other areas, at the time of maximum local prosperity, serves to underline firstly, that the objective aspects of the environment did not necessarily alter previous images of migration. Secondly, sectoral, and especially enclave growth, was associated with increased income disparities, not greater equalization. Thirdly, capital in the hands of people who already had a high propensity to migrate simply provided a greater opportunity for migration, not an alternative to it.

In St Vincent, the long-standing spatial disparities in income between south and north of the island were reinforced by the developments in tourism and manufacturing since the late-1970s. It was not so much that the south had become particularly prosperous as the fact that the north had stood still. Wage labour in plantation agriculture, in many cases only seasonally, still characterized the occupational structure of the north.

Neither from tourism nor from manufacturing was government revenue high enough to equalize the opportunities throughout the island. Like all economic ventures based on foreign investment attracted by tax-free concessions on imports, guarantees of low wages, and the facility to repatriate profits, the real impact upon the national economy was minimal. The lack of integration of tourism into the rest of the economy, especially the agricultural sector, together with the seasonal nature of the industry's labour requirements, have reduced the benefits accruing to the society. Besides, alienation of land in the case of St Vincent amounted to entire Grenadine islands. Meanwhile, tourism has had the effect of raising expectations with only limited direct benefits to the people themselves. Tourism in St Vincent, as elsewhere in the Caribbean, has made a decided impact on people's images of foreign countries especially the United States and Canada and heightened the dependency mentality in a number of direct and indirect ways.

In summary, it would appear that at the local level enclave industries have had a distorting effect upon the economy. Tourism, bauxite and manufacturing have, in various ways, exacerbated the problems in agriculture, increased wage discrepancies and inflated prices generally because of the pockets of prosperity associated with them. In addition to those persons directly employed by the particular industry, others, especially in business, have benefited indirectly. But the majority have had to bear the burden of inflated prices for basic goods with few, if any, other benefits. At the national level, as distinct from the immediate sites of these developments, the pattern of industrial growth has increased foreign exchange revenue and provided additional formal employment opportunities. On the other side of the balance has been the less easily measured impact of increasing the structural dependence of the economy as well as the increased psychological dependency fostered by foreign-oriented, capital intensive, or luxury industries. These attitudes have been consistent with a high positive image of the metropolitan countries and of migration as the means of achieving the benefits of those countries.

Economic performance in the Caribbean has been profoundly influenced by external factors, especially financial and commodity markets, international prices and technological developments. In that all Caribbean countries have been potentially in the same position *vis-à-vis* international trends, it has been evident from the wide variability in economic success that internal conditions have also been critical. Differences in economic performance have been to some extent determined by the location, size and natural resources of each country but, as the Caribbean situation has demonstrated, performance has been heavily dependent on other circumstances as well. These include the particular nature and combination of resources, the historical pattern of their exploitation and the balance between production for export and for home consumption. Performance has been further influenced by political systems and social structures and their implications for stability, confidence, societal order and organization, and the existence of an appropriate labour force.

Social structure

Given that the plantation was responsible for the social structure of the modern Caribbean in the first place, race was closely aligned to distinctions of economic wealth, political power and social status. The pervasiveness of the association between race and class has varied with the persistence of the plantation structure in different parts of the Caribbean. Thus Barbados, with its continued plantation presence has been associated with its somewhat anachronistic pattern of racial stratification, with the persistence of a small indigenous land-owning white elite. In the class hierarchy, this group has been of comparable status to the light-skinned (though coloured) elite of the commercial and financial sectors. However, to a varying extent throughout the Caribbean the white, brown, black hierarchical association with upper, middle and lower class has been greatly modified (Smith, 1984).

Racial minorities were outside the original race-related Creole class structure. In Barbados, the only significant minority was comprised of the poor whites or 'Redlegs' who had arrived in Barbados from Scotland prior to the development of sugar. Most Redlegs became assimilated into the urban middle-class society in the twentieth century or emigrated (principally to Canada). By the 1970s only a few remained in Barbados as part of the rural agricultural working class, chiefly residing in the eastern parishes of the island.

In both Jamaica and St Vincent the more typical association of ethnic minorities and post-Emancipation labour supplies for the sugar estates occurred. In the case of St Vincent the most significant ethnic minority was Portuguese, the descendants of indentured estate labourers from Madeira and the Azores, who were imported into St Vincent in the nineteenth century. In Jamaica the situation was more complex, with Indians and Chinese who came as indentured labourers, while Sephardic Jews and later, Lebanese, arrived as free traders.

Social stratification

Transformation in the social structure of Jamaica, Barbados and St Vincent, as in all Caribbean countries, has been strongly influenced by economic change. The original association of race and class which evolved as integral to the expansion of sugar production was greatly modified with the subsequent decline of sugar. In particular, the symbols of class status and the pattern of stratification became more intricate as the economy became more varied and complex. Nevertheless, despite significant change, there have been important continuities from the earlier patterns.

The recurrence of ascription 'from below' led to the merging not only of racial characteristics but also of cultural values and social institutions. Thus the increasing heterogeneity of class was accompanied by a blurring, if not an actual lessening of the distinctions of race. For all this class mobility and the broadening of the parameters of racial and cultural status with which class was associated, the middle-class lifestyles to which the upwardly mobile aspired were not accompanied by a commensurate increase in real income. This was highly significant in terms of the evolving class relations, for rising expectations could not be sustained by the less rapidly expanding economic base. Certainly, the disparity between those who were employed in the new industries and those who were not, increased considerably.

As already indicated, the capital-intensive nature of the new industries brought about a relative decline in the number of available jobs and the numbers entering the formal, non-unionized, lower income sector increased. With the exception of those who prospered from illegal activities, as in the sale of marijuana (ganja), which brought about its own tensions, rising expectations based on the signs of modern industrialization, accompanied by widening income gaps led, not surprisingly, to a greater sense of frustration and deprivation in the societies.

The dynamics of social relations in Jamaica, Barbados and St Vincent also had to absorb the tensions developing as a consequence of the changing social stratification associated with both economic and political change. Distinctions of colour were diminishing in their former clear alignment with status, and not only were elite groups no longer exclusively white but neither were they necessarily expatriate. The blame for local discontent began to include the internal elite groups and not solely or even primarily external colonial powers or multinational corporations. This has had a profound effect on the nature of class relations within Jamaica, Barbados and St Vincent in their post-independence period.

The spatial distribution of social class

The establishment of free settlements based on subsistence agriculture by colonization of the interior upland occurred in Jamaica and St Vincent soon after the emancipation of slaves. (The extent to which these ex-slave populations were reconstituted peasantries is discussed in Mintz (1974).) Former slaves moved to the back-lands which they had already cultivated during slavery and also to the marginal lands which became unprofitable and were abandoned by the estates. A third zone of colonization was comprised of the high and in many cases steep, wooded Crown lands of the interior. The Barbadian ex-slaves who remained in the island had few opportunities to go far from the plantations and settled along the roads and the coast, except those who moved to Bridgetown.

The emergent settlement pattern of highly dispersed mountain and upland villages in Jamaica and St Vincent contrasted with the linear pattern of settlement along the perimeters of the sugar estate lands in the case of Barbados. In Jamaica some settlements occurred in the marginal plantation areas as well. In all three islands settlement clusters and linear formations have been associated with the main lines of communication.

Besides the rural economies, there were also urban economies which developed from the seventeenth century around the centres of colonial administration, port facilities and commerce. Other, usually smaller, less prestigious towns grew up after Emancipation as market centres for peasant production. The towns have remained the chief places of residence of the commercial, administrative and professional groups – the core of the middle classes, while the rural areas have remained characteristically the location of the lower-class plantation wage earners and peasantry.

The spatial distribution of the social classes in Jamaica, Barbados and St Vincent has remained closely linked in each case to the island's economic structure. Whereas the former landed upper class was rural based, the pattern changed with the emergence of the new industrial and commercial upper class, which became almost entirely urban. The greatest concentrations of both the upper and the upper-middle classes occurred in the suburban areas of the capitals. Also located in the major towns were the urban wage labourers, the petty capitalists, self-employed and service workers of all types, as well as the scufflers and the unemployed.

In St Vincent and even in Barbados, the middle classes were virtually all based in the suburban extensions of Kingstown and Bridgetown. Rural centres were almost entirely inhabited by small entrepreneurs running the local commerce, together with the range of low-paid service workers, small farmers, rural wage labourers and unemployed.

In Jamaica there was greater social diversification in rural centres and, depending on the particular location, all or most of the components of the entire social hierarchy could be present. For example, in rural areas which were centres of the bauxite or tourist industries, the population included members of the upper class and representatives of virtually every other stratum down to the casual labourer and shopkeeper, the urban wage labourers, and the urban unemployed. The peripheral districts of these urbanized centres were inhabited by small land-holders, agricultural labourers, landless and unemployed agricultural workers.

In rural areas with an urban market town as its nucleus, the top of the hierarchy was missing or numbers in this group were so few and dispersed that they were hardly apparent. They met socially with people of their own class, sometimes in other parishes. This left at the top of the small town social hierarchy, the upper-middle class comprised of local professionals – lawyers, doctors, dentists and secondary school teachers, along with the most prosperous of the business community. Racially, this population was comprised of black and brown people, with an increasing tendency to be predominated by black. The lower-middle class in the small towns was comprised of the less prosperous business persons and those who had achieved wealth recently through ganja thus, despite auspicious evidence of wealth, they have not yet been accepted as being upper-middle class (though their children, with the benefit of secondary school education, will no doubt be so later on).

In rural districts, whether in Jamaica, Barbados or St Vincent, the population was almost entirely comprised of a rural lower class which had evolved from the original population of agricultural workers and semi-subsistence farmers, usually referred to in the Caribbean context as the peasantry. This was comprised of small farmers, agricultural wage labourers and the unemployed as well as tradespersons, chiefly carpenters, masons and plumbers, tailors and dressmakers and barbers and hairdressers, who combined this occupation with own-account or paid agricultural work.

Welfare

Education and health care in the Caribbean reflected both social and spatial variations in the accessibility of welfare provisions. While overall economic levels helped to explain the quantity and quality of welfare services in different countries of the region, there were a number of anomalies. For example, Jamaica with the second highest per capita income of the CARIFTA states, experienced some of the greatest inequalities in access to adequate education and health facilities.

The point was graphically made by the World Bank report of 1978, which showed that in educational attainment measured as a percentage of the total male working population not having passed any public school-leaving examination, Jamaica scored worst with 90.5 per cent, St Vincent, 89.4 per cent; and Barbados, in a much better position, recorded 83.0 per cent (Chernick, 1978: 269-71). For a similar period in the early-1970s child mortality rates in Jamaica were 45 per 10,000, whereas the figure for Barbados was 22 while the average for the CARIFTA states was calculated at 27.9 per cent. The rate for St Vincent's child mortality was not available, although in other aspects of health care it came lowest of the three countries (Chernick, 1978: 269-70).

Education

The reputation of elitism in the Caribbean education system was true of the secondary schools of colonial tradition. To such schools, of which there are now relatively few, only a small minority of the total population had access. In both content and method, the education traditionally provided by them prepared its pupils for elitist occupations and aspirations, metropolitan lifestyles and values (Baksh, 1984; Cross and Schwarzbaum, 1969). This form of education steered those who received it towards an easy, almost natural transition to further education and careers in the metropolitan countries (Tidrick, K., 1971).

The pre-independence period in Caribbean countries was characterized by only upper and upper-middle class access to this type of education. Its exclusivity was maintained by a process of social selectivity together with the payment of fees which were outside the range of the majority. Only gradually did these schools begin to take a small number of non-fee paying children, who gained access through government scholarships.

Ironically, it was in the post-colonial era in Caribbean countries that the elitist type of educational curriculum became more widespread with the new educational policies for increased access to secondary schools. This increased the opportunities but it also raised the aspirations relating to education and the high status occupations which it was seen to afford. To add to the supply of secondary school opportunities, the traditional schools were made accessible through a major increase in the number of free places to be won by examination at age eleven. In Jamaica and Barbados capacity was further expanded through the construction of new secondary schools.

In Barbados and Jamaica, the rising expectations of obtaining a secondary education, in excess of the increased number of places, led to the growth of a range of privately run institutions. These schools attracted those who, though failing the government free place examination, could afford the relatively low fees demanded. Those who failed to reach the standard either to pass or even to sit the secondary school free place examination and who could not afford the relatively low fees of the independent schools, have felt an even greater sense of deprivation.

In the newer secondary schools, teacher qualifications were generally inadequate, resources limited and rates of success in achieving traditional standards extremely low. The Jamaican 1978 Five Year Plan for Education identified the main problems of the system as a significant shortage of school places at both the primary and secondary levels, a shortage of trained teachers and the need for improvement in the quality of programmes being offered. The aim was to provide 12,000 additional primary places and 43,000 additional secondary places (National Planning Agency, Economic and Social Survey, Jamaica, 1978: 19.1). This came after a decade of major increases in school places.

The aspirations raised by the post-war and post-independence developments in the educational systems have left a large proportion of the populations, especially in Barbados and Jamaica where most developments have taken place, of the opinion that educational opportunities and their occupational advantages were much more accessible than they were in reality. For a large proportion of the population, the only provisions available were government primary or 'all age' schools. The removal of the more gifted or motivated students to the secondary schools from the traditional elementary schools, as they were formerly termed, left the primary schools attaining much lower standards, even though numerically the provisions increased dramatically in the post-independence period.

The educational system has contributed to the potential for migration as well as facilitating actual moves in a number of ways. The traditional education of the upper and middle classes has encouraged the movement to metropolitan centres in order to achieve at levels to which aspirations have been raised. The system in the Caribbean – both educational and cultural – has provided the foundation for an easy transition to those centres. For those who aspired to high status occupations but who could not achieve them because of the low level of their educational opportunities, migration has provided the substitute for scholastic achievements and the means to improve their status and life chances through this alternative avenue.

Health care

A high level of health care was available to those who could afford it, and in the case of St Vincent, specialized treatment was obtained by going to an island with a larger, better equipped hospital than could be maintained locally. In any case, such levels of medical facilities were available only to the upper and upper-middle classes who took out private insurance to cover treatment. For the majority of the population, specialized medicine was available in the government hospitals. Difficulties arose because such provisions fell far short of the demand in every respect and, as a result, access of people in the lower classes to such treatment was highly problematic and primarily determined by their residential location. Remote rural areas were particularly poorly served.

Inequalities also characterized the primary sector of health care services. A national health service in all three islands made basic provisions, but these were not adequately financed in relation to the demand. In Barbados the number of persons per doctor was 1,167 in 1982; in Jamaica the figure was 2,800 in 1979, increasing to 5,876 in 1984 (Europa Yearbook, 1987). This indicated for Jamaica not just the increase in total population, but the loss of medical personnel from the labour force, chiefly through migration. Private medical facilities were utilized even by the relatively poor to fulfil their perceived need. The pattern of health care undoubtedly reflected the more general social and spatial inequalities within each island, as well as the differential in levels of development between the more buoyant economies of Jamaica and Barbados in contrast to the relatively poorer economy of St Vincent.

Despite the deficiencies in the provision of medical services, all three societies have enjoyed improved standards of public health. The associated improvements in nutrition, hygiene and health education have also contributed to a reduction in malnutrition, infant mortality and parasitical diseases. These have had significant implications for the overall demographic structure of the islands' populations, particularly through the decline in fertility and mortality which have ensued.

Demographic characteristics

Population trends

The low inter-censal population growth rates throughout the twentieth century in Jamaica, Barbados and St Vincent reflected not only the reduction in fertility rates since 1946, but also the fact that the decline in mortality rates was offset consistently by high net migration (Table 2.3). The reduction in mortality meant that by 1970 life expectancy at birth was 70.9 for Barbados, 70 for Jamaica and 63.2 for St Vincent (Chernick, 1978: 240). The life expectancy figures for Barbados and Jamaica were comparable with the average of 71 years for the developed countries.

Taking each age group as a proportion of the total, the impact of low fertility upon the under-15 age group has been offset by the out-migration of the middle groups. In Jamaica and St Vincent some 50 per cent of the total populations were under 15 in 1982, while in Barbados it was approximately 40 per cent. The reduced mortality rates had the effect of increasing the 55 and over age group, which was further exaggerated as a percentage of the total population because of the reduced size of the younger adult groups through migration plus some return of the older migrants from abroad.

This pattern of population growth resulted in very large dependency ratios. They were particularly high in St Vincent where the figure was 127 by 1970. In Jamaica, the dependency ratio was 107 by 1970 and, though relatively lower in Barbados, even then it was 84. These figures reflected the general trends in the region as shown by the mean of 103 for all CARICOM countries (Table 2.4).

Table 2.3 Inter-censal population growth rates

	(Per cent per annum)				
	1911-21	1921-46	1946-60	1960-70	1970-80
Jamaica	+0.3	+1.6	+1.6	+1.4	+1.40
Barbados	−0.9	+0.8	+1.3	+0.2	+0.42
St Vincent	+0.9	+1.0	+1.7	+1.5	+1.19
CARICOM (Mean)	+0.2	+1.3	+2.2	+1.4	+1.23

Sources: 1970 Population Census of Jamaica, Barbados and St Vincent; 1980-1981 Population Census of the Commonwealth Caribbean; 1982 Population Census of Jamaica.

Table 2.4 Population dependency ratios

	Proportion under age 15	Proportion over age 64	Dependency ratio (per 100)
Jamaica			
1960	41.2	4.3	83
1970	46.1	5.5	107
1985	31.35	5.2	74
Barbados			
1960	38.3	6.4	81
1970	37.1	8.3	83
1980	29.5	10.4	66
St Vincent			
1960	49.2	4.2	115
1970	51.2	4.8	127
1980	n.a.	n.a.	n.a.
CARICOM (Mean)			
1960	44.3	3.5	92
1970	46.4	4.4	103

(n.a. = not available)
Sources: 1960, 1970, Population Census of Jamaica and Barbados; 1980 Population Census of Barbados; Economic and Social Survey of Jamaica 1986.

The high proportion of dependants in the population of Jamaica, Barbados and St Vincent has had serious consequences for the economically productive age groups (those between 15 and 64). With at best only the most rudimentary of social security systems in any of these countries, the burden of high dependency ratios was most acutely felt at the household level. Household strategies for coping economically, let alone for improving circumstances or achieving any measure of upward mobility for its members, have had to adapt to the pressures and operate within the constraints resulting from the household's demographic characteristics. Migration has been a major component of these strategies. At the national level the islands' demographic structures have affected not only the demands placed upon social services, especially medical services and education, but also they have determined the size (and to some extent the composition) of the labour force with its associated implications for employment.

Labour force and employment

The direct and indirect impact of low natural increase of the population coupled with high rates of migration occurred alongside reduced participation rates in the labour force of Caribbean countries since the 1960s. Jamaica was particularly affected in this way, with a decline in both male and female participation.

The recorded unemployment rates in 1970 were 18 per cent for Jamaica and 9 per cent each for Barbados and St Vincent. By 1986 there had been a significant increase in each case. Rates were estimated at 17.7 per cent for Barbados, 22.3 per cent for Jamaica and 30 per cent for St Vincent. These rates masked the additional factor of underemployment. Of those employed, only 58 per cent were in full-time work in St Vincent. The figure for Jamaica was 66 per cent and Barbados had a better record at 75 per cent of those employed being in full-time work (Chernick, 1978).

Undoubtedly, some of the recorded unemployment and underemployment could be accounted for by the number of women engaged in 'home duties', and also by the involvement of a large proportion of the labour force, especially women, in the informal commercial sector, most particularly in Jamaica.

Local labour markets in Jamaica, Barbados and St Vincent have been closely allied to the structural constraints of their economies. The high proportion of workers employed in primary economic activities and services and the low proportion in manufacturing, commerce and public utilities, has reflected the traditional structure of underdeveloped economies. In this respect St Vincent has been in a particularly disadvantageous situation, though relative to population size the situation has been similar for Jamaica and Barbados as well.

The problem of obtaining full-time employment has arisen chiefly in the lower levels of skill, but also among the professional and highly skilled groups there have been limitations to pursuing careers in specialized areas. Furthermore, because the education systems have encouraged participation of the successful in the wider regional and international labour markets, there has been an even greater potential for migration among the educated and highly skilled sectors of the population and thus a loss to the national labour force (Harewood, 1983; Palmer, 1983; Thomas-Hope, 1983).

Scarcity of skilled workers has combined with a surplus of unskilled. Despite relatively low wages for unskilled labour, the costs of capital have been lower than that of labour in the formal sector and especially in the enclave industries. Income differentials have been wide between employment in the formal and informal sectors and particularly wide between the enclave industries and other activities. There have been no reliable data on income levels but some evidence has suggested discrepancies of some three to five times the earnings of semi-skilled and unskilled workers in bauxite and luxury tourism as in similar work in other sectors (Chernick, 1978: 86). This was partly explained by the fact that the bauxite industry has been capital intensive, thus employing a disproportionate amount of highly skilled labour. In addition, the wage scales have been higher. Since local labour has been employed in very small numbers, the situation of wage discrepancies in the locality of bauxite and tourism has been exacerbated even further.

Migration

Workers from Jamaica, Barbados and St Vincent have participated actively in international labour markets, both within the circum-Caribbean region and outside it. The precise pattern of the migrations and migration fields has varied between islands over time. In the late-nineteenth and early-twentieth centuries, Jamaicans and Barbadians were heavily represented in the labour force of the American Fruit Company operations and railway construction in Central America, the cutting of the Panama Canal and in the United States' sugar plantations in Cuba in the 1910s to 1930s. Movements from St Vincent in the early decades of the twentieth century were chiefly to the oil companies active in the Netherlands Antilles of Aruba and Curaçao.

Since World War II, short-term labour migrations have again shown a more localized pattern for Vincentians and a more long-distance movement for the Jamaicans and Barbadians. There has been a regular seasonal migration from St Vincent to Barbados to cut cane whereas Jamaicans and Barbadians have been involved in cane cutting and other fruit harvesting operations farther afield, in Florida and the mid-Western states of the United States as well as in Canada (Marshall, 1984; McCoy and Wood, 1982; Thomas-Hope, 1985).

People from all three islands have participated actively in the movements to Britain (1952-62) and North America (from 1965). Even relatively small numbers of migrants to those countries have represented a significant proportion of the island populations. Between 1956 and 1960 the migration to Britain accounted for 11.2 per cent of the Jamaican population, 9.1 per cent of the Barbadian population and 13.3 per cent of the Vincentian population (UK, The Home Office, cited in Peach, 1968).

In detail, migration flows have been difficult to monitor. The official migration data consistently have missed an unknown percentage accounted for by leakages which have occurred through those who leave on temporary visas. This has included some who initially travelled from Jamaica, Barbados and St Vincent on visitor or student visas and later obtained longer-term permits to stay at their destination. For example, the number of Jamaicans obtaining immigrant status in the United Kingdom in 1989 was 520 whereas the number who entered the United Kingdom in that year was 32,200 (UK, Home Office data). The number of Barbadians obtaining immigrant status in 1989 was 40, while the number entering the country was 9,510. Vincentians were not recorded separately in the United Kingdom immigration statistics and were included in figures for the West Indies Associated States until this Association ceased to exist in 1983.

While accurate figures for migration cannot be deduced from the official figures, taking either immigrant status or entry figures as an indication of comparative flows, it is clear that the dominance of the United Kingdom as the destination of Jamaicans, Barbadians and Vincentians (as was the case for all citizens from the former British West Indies) in the late-1950s and early-1960s was replaced by the United States since the mid-1960s. For example, through the 1970s the number of Jamaican immigrants admitted to the United States was lowest at 9,026 in 1976 and highest at 19,265 in 1978. In the 1980s numbers peaked to 23,569 in 1981 and were maintained at an annual rate of between 16,000 and 20,000 for the rest of the decade (Jamaica, *Economic and Social Survey*, 1978, 1986, 1990). This level of entry has continued into the 1990s.

The importance of Canada as a destination of persons from Jamaica, Barbados and St Vincent surpassed the United Kingdom by the late-1960s and Canada has remained the second most important destination since that time. Landed immigrants in Canada from Jamaica ranged from 3,000 to 11,000 per annum through the 1970s and from 3,000 to 5,500 through the 1980s. Landed immigrants in Canada from Barbados numbered approximately 300 per annum in the 1980s; those from St Vincent, at about 200 per annum (Canadian Government employment and immigration statistics, personal communication).

Numbers of persons obtaining Landed Immigrant status at any migration destination do not reflect those short-stay migrants who circulate between the home country and the overseas country without the necessity of obtaining a permanent migrant visa. In addition, return migration figures have been subsumed in the official net migration data. It is impossible from these figures to deduce whether a reduction in numbers has been due to a decline in outward movement or an increase in return flows.

The shift in the destination of people from the Caribbean was accompanied by significant changes in the selectivity of migrants by occupation. The open entry policy of the United Kingdom in the 1950s and up to the passing of the Commonwealth Immigrants Act of 1962, permitted the entry of large numbers of both skilled and unskilled workers. By contrast, the movement since the 1960s to the United States and Canada has been characterized by a predominance of professional, administrative, managerial and other white collar workers. In 1977, 21 per cent of the Jamaican migrants to the United States fell into these categories and of the further 55 per cent which was classified as dependants having no stated occupations, many were the family members of those white collar workers. The implications of the loss of highly trained personnel from the labour force of the islands have been considerable.

Migrant flows have also been dominated by people in the young adult groups, thus the movements have made an important contribution to demographic trends in Jamaica, Barbados and St Vincent, as they have throughout the Caribbean. Migration has not only reduced the effect of declining fertility rates but also, as indicated above, it has contributed to that reduced rate through the decrease in the proportion of the population of reproductive age. Migration has thus influenced the demographic structure of the islands.

Return migration has been less generally recognized for its impact on the demographic pattern. In the 1930s and 1940s the return of people who had migrated in the preceding two to three decades was significant. Likewise, the return of people who went to the United Kingdom in the 1950s and 1960s continued throughout the 1980s and can be expected to continue in the 1990s. Most of these returning long-stay migrants will not enter the labour force on their return, for they will have reached the age of retirement. Those long-stay migrants who return to work will be joined by larger numbers of short-stay migrants from destinations in the United States, Canada and even other Caribbean countries, who have re-entered the labour force each year.

Conclusion

Economic developments, and the part Jamaica, Barbados and St Vincent have played in the global economy, have been basic to their underdevelopment. Furthermore, despite the variation, all three islands are characterized by small size, the associated limitations in physical and human resources and the inevitable dependence on extra-regional markets and suppliers. The continued structural dependence of their economies upon the outside world is matched by the extent of psychological dependence of their societies. The resulting external, and invariably metropolitan orientation, constitutes a major factor in helping to perpetuate a migration mentality which has become deeply rooted in the social institutions and culture. Yet within this context of shared structures there is considerable diversity both within and between Caribbean countries, as exemplified by Barbados, Jamaica and St Vincent. This diversity at the micro level must be taken into account in attempting to understand the nature of the localities which reflect the way people express their culture, make decisions and live out their lives.

Notes

1 Alumina is one intermediary stage in the refinement of aluminium from bauxite ore. Future references will refer simply to the bauxite industry.

CHAPTER 3
The micro-environments of migration

Size, location, physical structure and related socio-economic developments combine to produce the distinctiveness of each Caribbean country and, within each, the intricate variability at the micro scale. The legacy of a plantation history and the nature of the plantation-peasant dichotomy formed the basis of each island landscape.

In Barbados virtually all lands provided prime environments for sugar, leaving none of the island outside its scope. The physical landscape favoured no free settlements after Emancipation; there were no mountains to which ex-slaves could retreat. Everywhere the flat sugar lands dominated the landscape. The economic monopoly of sugar was directly reflected in the social pattern, the settlement pattern, and the characteristic chattel house, a house without permanent foundations which just rested on land owned by the plantation. The chattel houses reflected the extent to which people were alienated from the land.

Jamaica was well endowed with land suitable for sugar production, while still leaving relatively large tracts of high plateau or mountainous interior. There, free villages were established by ex-slaves in the mid-nineteenth century, thus forming the first generation of the re-constituted or proto-peasantry.

By contrast, St Vincent, with a less appropriate environment for sugar, was always economically marginal in colonial terms. The spatially meaningful distinctions, therefore, have been determined not by the distinctiveness of mountain and plain landscapes, but by the separation of the Leeward and Windward sides of the island and, even more, by the separation and separateness of the northern volcanic region. The physical inaccessibility of the north has been reinforced by its perceived remoteness on account of the threat of volcanic eruption, and socially on account of the resulting isolation and pervasive poverty. Not only was wage labour traditionally based solely on coconut plantations, but peasant livelihood was poor in the extreme. A living has had to be eked from a wind-swept coast or else from steep slopes, denuded land and soils perpetually overlain by new layers of volcanic ash in an area under the ever-present threat of eruption.

Superimposed upon the earlier structures are the effects of urban growth with manufacturing, tourism and, in Jamaica, bauxite. These developments have fundamentally altered the material landscape of those areas affected by them. The modern industries have also had a major impact upon the socio-cultural systems associated with them through the effects upon infrastructure and accessibility to the outside world. But they have had an inflationary effect upon land and services as well as upon the expectations and aspirations of the local people.

The configuration of settlements and the districts of which they are comprised, reflect variations in the work and lifestyle as well as the opportunities and constraints of communities associated with the plantation, peasant or urban circumstances, or those of the newer extractive and tourist industries. The spatial variation in class, with the high concentration of the middle class in urban centres, has also made its impact upon the material and cultural landscapes. The most cogent material expression of this social history is the pattern of settlement and the nature of house and yard.

While districts have been a material expression of the socio-economic environment, house and yard units have been tangible symbols of the cultural landscape comprised of institutions, values and status symbols. For the yard, as 'a geo-social entity of special significance' according to Brodber (1975: 1), has been a delineation not only of territory, but also of the community which inhabited the district and which provided mutual support, protection and practical assistance.

Furthermore, differences in the nature and use of household space were associated with a distinct class-related pattern of behaviour. Yards with open spaces for most domestic activity and social interaction contrasted with the enclosed units of those households whose domestic and social activities were all carried out indoors. Not only have the characteristics of social and economic behaviour typically differed between classes but, as Austin (1984: 41) pointed out, 'the mode in which they are realized – through a public street and yard life – were peculiar to the working class'. The containment of household activities within the house were characteristic of the upper and middle classes. As households become upwardly mobile, so more activities occur 'inside' rather than 'outside', and the enclosed structure is enlarged to accommodate this change.

The pattern of social and economic developments is reflected in the cultural landscape which has evolved, as well as the meaning, symbolism and associations conveyed by each type of place. Each has brought its own particular opportunities and psychological orientations fixed upon new expectations and goals. For this reason, explanation of migration behaviour must be sought with reference to the socio-economic and cultural experience of people from the range of micro-environments which signify different types of places or localities and societal situations. This is done here in the case of Jamaica, Barbados and St Vincent respectively.

Representation of localities

To ensure a balanced perspective, the experiences of people from the range of localities within Jamaica, Barbados and St Vincent were examined with respect to individual and household migration behaviour. The varying environmental situations existing in the three islands meant that different criteria had to be used in establishing a stratification meaningful for each island. (The stratification is outlined in the Appendix, p.168).

In the case of Jamaica, five broad strata were identified: the Kingston Metropolitan Area (KMA); an urban zone (excluding the KMA); a plantation zone; a bauxite zone; a mixed farming zone (Figure 3.1a). Because of the urban concentration of centres of tourism, they were not treated separately. In Barbados, three broad zones were identified: Bridgetown, the area of tourism development and the sugar plantation zone (Figure 3.1b). In St Vincent, location, rather than economic and livelihood criteria, provided the basis for regional differentiation and three strata were identified: Kingstown, the South (excluding Kingstown) and the North (Figure 3.1c). Two localities were selected to represent each area (Figures 3.2a, b, c).

JAMAICA
Some of the fundamental contrasts in the **Kingston Metropolitan Area** were represented by Harbour View, a middle-class suburb and Grant's Pen, a low-income district.

Harbour View, as a residential area, only dated back to the 1950s. It was the second of the private, middle-income, housing developments to be established in Jamaica, located, as its name suggests, overlooking Kingston harbour and east of the city itself. Though each bungalow in the development was very small, nevertheless, they had all the ingredients of middle-class residence. In most cases, each dwelling housed a single family unit whose domestic and social activities were contained within the dwelling. Children went to the nearby primary school or to private preparatory schools, then to secondary school in the city with some proceeding to college or university; most residents were white-collar workers and their lifestyle, attitudes and expectations were characteristically middle class.

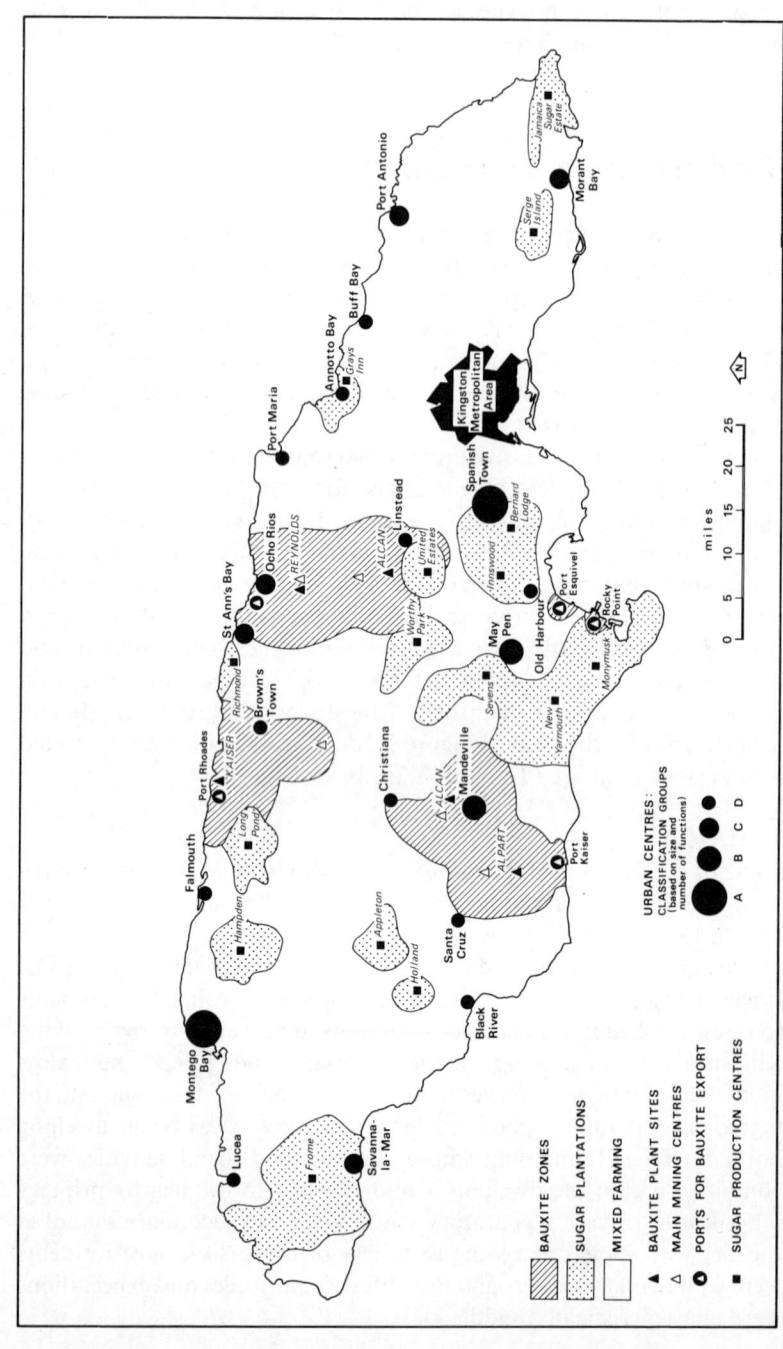

Figure 3.1a Jamaica: Stratification of socio-economic zones

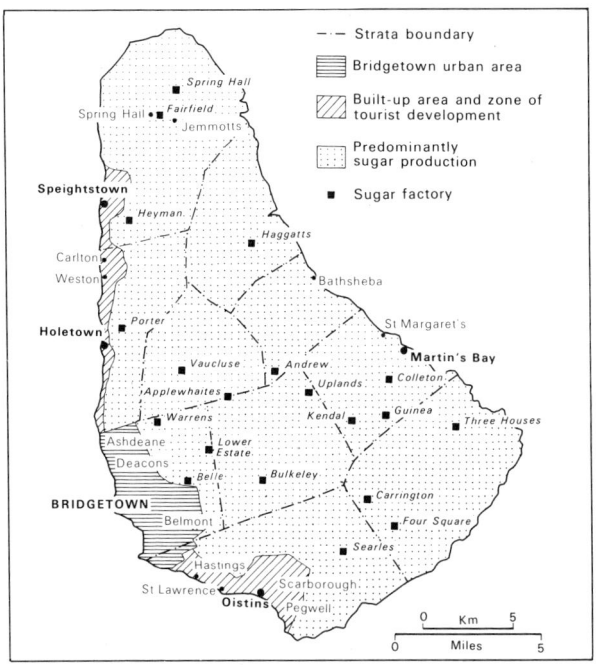

Figure 3.1b Barbados: Stratification of socio-economic zones

Figure 3.1c St Vincent: Stratification of socio-economic zones

68 Explanation in Caribbean migration

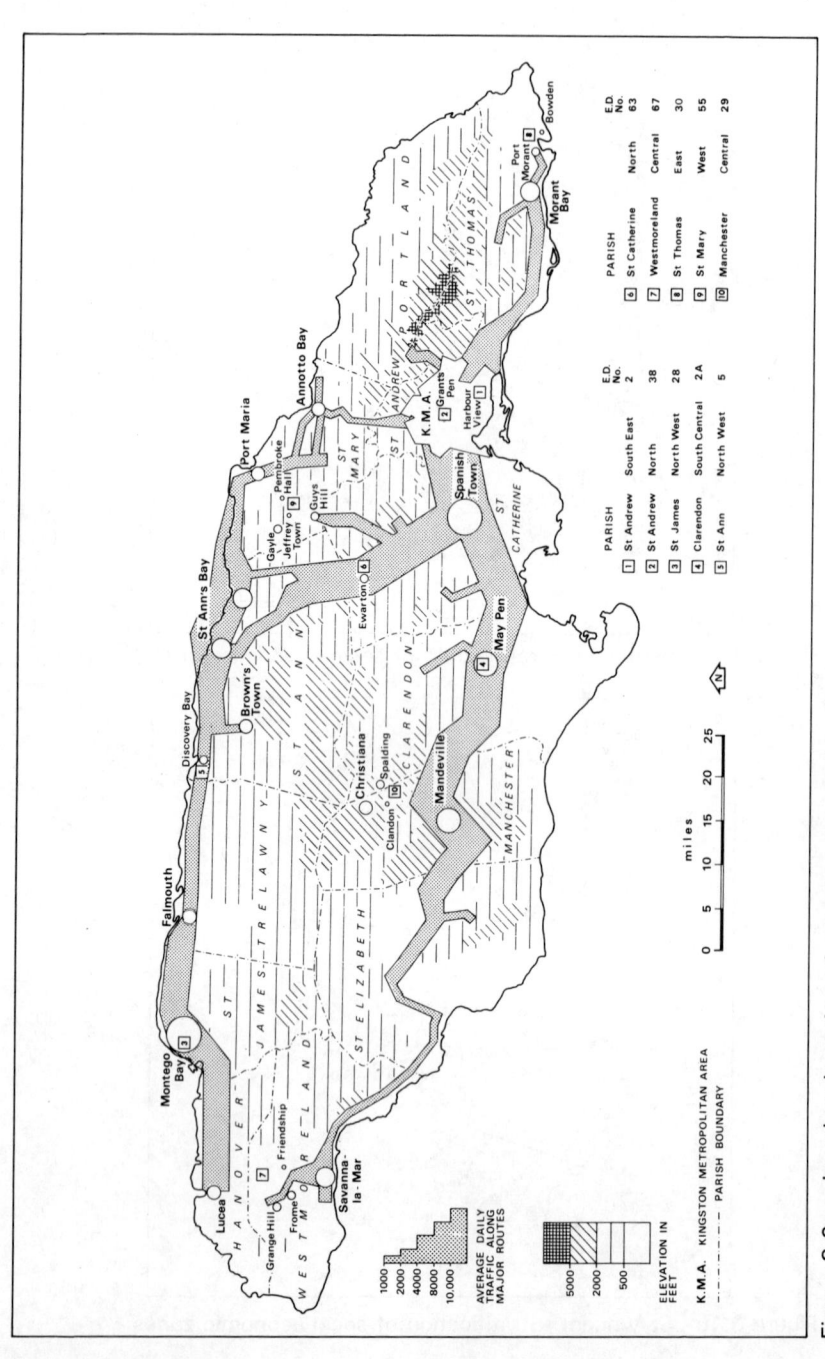

Figure 3.2a Jamaica: Location of sample areas and major routes

The micro-environments of migration 69

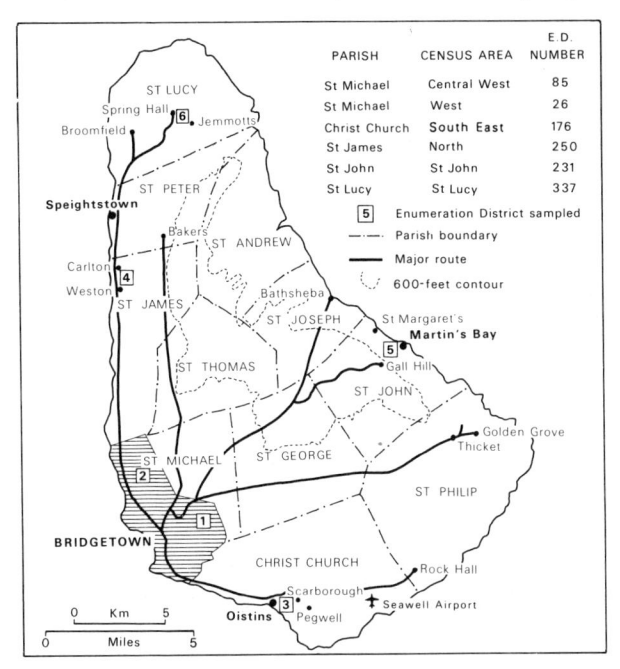

Figure 3.2b Barbados: Location of sample areas and major routes

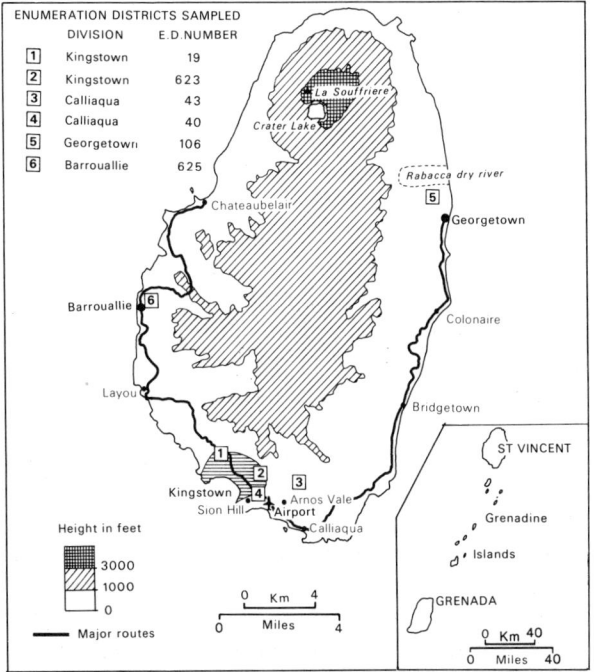

Figure 3.2c St Vincent: Location of sample areas and major routes

By contrast, Grant's Pen, like other older, low-income areas in Kingston, was characterized by a mix of dilapidated, older wooden houses of neat and interesting design and tenement yards which had developed between them. Unlike the middle-class districts, there were no gardens in this area. Space was at a premium and the yards provided an extension of household space. Unemployment in the area was widespread, but there was a high level of participation in the informal sector. Other members of the community were employed in factories, construction and low-paid service jobs in other parts of the city.

Other urban areas were represented by the low-income district of Catherine Mount in Montego Bay and the Pennant Wood Road-Weston Park Road area of May Pen. With a population of 71,000, Montego Bay was a major centre of the north coast tourist industry. The smaller town of May Pen, with a population of some 41,000, and located in the Parish of Clarendon, forty miles from Kingston, had its origins as a market centre. Based on its accessibility to the Spanish Town-Kingston manufacturing corridor, May Pen became the location of some light manufactures and the town grew during the phase of import substitution in the 1960s. Like many districts of smaller towns, those of May Pen comprised a heterogeneous area of more than one community and consisted of a range of low-income and middle-income households.

The areas directly influenced by the bauxite industry in Jamaica were characterized by one or a combination of mining, port facilities or the processing of the ore to alumina powder. The village of Ewarton in the Parish of St Catherine was dominated by the processing plant of the ALCAN Bauxite Company, while the settlement in the western section of Discovery Bay was the site of the Kaiser Bauxite Company storage, drying and port facilities. Both villages were highly accessible, juxtaposed along major routeways. Ewarton lay only thirty miles from Kingston on a major south-north artery across the island, and Discovery Bay on the main tourist route of the north coast.

In Ewarton and Discovery Bay the semi-subsistence economy and lifestyle of rural populations, based on farming or fishing, existed next to the capital-intensive, export-oriented bauxite industry. In some respects the two types of economic activity existed in a symbiotic relationship, forming their own particular type of ecology. But in other respects there was an underlying sense of alienation on the part of local residents who felt they had lost more than they had gained from the presence of bauxite operations. Ownership by the companies of most of the surrounding land, the negative environmental effects of caustic waste and red bauxite dust and, in the Discovery Bay area, the perceived loss of livelihood in fishing caused by the establishment of a shipping channel through the coral reef, were reflected in widespread disappointment and a mood of resignation. Yet this prevailed alongside the satisfaction of a small minority who benefited directly from the company or who still hoped that they might. The company was still perceived as providing the ideal form of employment which was potentially available, even though few local residents had been employed once the initial construction of the plants had been completed some twenty years previously.

The plantation and small-farming areas comprised the entire landscape other than those areas delineated as being urban or within the direct ambit of bauxite operations. Each locality within these areas thus differed according to the specific location relative to the national infrastructure, especially with respect to urban centres. The small-farming areas in particular, took on quite specific characteristics on the basis of altitude, slope, soil type, and rainfall, all directly affecting the opportunities for farming.

A district in the parish of Westmoreland on the margins of Frome sugar estate, and a second district which was part of Port Morant in the parish of St Thomas, close to the Bowden sugar estate, exemplified some of the variation in level of accessibility of **plantation communities**. This meant that the limitations in occupational opportunities and the conservative nature of communities associated with plantation agriculture were compounded in areas remote from alternative employment opportunities or ease of access to schools and urban life.

Not only was the parish of Westmoreland relatively remote from the centralized activities of Kingston, but also much of the area was comprised of scattered settlements between the village of Friendship and Callaloo Gutter. This was a generally poor area, reflected in the quality of the predominantly small, wooden houses and lack of household amenities. There was only a very basic infrastructure of partially paved roads, no electricity or mains water supplies. The few trucks and buses which serviced this area provided some motorized transport to and from the nearest town of Savannah-la-Mar.

Port Morant, in contrast, was a large village located on the main south coast road and was only seven miles from Morant Bay and forty miles east of Kingston. Accessibility and the range of opportunities were much greater in the Port Morant area than was the case in Westmoreland. Nevertheless, the sugar plantation was not the occupation which people perceived to be the ideal and their references were based upon urban lifestyles.

In the marginal sugar areas people generally shunned the available agricultural work on the plantation, though many households were involved in sugar share-cropping. Part of the marginal sugar lands in the parish of Westmoreland had been divided in the government's Land Lease programme of the 1950s and distributed in 5 acre lots on lease to some of the many landless peasants and former sugar workers in the area. Much of this land lay idle but some sugar cane was grown by the small-farmers who utilized household labour for planting, weeding and cutting the cane. As a consequence, children attended school only intermittently and in many families, hardly at all at times of harvesting.

Likewise, in Port Morant, the proximity of Bowden estate was not perceived to be an advantage in terms of work opportunities. Instead, people wished for manufacturing plants to be located nearby, which would provide, in the words of one resident, 'clean and dignified employment, so that young people could be seen each day going to work, respectably dressed'.

Central Manchester, in the Clandon area and central St Mary between Pembroke Hall, Lucky Hill and Jeffrey Town districts typified **small-farming, upland environments**. Despite the similarities in the ecological characteristics of these two districts, the fundamental contrasts, as in the case of the two plantation areas, were the result of their different locations. In the one case the area lay astride the main north-south routes through the island, on the Christiana-Mandeville road and was, therefore, highly accessible. The central St Mary districts, by contrast, were relatively inaccessible and considered by inhabitants of the area and outsiders alike to be remote. Nevertheless, there was regular contact with Kingston, especially by higglers whose chief market outlet was in the city.

The level of prosperity of small-holders within each community varied but, overall, there was more land ownership among the Manchester farmers than was the case in central St Mary. Furthermore, the accessibility of the Manchester communities to alternative sources of employment in Spalding and Mandeville was associated with the prosperity of this rural area.

The only supplement to domestic food production in central St Mary was cash earned through the cultivation of bananas for export, an activity to which people were resigned for want of a better alternative. There was a general sense of frustration associated with the high level of rejection of fruit by the Banana Marketing Board coupled with the low prices paid to the growers.

The greater prosperity and accessibility of central Manchester was evident in the larger number of children attending secondary school in nearby Spalding. In the case of the central St Mary communities, most children in the district went only irregularly to school, attending when their labour was not required for domestic or farming chores.

Very few reached the end of the primary school course or were entered for any public examinations.

The distinctive characteristics of each place or locality was influenced as much by dominant economic activity as by its accessibility to the main centres of population, in particular Kingston, the primate city. Opportunities for work, education and welfare facilities varied with each type of place, and so too did the base line against which people pitched their expectations. A very similar range of livelihoods and accessibility factors conditioned the characteristics of localities in Barbados and St Vincent.

BARBADOS

In **Bridgetown**, the capital of Barbados, Belmont to the north of the city centre and Ashdeane-Deacons to the west, exemplified much of the variation found in this urban area. Both districts comprised a mix of middle and lower-class households. The middle-class houses were of the standard concrete type located in small lots of land enclosed by a low wall and hedge. Some of the older middle-class houses were of a more ornate wooden style. Virtually all the lower-class houses were wooden and of the chattel house kind, typical of Barbados.

In the lower-class districts the housing density was everywhere high, with dwellings located along the small tracks leading from the main roads which bordered the district. Only in the area of Deacons was there a small development of apartment blocks containing flats for rental to higher-income working-class households.

The entire **tourist zone** was situated along the coast of the parishes of Christchurch to the east and St James to the north-west of Bridgetown. Both were highly accessible to Bridgetown itself. The high density tourist developments in Christchurch contrasted with the quieter, lower intensity of tourist activity in St James. But even in Christchurch the seasonal nature of the industry and the large number of self-catering accommodation units in the area kept the opportunities for employment relatively low.

The number of commercial and service facilities was greater in these areas than elsewhere outside of Bridgetown and employment was available in the various aspects of tourism or related commercial activity. Thus, despite the disenchantment among those who benefited little in a direct way from tourism, there was an aura of general prosperity which had many indirect effects upon the inhabitants. In particular, the very high level of expectations which existed among the young was far greater than the opportunities for fulfilling them.

Proximity to Bridgetown brought the potential for urban employment, schools and medical facilities to the populations of this area with no difficulty. However, in Bridgetown the people from St James necessarily competed for work with the rest of the labour force and the opportunities fell far short of the high levels of expectations and ambitions which existed, especially among the youth of this area.

Apart from the Bridgetown-St Michael urban area and the coastal tourist zone of Christchurch and St James, the rest of the island was dominated by sugar plantations. Linear settlements were located at intervals along the roads which bordered the cane fields and a few such settlements were included within each district.

The districts studied in the **sugar zone** in the sample were in the parish of St John on the east side of the island and in St Lucy, the northernmost parish. By contrast with the areas in Bridgetown and the tourist zone of the south, the communities in the plantation zone were much poorer.

The area of St John, from St Margaret's Chapel in the north to Martin's Bay in the south, comprised a rocky coastal strip about a mile wide which descended steeply to the beach. Unsuitable for sugar cane, it provided, instead, a location for the houses of plantation workers. Residents bemoaned the fact that they had no tourist attractions or recreational facilities. Although Bridgetown was only 25 miles away, a journey which took less than an hour by public transport, there was a sense of being peripheral on account of the lack of visitors to the area and the virtual absence of foreign visitors. There was widespread disinterest in plantation work and people only engaged in such work out of necessity, not ambition. The proximity to the sea allowed some people the opportunity of fishing as an alternative, more independent livelihood.

In other areas dominated by the sugar plantations, as exemplified by the Jemmots district in the parish of St Lucy, there was an even greater sense of isolation and virtually no alternative form of livelihood in the locality.

Transport in the parish was poor and access to Bridgetown involved changing buses at Speightstown, in the neighbouring parish of St Peter. The frequency of buses during the daytime or late in the evening was very low, but a more frequent service to coincide with the travel of children to school and workers to the west coast and Bridgetown made daily commuting out of the area possible. This provided an alternative, although not an easy one, to plantation life. The establishment of a garment factory in the parish served to encourage the notion that an alternative to sugar was a possibility and this helped to fire the already high expectations which existed among young people who had rejected the plantation as a means of employment and as a way of life.

ST VINCENT

Kingstown, the capital of St Vincent, was focused around the harbour. Rising steeply from the small flat coastal area were the residential districts housing the town's population of 16,530.

Murray Village, one of the low-income districts of the town, was only semi-urban in character. Access was by means of a loose network of unpaved tracks which dwindled to isolated paths at the higher elevations, where settlement became increasingly sparse and eventually gave way to woodland and bush.

Houses varied in quality and though on the lower slopes of the hill there were a few large concrete houses in gardens belonging to middle-class families, in most cases the houses in this area were small, wooden constructions set in yards. The urban location of Murray Village lent itself to the need for rented rooms which frequently formed separate household units as infill within existing yards.

Despite the high concentration of housing in this district, a number of fruit trees and other tree crops such as breadfruit and pear (avocado) grew profusely. Little else could be grown because of the rocky nature of the area. There was complete reliance upon Kingstown itself for economic activity and the general poverty of the district reflected the difficulties in obtaining substantial employment.

The traditional middle-class suburb of Montrose, also set on hill slopes, in this case on the west side of Kingstown, stood out in contrast to Murray Village. Most Montrose residents were white collar workers with jobs in Kingstown. Their children went to the primary schools or to private preparatory schools. They nearly all proceeded afterwards to one of the main secondary schools in the island, located in Kingstown.

In **the south**, east of Kingstown, were the populated areas of Arnos Vale and Belair-Calliaqua; the former a virtual extension of Kingstown and the latter, a relatively prosperous farming area.

Though there was some variation, for the most part, this was a low-income area. The southern part of the district close to the airport, represented an overspill of Kingstown itself. Spontaneous in its growth, this area was serviced by no roads and small tracks gave access by foot. Though many of the dwellings had been upgraded by their occupants, there had been continual infill of flimsy shacks constructed by recent arrivals. In the northern, more prosperous extension of the district were located a number of substantial concrete houses.

Apart from the airport, a few factories in Arnos Vale provided some employment, together with that available in nearby Kingstown and in the tourist developments on the south coast. Even with all these combined, the opportunities for employment were very limited.

The fertile hill district of Belair just seven to ten miles away from

Arnos Vale, was in marked contrast to the built-up environment close to town. The economic mainstay of this locality was farming and a variety of food and fruit crops were grown for the domestic market, for which the chief outlet was Kingstown. Much of the land was owned by people living outside of the area who hired labourers within the district to work the land. However, in addition, the plots around the small houses of the local farmers were intensely cultivated and a variety of fruit and other tree crops were grown.

This rural situation was in many respects similar to that in Jamaica. Multiple occupation wass common; tradespeople could rarely make a living from their trade in a rural community and usually engaged in some cultivation as well. Standards of living varied considerably from one household to another and small-holders with only a quarter of an acre of land were next to prosperous farmers with 5 to 10 acres. In all cases, the entrepreneurs in the district had the highest living standards and owned the large concrete houses. Chief among these were the shopkeepers and the mini-bus owners.

A local primary school provided a basic educational facility. Few children from the district went to secondary school and those who did, had to travel to Kingstown to which there was easy access.

Barrouallie on the **Leeward coast** of the island was only 12 miles north-west of Kingstown, yet it was considerably isolated. The limited transport service along the narrow, winding Leeward road, was chiefly provided by the mini-buses and trucks transporting agricultural produce.

Some wage labour was available on properties growing arrowroot (Casson) or cocoa (Wallilabou), although this was not regarded as being a desirable occupation. Other cultivators grew vegetables for the household on the tiny plot (usually less than a quarter of an acre) around the house or 'in the bush'. The more prosperous farmers owned or rented up to 3 acres which was sufficient to provide for the household with some surplus to sell in Kingstown market.

The value of this sea-shore location was in the livelihood many derived from fishing and the major contribution fish made to the local diet. Other occupations of Barrouallie residents included tailoring, dressmaking either full-time or part-time in combination with farming. Clerical jobs were the most prestigious, although there were only minimal opportunities for such work in the magistrates court and post office for those with an appropriate educational background. The most prosperous residents of the town were, as elsewhere, the entrepreneurs. Some nine major shops were located around the central square and between them they sold a range of groceries and basic dry-goods provisions.

There was a primary school and an infant school in Barrouallie but no secondary school The few families who could afford to do so sent their children to secondary school in Kingstown. A minimal health service was provided at the local clinic which was staffed by a nurse and a doctor who visited weekly.

Chapman's Village on the **Windward side** was one of the poorest areas in the Caribbean in terms of material circumstances. There was a general appearance of poverty and a sense of marginality in this weather-beaten Atlantic shore and volcanic hazard zone. The volcanic cone of Soufrière was only out of sight when hidden by cloud; the Rabacca dry river valley which separated the community from the volcano conjured up the deepest fears because of its association with the overflow of molten lava or of flood waters from the mountain. Everyone knew someone, or knew about someone who had met a tragic death at Rabacca. If there was not the volcano then there were the hurricanes to remind people constantly of their precarious environment; this area, its houses and crops, had been ravaged at least once in everyone's living memory.

All the houses were typical one or two-roomed board constructions, with wooden windows. But in this district there was also a larger proportion of poorer style wattle and daub ('trash') houses than usual. In neither type of house were mains electricity or water found. As in all districts of this type, lifestyles were well adjusted to the material limitations. The problem was not so much that they needed, or, were it available, could afford electricity, but that they knew other people, those in the towns and abroad in 'Trinidad, America and England', who had it. This was important, for it had become their frame of reference.

It was not surprising that most people in the district were poor, for most were agricultural wage labourers. Coconut and banana properties (and, for a while, sugar) were located nearby and provided a minimum livelihood. This was supplemented by food grown and livestock kept in the limited space around the house or on the mountainous Crown lands.

Basic services were available in the nearby settlement, Georgetown. Like Barrouallie, Georgetown provided a limited range of welfare and commercial services but very few employment opportunities. An infant and primary school provided only basic educational facilities. Access to town by local mini-bus was limited to the early morning with return in the evenings. As in the case of transport to Barrouallie on the Leeward, so along the Windward road the buses restricted themselves to the peak travelling times for making the one-hour journey.

Characteristics of the populations

The range of localities included in the study and the random sampling procedures employed ensured the representativeness of the populations.[1]

Table 3.1 Characteristics of the sample populations: age distribution

	Age Groups		
	15-29	30-44	45-64
	(Percentage of total population)		
Jamaica			
Sample population	**48.8**	**27.2**	**24.0**
Global population (1970)	47.3	26.7	26.0
Global population (1982)	52.7	25.3	22.0
Barbados			
Sample population	**51.4**	**22.5**	**26.1**
Global population (1970)	44.5	24.5	31.0
Global population (1980)	50.3	25.1	24.6
St Vincent			
Sample population	**53.1**	**17.4**	**29.5**
Global population (1970)	49.5	25.0	25.5
Global population (1980)	57.1	21.7	21.2

Table 3.2 Characteristics of the sample populations: sex distribution

	Female	Male
	(Percentage of total population)	
Jamaica		
Sample population	**57.1**	**42.9**
Global population (1970)	51.3	48.7
Global population (1982)	51.4	48.6
Barbados		
Sample population	**56.5**	**43.5**
Global population (1970)	53.5	46.5
Global population (1980)	52.8	47.2
St Vincent		
Sample population	**58.5**	**41.5**
Global population (1970)	58.5	41.5
Global population (1980)	52.8	47.2

Table 3.3: Characteristics of the sample populations: education

	No school	Primary without exams	Primary with exams	Secondary without exams	Secondary with exams	Tertiary
			(Percentage of sample population)			
Jamaica	0.8	8.6	16.4	38.4	35.7	0.1
Barbados	1.8	9.0	26.3	48.1	14.6	0.2
St Vincent	3.5	11.6	17.1	31.8	36.0	0.0

Table 3.4: Characteristics of the sample populations: occupation

	Occupational groupings				
	1	2	3	4	5
		(Percentage of sample population)			
Jamaica	0.5	11.7	15.7	37.7	34.4
Barbados	2.2	15.3	24.5	39.3	18.7
St Vincent	1.2	14.7	30.2	22.9	31.0

Occupational groupings
1 High level managerial and professional
2 Skilled workers, clerical workers, teachers, nurses, medium-sized landowners and entrepreneurs
3 Semi-skilled workers, commercial small-farmers, other small-scale entrepreneurs
4 Unskilled workers
5 Unemployed and casual labourers

A high proportion of the population was in the young adult group (15-29 years). This was particularly true of St Vincent, where more than 57 per cent of the population were in this category at the time of the 1980 census (Table 3.1). A further demographic trend in each of the islands was reflected in the large number of females to males in each of the age cohorts (Table 3.2).

Levels of educational attainment varied between islands, but in general there was a high proportion of each of the island populations, and especially that of St Vincent, without any formal school-leaving qualifications. Nevertheless, there was a significant percentage of the populations, principally in the urban centres, with some secondary education and many with formal certificates. A very small percentage of the island populations had had the opportunity of attending a tertiary institution and, in the case of St Vincent, the number in this category was negligible (Table 3.3).

The high level of unemployment, under-employment and casual labour characteristic of the region was particularly evident in Jamaica and St Vincent. The general occupational profile of each of the islands demonstrated the large percentage of the population in unskilled and semi-skilled types of work (Table 3.4).

The representativeness of the sample was vitally important in that it permitted generalizations to be made about the overall adult populations of Jamaica, Barbados and St Vincent.[2]

Notes

1 All census enumeration districts of the three islands were included in the stratification, and because of the spatial distribution of social classes, the sample represented the range and the proportion in which people of different classes were distributed.

Stratification of the islands into broad socio-economic zones provided the framework within which was drawn a three-stage random sample comprising localities – represented by census enumeration districts (EDs) – households and individuals. All EDs, and thus all individuals, had an equal probability of selection. Using a random sampling procedure, EDs were selected from the total of EDs in each stratum and accumulated population totals ensured the statistical representation of each. A random sample was taken of households from the selected EDs and of individuals (in the age category 14-64) from the sample of households. The total sample populations comprised 750 individuals in Jamaica, 450 in Barbados and 300 in St Vincent.

2 A 95 per cent level of confidence was achieved in the representativeness of the sample taking the critical values for t using the Student's t distribution with two degrees and one degree of freedom in the case of the age-group and sex variables respectively.

Figure 3.3 An urban yard, Kingston, Jamaica

Figure 3.4 Marginal sugar cane area, Westmoreland, Jamaica

Figure 3.5 Chattel houses, Bridgetown, Barbados

Figure 3.6 Sugar plantation, central Barbados

Figure 3.7 The main street, Kingstown, St Vincent

Figure 3.8 General view of Barrouallie, St Vincent

CHAPTER 4 | Migration and the propensity for migration

The propensity for migration is related, in the first instance, to the perception of migration and the benefits and risks involved. In the light of these perceptions. places experienced and information about places not known take on meaning in the context of migration behaviour. Thus the image of migration itself is the first stage in the perception of opportunity and of migration propensity. The propensity for migration may or may not be followed by actual moves, depending on the nature of prevailing practical circumstances of finance, freedom to move at the level of the household and immigration legislation at the level of international relations.

The perception of migration

Evaluations of migration accorded closely with the ways in which people translated the 'evidence' which they saw from other people's migration experience. Based on what they believed about migration in the first place, the benefits were assessed and the time in people's lives when it was deemed appropriate for migration was evaluated.

The criteria of success varied in detail from one social sector to another, chiefly on the basis of class. But for all groups there was fundamental consensus that migration success related to a combination of material and cultural improvement. Material gains were evaluated in relation to the migrant's circumstances prior to migrating, thus there was nothing absolute about the measure of material success. The more an individual possessed before migrating the more affluent he or she would be expected to become. The perceived indices of affluence were measured by factors ranging from manner of dress, size and quality of housing which the migrant could afford, the possession of luxury items – especially electrical and electronic appliances, the person's ability to make frequent visits home, to distribute gifts of various kinds to relatives and to entertain friends and acquaintances.

The displays of material wealth were enhanced by evidence of cultural gains. These included perceived improvements in the ability to speak grammatically or, even more impressively, the ability to speak with a foreign accent, to the evidence of improved decorum (referred to as good manners), good taste and enhanced social status and prestige. One respondent voiced what appeared to be a widespread view that those who returned from abroad 'look better in every way'.

The chief exception to this positive view about the benefits of migration was felt to be exhibited by those persons who had returned from Britain and about whom there was the general feeling that 'they come back from England crack'. The onset of a high incidence of neurosis, described as 'nerves', was believed to occur among those who went to Britain. It was concluded that this situation was brought about by stress on account of the difficulties under which the migrants worked and lived and, in particular, the problems they faced in coping with the weather. In addition, there was some question about the true level of material prosperity achieved by migrants to Britain. Thus the high stress factor was also attributed to the frustration of not succeeding quickly. It was observed that it took a much longer time for migrants in Britain to acquire the same level of prosperity as those who went to North America.

The overall view took into consideration the various aspects of successful and unsuccessful outcomes of migration as perceived by the Jamaicans, Barbadians and Vicentians. Taking all things into consideration, the vast majority of people estimated that the migrants known to them had definitely improved as a consequence of their migration. The Vincentian responses were vague but in Jamaica the views held indicated that there was overwhelming emphasis placed upon the advantages which had been derived from migration both among those persons known to them and, where relevant, from their own experience. The Barbadian's views, though positive, were less clear cut (Table 4.1a).

The variation between the three islands raised a number of fundamental questions. The lower evaluation accorded migration by the Barbadian sample was puzzling in the light of the consistently high migration rate from Barbados. There was no evidence to suggest that returnees to Jamaica showed evidence of greater success than the returnees to Barbados. Nor was there any apparent reason why the Vincentian sample should be so non-committal on the question of the benefits of migration. Though the Barbadians were more conservative in their evaluation of their migration success, they were more certain that migration was recommendable for young people. The temporal aspect of the image of migration played a very important part in the perception of migration and its value. Whether or not it was expected to be a resounding success, it was still regarded in a positive light and as an integral part of the life experience.

Table 4.1 Assessments of the value of international migration

a) **Evaluation of the change in other people as a consequence of migration**

	Definitely no improvement or negative change	No positive change if any	Not clear if any negative or positive change	Some positive change	Definitely much positive change
	(Percentage of the sample population)				
Jamaica	0.7	10.3	8.6	8.7	71.7
Barbados	0.2	2.8	20.6	20.4	56.0
St Vincent	0.0	7.7	15.4	15.4	61.5

b) **Perceived desirability of migration for young persons**

	Definitely undesirable	Not particularly desirable	Neither desirable nor undesirable	Quite desirable	Definitely desirable
	(Percentage of the sample population)				
Jamaica	10.6	5.5	12.9	6.4	64.6
Barbados	33.9	2.0	8.8	4.7	50.6
St Vincent	15.1	1.2	4.7	6.2	72.8

Evidence of migration success

A large proportion of the populations had strong positive views about the benefits to be derived from international migration. (Migration within one's own Caribbean country was seen in a much more varied light and its benefits evaluated as subject to a number of conditions.) The views on the beneficial effects of observed or experienced migration did not vary with the age or sex of the individual nor with levels of personal satisfaction, for example whether the individual was engaged in preferred employment. However, there was a significant, though fairly weak, association with occupation and education, the more educated being more discriminating in their views.

Contact with places and people abroad tended to enhance attitudes towards migration, and there was a tendency among those who had not been abroad themselves to hold a more positive view on the matter.

This suggested that believed success was more important than actual information or experience of migration. Despite the slight variability in views held, the value of migration was shared to a greater or lesser extent by young and old, professional and skilled, as well as unskilled and unemployed, male and female. Furthermore, the observation that international migration was evaluated quite differently from that of internal migration, indicated that the related decision-making and behaviour were based upon quite different values and criteria.

The conditional aspect of the image played a limited role in the evaluation of international migration. If migration were to occur, it was overwhelmingly believed that it would provide opportunities inherently beneficial to the individuals engaged in it and, by extension, to their family and household.

A further indication of the image of migration was evident in the perception of the risk involved in the process.

Perception of risk in migration

Evaluation of the risk factor in migration was minimized by most people on account of the optimistic view of the material wealth of countries abroad, especially the metropolitan countries or other centres of metropolitan economic activity. Migration to any other place other than the North American or West European metropolises was regarded to be of quite a different order and was perceived to contain a major degree of risk. But most people did not even think of countries outside the traditional migration destinations or areas of North America or European economic activities.

The image of risk in migrating was of a low priority and played a minimal role in determining the value of migration. In St Vincent respondents had little or no idea about whether or not there was significant risk in migrating and did not see the point of considering the matter, since it was not perceived to be relevant to their views about migration, hence no figures (Table 4.2).

Table 4.2   Perception of risk in migrating

	Very high	Fairly high	Non-committal	Not very high	None at all
	(Percentage of the sample population)				
Jamaica	30.3	9.3	12.1	14.2	34.1
Barbados	16.3	13.0	32.5	20.7	17.5
St Vincent	—	—	—	—	—

To many people the risk in migrating was assumed to relate merely to the possible danger involved in travel by air; not the problems of adjusting to, and making a success of migration. The expected success of migration was virtually taken for granted. It was felt that only the foolish were at risk. 'It is only the lazy and idle who don't make it over there', was a frequently voiced opinion.

There was no significant association between occupational status and perception of risk in migrating. Nor could the variation in perception of risk in migrating be accounted for by differences in age or sex. There was not even any significant association between those who had been abroad and those who had not been abroad in the perception of risk.

One might have expected the prior experience of having been abroad to have had a consistent relationship to the perception of risk, but this was not the case. In Jamaica, those who had not previously been abroad had a more optimistic perception of the risk factor in migration than those who had been abroad. In the Barbadian case the reverse situation occurred, with those who had already been abroad perceiving the risk element to be lower than those who had never travelled.

To some extent, the more mobile persons were those with the least concern about the problems of risk in migration, whereas those who moved around little tended to be the more cautious. Those who held a valid passport were those least of all concerned about risk. This again suggested that the disposition towards migration led to, or was associated with, an optimism that brought about the favourable interpretation of information, almost irrespective of the nature of that information. Those who themselves were not keen on migrating or had a low propensity for, or poor image of migration, were also those who were aware of the risk and the negative aspects of the process. This reflected not so much the actual circumstances as it did the image of migration itself.

The issue which this underlined was the need for explanation of the factors which conditioned the image. This was essential in order to understand the implications of the image in migration and so to explain the uneven distribution of decisions and behaviour involved in the migration process.

Components of the migration process

Migration behaviour may be abstracted to include the two major components of the migration process – the propensity for movement and the actual move. Propensity is the most appropriate primary indicator as it is the first stage in the individual's decision-making procedure. It reflects the stage at which the meaning of migration is translated by the individual into a form of behaviour which is perceived to be relevant to his or her objectives or goals. Whereas the actual moves vary in their volume and timing as well as the combination of destinations included, the propensity varies in its intensity. The migration landscape is an expression of the spatial variation in both these phenomena.

The propensity for migration

The propensity for migration is defined here as the orientations which favour, or are conducive to migration, as well as the desire or intention to migrate.

Orientation towards migration

Indicators used to measure orientation towards migration included the preference for migration over alternative means of improving personal circumstances, and engagement in actions focused upon migration as an objective, such as the possession of a valid passport.

Migration as preferred option

The extent to which people themselves would choose to migrate if the opportunity were to arise, was a further indication of the aspect of value in the image of migration. It related to questions of whether migration was more or less preferable to other options in the course of one's life; whether it was more or less dependable as a means of achieving particular goals. People evaluated migration in relation to the purchase of a house, a car and other consumer goods. Above all, migration was valued as an investment for the future, with long-term exponential benefits and not simply as the means of immediate financial reward. Migration was seen as the essential first step if home ownership and the acquisition of consumer durables were to follow. The conditional aspect of the image was dominant and worthy of short-term hardships, even considerable sacrifice, for the sake of the long-term advantages.

Approximately half the populations interviewed stated that they would most definitely choose to migrate if the financial constraints were removed, and a further 15-27 per cent indicated that they would most likely elect to migrate (Table 4.3a). The variation between Jamaica, Barbados and St Vincent in terms of migration as a preferred option not surprisingly replicated the pattern of variation in perceptions of the desirability of migration: the Vincentian population demonstrated

Table 4.3 Migration orientation

a) Migration as preferred option

	Definitely no	Not likely	Not sure	Most likely	Definitely yes
			(Percentage of the sample population)		
Jamaica	20.7	6.7	10.2	12.2	50.2
Barbados	22.8	8.8	6.5	15.5	46.4
St Vincent	0.0	0.0	18.2	27.3	54.5

b) In possession of a valid passport

	No	Yes	No response
		(Percentage of the sample population)	
Jamaica	73.7	24.6	1.7
Barbados	68.3	31.7	—
St Vincent	65.9	34.1	—

the greatest interest in migration, the Barbadian population, the least. Yet when the number of those indicating they would definitely choose to migrate if financial constraints were removed was combined with those who would most likely choose to migrate, there was only a negligible difference between the Jamaican and the Barbadian cases (with 62.2 per cent and 61.6 per cent respectively).

There was no significant relationship between the perception of migration as desirable option and the fact that individuals were engaged in the employment of their choice. Nor was perception of migration related to the occupational status, educational background or age of the person. However, there was some association by gender, women showing a greater propensity than men for taking up migration opportunities. There was also a much greater tendency for migration to be the preferred option among those persons who had several relatives and friends abroad, especially from their own household. A larger proportion of those who had never been abroad would regard migration as a priority if there was an option, but even among those who had already been abroad 40 per cent of the Barbadian and 59 per cent of the Jamaican group would take the option to go again.

Possession of a valid passport

More than a third of the Vincentian population, just under a third of the Barbadian, and a quarter of the Jamaican population were in possession of an up-to-date passport. There was no significant association between holding a valid passport and social characteristics measured in terms of occupation or education.

The strongest relationship was with age, a larger proportion of the population in possession of a passport being among the age groups over twenty-nine years. Of those Barbadians who had already been abroad, 75 per cent were in possession of an up-to-date passport and 25 per cent were not, whereas of those who had never been abroad, though 87 per cent had no valid passport, 13 per cent did. In the Jamaican case, the pattern was similar, with 70 per cent of those who had already been abroad still holding a valid passport, 30 per cent not; of those who had never been abroad, 80 per cent had no up-to-date passport but 20 per cent did have one (Table 4.3b). These factors were clear indication of a strong orientation of the three islands' populations towards migration and considerable experience of migration as well.

The intention to migrate

The Vincentian population demonstrated by far the strongest desire or intention to migrate. The Jamaican population was a close second, followed by the Barbadians who recorded a much weaker intention to migrate (Table 4.4).

Table 4.4 Intention to migrate

	Very high	Medium	Low
Jamaica	68.3	10.8	20.9
Barbados	56.9	10.1	33.0
St Vincent	71.7	8.1	20.2

Note: An index of migration intent was derived by combining a number of measures of the strong wish or intention to migrate determined from the interviews. The migration intent was taken to be reflected in the individual's decisions about the desirability of migration generally, as well as his or her personal wish to migrate, whether for a brief period of about one year or for an indefinite period. The scores were measured on a seven-point scale, then summarized to present three categories, little, medium and great desire to migrate.

The most consistent feature of the three islands was the lack of significant association between the extent of the desire to migrate and any particular social and demographic characteristics, apart from the tendency for women to show a slightly stronger intention to migrate than men. Furthermore, the association between the desire to migrate and other variables reflected a very high level of variation occurring between the three islands.

The difficulty of finding a job and prior experience of having been abroad were important in the Jamaican case; evidence of the benefit derived from migration, the number of members of the household abroad and, related to this, the extent of correspondence with people abroad ranked high among the Barbadian population; problems of access to town was the most relevant issue in the Vincentian case. This high degree of variability between Jamaica, Barbados and St Vincent in the factors associated with the current desire to migrate was a very important factor. It reinforced the idea that explanation does not lie in any single or simple set of negative characteristics of the locality or country and reflects a much more variable and complex set of processes.

Meanwhile, the lack of explanation based on occupation, educational background or age were also of major importance. Before pursuing this question, the rate and variation between islands in actual outward movement needs to be described.

Actual migration

A comprehensive definition is here used to include the overall outward movement of household members at all stages in the emigration process – those just gone, gone for a long time (using 1955 as the limit), gone and returned, gone and about to return, whatever the duration of absence or sequence of return (Table 4.5).

Whereas only 13.3 per cent of the Jamaican population sample had previous experience of having been abroad, 29.7 per cent of the Barbadians and 47.7 per cent of the Vincentians had been abroad for varying durations at some time in the past. Of the Barbadian sample, 17.8 per cent had been abroad more than once, of the Jamaican sample, 9.4 per cent had been away more than once and of the Vincentian sample, this was the case for 33.3 per cent.

There was no significant association between the number of times respondents had been abroad and any characteristics of the respondents themselves, whether social or demographic. Nor was there any relationship between travel abroad and the perceptions or experience of individuals.

Table 4.5 Actual migration

a) Been abroad and returned

	Number of times abroad			
	None	1 – 5	6 – 10	More than 10
	(Percentage of the sample population)			
Jamaica	86.7	11.7	1.5	0.1
Barbados	69.4	24.4	4.1	2.1
St Vincent	52.2	35.7	9.3	2.8

b) Household members abroad

	Number of household members abroad			
	None	1	2 – 6	More than 6
	(Percentage of households in the sample)			
Jamaica	39.8	28.5	30.8	0.9
Barbados	35.8	26.4	36.4	1.4
St Vincent	31.7	24.7	42.0	1.6

Consistent with the strong positive image of migration demonstrated by the Vincentian population, there were more than two-thirds of the households in the sample with at least one member abroad. In Barbados, there were 64.1 per cent of households with at least one person abroad and in Jamaica there were 60.1 per cent in this situation. Some households had more than one member abroad, in a few cases even as many as ten.[1]

Locational variations in migration and propensity for migration

Rates of actual migration[2]

The greater variation in emigration occurred not between islands but within them. Overall emigration rates for Jamaica, Barbados and St Vincent were respectively, 121.8, 144.0 and 152.6 for every hundred persons in the total population (Table 4.6). The differences between islands were small by comparison with the differences within each of the three islands. For the Jamaican sample, the standard deviation of the emigration rates from different areas was 35.7 and for Barbados 31.5. The St Vincent case, with a standard deviation of 54.6, indicated a much wider discrepancy in emigration rates from different parts of the island than was the case for Jamaica and Barbados.

Table 4.6 Actual migration and propensity for migration

	Actual emigration rates	Potential for emigration indices
JAMAICA		
Kingston Metropolitan Area		
Harbour View	144.0	226.0
Grant's Pen	130.6	373.3
Other urban		
Montego Bay	87.1	345.7
May Pen	153.4	363.5
Rural: bauxite		
North West St Ann	122.1	363.0
Ewarton, St Catherine	193.2	348.0
Rural: plantation		
Central Westmoreland	81.3	385.3
Port Morant, St Thomas	117.3	377.3
Rural: mixed farming		
Western St Mary	109.3	377.3
Central Manchester	80.3	380.3
MEAN	121.8	362.7
BARBADOS		
Urban: Bridgetown		
Belmont, St Michael	176.0	147.8
Deacons, St Michael	168.0	139.0
Rural: tourism		
Oistins, Christchurch	176.2	286.0
Weston, St James	107.4	267.9
Rural: plantation		
St Martins Bay, St John	111.6	333.8
Central St Lucy	145.3	345.3
MEAN	144.0	253.4

	Actual emigration rates	Potential for emigration indices
ST VINCENT		
Urban: Kingstown		
Montrose	119.6	302.2
Murray Village	164.6	389.6
Rural: South		
Belair	96.8	403.2
Sion Hill/Arnos Vale	129.2	414.6
Rural: Windward and Leeward		
Chapman's (Windward)	153.6	448.7
Barrouallie (Leeward)	252.9	407.8
MEAN	152.6	394.3

The distribution of out-migration rates showed that in Jamaica, the bauxite area in the parish of St Catherine, near Ewarton, recorded the highest emigration figure, with a large difference between this area and the rest. The sample in May Pen, an urban population, was second after Ewarton in rate of emigration. There was no apparent consistency among the urban areas since Montego Bay had an even lower emigration figure than most of the rural places, while May Pen showed a strong similarity to the situation in the Kingston Metropolitan Area (both for the middle class of Harbour View and the lower class of Grant's Pen). Likewise, bauxite areas were not similar in their emigration rates. In the Discovery Bay bauxite area emigration was considerably lower than in the Ewarton bauxite area.

In Barbados, central St Lucy was an anomaly in the overall trend. St Lucy, the least accessible parish, had an emigration rate much higher than those areas located in the capital Bridgetown and of a similar social composition. This exception apart, high emigration rates occurred principally from Bridgetown, or areas close to it. Despite the very different locational aspect of Martin's Bay, in the parish of St John and Carlton Weston in St James, the emigration rates from these areas were surprisingly similar. In both, plantation work together with fishing formed the chief means of making a living, although in St James additional seasonal employment was obtained in the tourist industry.

A comparison of the situation in Christchurch with that in St James showed the reverse situation. There was a considerably higher rate of emigration in Christchurch, although in many respects these areas were very much alike in socio-economic structure. The two sample populations in St Michael had a very similar breakdown of social groupings so that the existence of only negligible differences in their emigration backgrounds was easily explained. Migration rates in both Deacons and Belmont in St Michael were very high (176.0 and 168.0 respectively). However, when these two samples were broken down along class lines (taking 'occupation' as the criterion), the emigration patterns were similar to those of middle and lower-class samples in both Kingston (Jamaica) and Kingstown (St Vincent) with slightly higher rates with respect to the middle-class populations.

St Vincent presented a third variant in the Caribbean emigration pattern. Barrouallie had by far the highest rate of outward movement for any of the areas, with an emigration of over 250 per cent of the population. Like central St Lucy in Barbados, so Barrouallie appeared to have been an anomaly in St Vincent, which raised the question of whether these particular types of rural areas shared some common features which may have helped explain their particularly high emigration rates.

In St Vincent's capital, Kingstown, the middle class of Montrose differed appreciably from its social counterpart in Jamaica – namely, Harbour View. In Montrose, the 119 emigrants for every 100 persons was lower than for most other areas in the same island. (Belair was the only area with a lower departure rate, at 96 per cent). Most of the earlier repatriates from Curaçao and Aruba (some of whom were born there of Vincentian migrants) were among the urban middle classes of St Vincent. Such repatriates were very rarely encountered among the lower classes, indicating the inter-generational upward social mobility that has been associated with the migrations both to Central America and to the Netherlands Antilles. Parallels were found in Jamaica in the case of Harbour View where there were some repatriates – or their descendants and relatives – from Panama and Costa Rica. A similar situation pertained among the return migrants from Venezuela in Trinidad and the return migrants from Cuba in Barbados. As in the Grant's Pen district of Kingston, Jamaica, so too in the lower-class population of Murray Village in Kingstown, St Vincent, the rates of outward movement (130.6 and 164.6 respectively), were above the island averages but not by a large amount.

The two areas closest to the capital, namely Sion Hill and Belair, both recorded the lowest number of emigrants which was in contrast to higher departure rates recorded for Barrouallie and Chapman's, situated farther from Kingstown. Perhaps the significance was that apart from economic prosperity, distance from the capital may also have been important in generating wide variations in migration behaviour. By comparison with Sion Hill, St Vincent, none of the Jamaican or Barbadian districts was situated in such close physical proximity to the capital, yet in a social and economic sense largely marginal to the activities of the town. This example, together with others cited as irregularities in the pattern of emigration, could not be explained solely by variation in economic or social characteristics.

Indices of migration propensity[3]

The intra-island discrepancies between the indices for migration propensity were, in general, greater than the inter-island differences (Table 4.6). Whereas in the case of the actual migration rates St Vincent had the largest range, in terms of the propensity to migrate, it was Barbados which recorded the widest variance between different parts of the island. (The standard deviation for Jamaica was 16.4, for St Vincent 37.5 and for Barbados 89.9). One would not expect that the widest intra-island differences in both migration propensity and rates of actual departure would occur in the smallest of the territories, since in these one would assume greater uniformity of circumstance and attitude. This gave increased weight to the notion that relatively small-scale environmental differences had a critical influence upon the migration pattern.

In each island communities could be identified on the basis of two broad categories with respect to propensity for migration: rural communities with generally high levels and the urban populations which recorded appreciably lower ones. Exceptions to this trend were found in the plantation area of Westmoreland which recorded a relatively low index. Westmoreland, it will be recalled, was also irregular with respect to the pattern of actual departure rates from Jamaica. Montego Bay recorded the lowest index in the urban group, a situation which was true also for the actual departure rates.

The disparity between the low and middle-class income groups within the city reflected a similar situation to that of the rural-urban dichotomy in the overall island pattern. This was significant because it reflected the combined effect of location and social class in determining the differences which occurred in these two aspects of the migration process.

Emigration rates and type of locality demonstrated little correspondence at first glance. Plantation areas, for instance, could not be distinguished by their emigration pattern from small-farming districts; capital investment in rural industry had not affected the emigration of different areas in the same ways; the departure rates from towns were not solely related to the characteristics of urbanization but apparently were affected also by other variables, principally relating to accessibility.

The migration landscape

The importance of extrapolating a picture of the migration landscape lies primarily in the contribution it makes to examining the migration experience of specific places, or points in space, in the wider relational context of island-wide trends. Where did the peaks and ridges lie in the general topography of migration sources? To identify the watersheds which differentiated areas of high from low migration, was to establish a basis from which questions could be raised concerning the process and its explanation. The variables which coincided with, and possibly accounted for, the breaks of slope in the configuration of migration source areas, could be more easily detected.

The potential for migration and the actual flows are always present in the Caribbean. They are not always present to the same extent and in the same places, however, nor are they necessarily co-ordinated in time. It was most usual for the actual locational displacement of an individual to be preceded by the desire to move, though exceptions occurred in the migration of dependants, especially children: for while constituting an important sector of the latter phases of a migration stream, dependants rarely played any active decision-making role in the move. Nevertheless, they constituted an important factor taken into consideration by the active decision-makers of the family or household unit. Very much more common than emigration occurring without preliminary decision-making activity was the reverse situation, where the first stages of decision-making occurred without the final decision, or the opportunities, which brought about the actual displacement of the individual.

Indices of propensity for migration and actual migration measured different aspects of the migration process, and the coincidence or non-coincidence of the two patterns in no way negated the reality of the other's existence. In examining the migration process not only was it necessary for both components to be described but also their inter-relationship under varying circumstances had to be understood. Thus central issues concerned the nature of the gap between actual population displacement and the potential for migration, the distribution and changes in the differential between the two variables and explanations for the existing pattern.

The pattern of migration behaviour in relation to transport routes and the capital town or city, reflected – in the case of Jamaica – a corridor of high migration volume from south of Mt Diablo through the centre of St Catherine, following the main road which connects Kingston with the north, incorporating Spanish Town and the bauxite area centred on Ewarton; from there the emigration rate diminished towards the Kingston Metropolitan Area. The metropolitan area itself shared a similar emigration pattern with communities westwards along the main communication routes to Clarendon, including the town of May Pen. In the eastern third of the island the emigration was generally greater than for the west, a situation which was as true for small-farming areas as for the plantation zones.

The channels of information and corridors of movement and thus greater accessibility to Kingston, appeared to have been critical variables in the actual emigration. Contrasts were greatest between east and west, and between the areas of high and low connectivity with Kingston. For example, of the sugar estate areas it was the location in St Thomas (just east of the capital) which had the larger emigration volume as compared with an estate area in Westmoreland; the urban area of May Pen greatly exceeded westerly located Montego Bay in actual emigration. Of the bauxite areas, emigration was higher from Ewarton, less than 40 miles from Kingston, than it was from Discovery Bay, a similar type of area but on the north coast. Similarly, rural St Mary rather than rural Manchester had a high emigration rate, although in terms of social and economic structure both areas were remarkably similar (Figure 4.1a).

The out-migration rates in the case of Barbados decreased away from Bridgetown in a general north-easterly direction. Despite the small size of this island and the relatively high level of connectivity between most areas and the capital, distance and accessibility still appeared to affect emigration rates (Figure 4.2a).

The existence of the principal communication lines along the Windward and Leeward coasts of St Vincent was an important factor in the emigration pattern. At the same time, distance from Kingstown seemed to have been associated with diminishing emigration rates. This is a situation similar to that pointed out for the rural areas of western Jamaica and north-eastern Barbados. But in the case of those areas astride the main Windward and Leeward roads, there was a considerably higher rate of out-migration as exemplified by that for Chapman's village and Barrouallie (Figure 4.3a).

In all three cases – Jamaica, Barbados and St Vincent – accessibility appears to have played a significant role in influencing the configurations of migration rates. However, the relationship between emigration and accessibility was not immediately evident, nor was it clear what other factors played a part in producing either the consistencies or the inconsistencies in the association. The nature of the interrelationship thus required further scrutiny.

Migration propensity and actual migration compared

The surfaces which described variations in Jamaica, Barbados and St Vincent in propensity to migrate, demonstrated an almost opposite trend to that of actual departures. The corridor of high emigration rate stretching north and south from the metropolitan area in Jamaica was at the same time a zone of relatively low propensity for emigration. High indices for the propensity to emigrate could be described according to a west to east trend as increasing eastwards with the exception of the central area where the major routes going north and west from Kingston were located. Along a north-south axis the demand for emigration showed an overall decrease towards the metropolitan area (Figure 4.1b).

In Barbados the reversal of the general trend of actual migration rates was again evident in the desire to migrate configuration, with the demand for migration higher towards the more inaccessible north-east. Along a horizontal axis through the island's central section were increasing values, also in the direction of lessening accessibility with the capital. St Vincent was no exception to the pattern as described for Jamaica and Barbados, showing a diminishing propensity to migrate towards the capital and areas most accessible to it (Figure 4.3).

The relationship between migration rate and migration propensity in Jamaica, Barbados and St Vincent strikingly illustrated the key importance of locality in migration behaviour.

The populations of rural St Mary, St Thomas and Manchester (all in Jamaica), Belair and Sion Hill in St Vincent and St James in Barbados, were very similar in migration behaviour. There was a pairing, rather than clustering of other places. The central Westmoreland and Montego Bay samples in Jamaica had widely disparate economies, the one being in a rural plantation zone, the other in an urban centre. Yet locationally within the island they were both relatively distant from Kingston. St Lucy and St John had a similar economic structure and also relatively similar locations with respect to Bridgetown. It should be noted, however, that the St Lucy population, with the higher emigration rate, had greater access to Bridgetown than did that of St John. The Belmont and Ashdeane districts of St Michael, Barbados, experienced above average actual emigration rates and below average desire to emigrate. The Montrose district in Kingstown, St Vincent, was as extreme in its potential for emigrationas the rural areas mentioned above, but

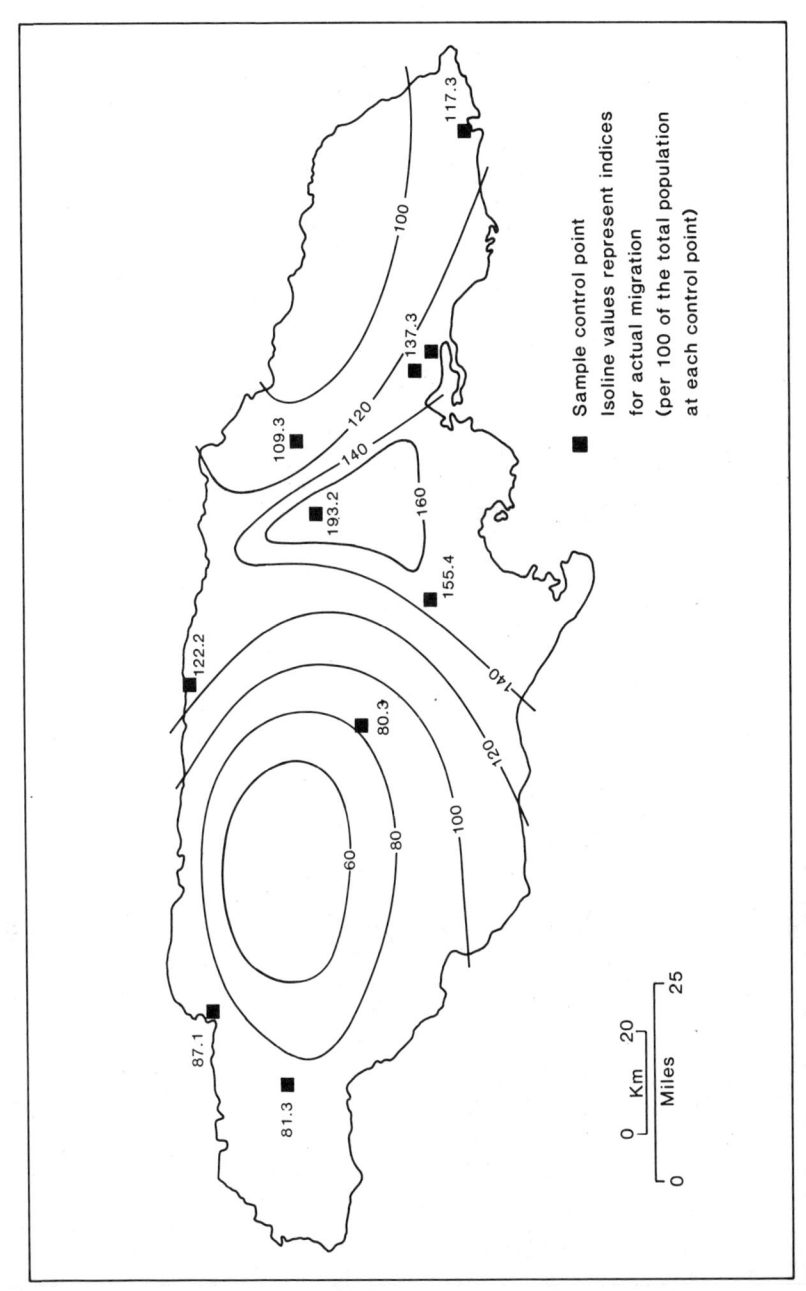

Figure 4.1a Jamaica: Actual migration

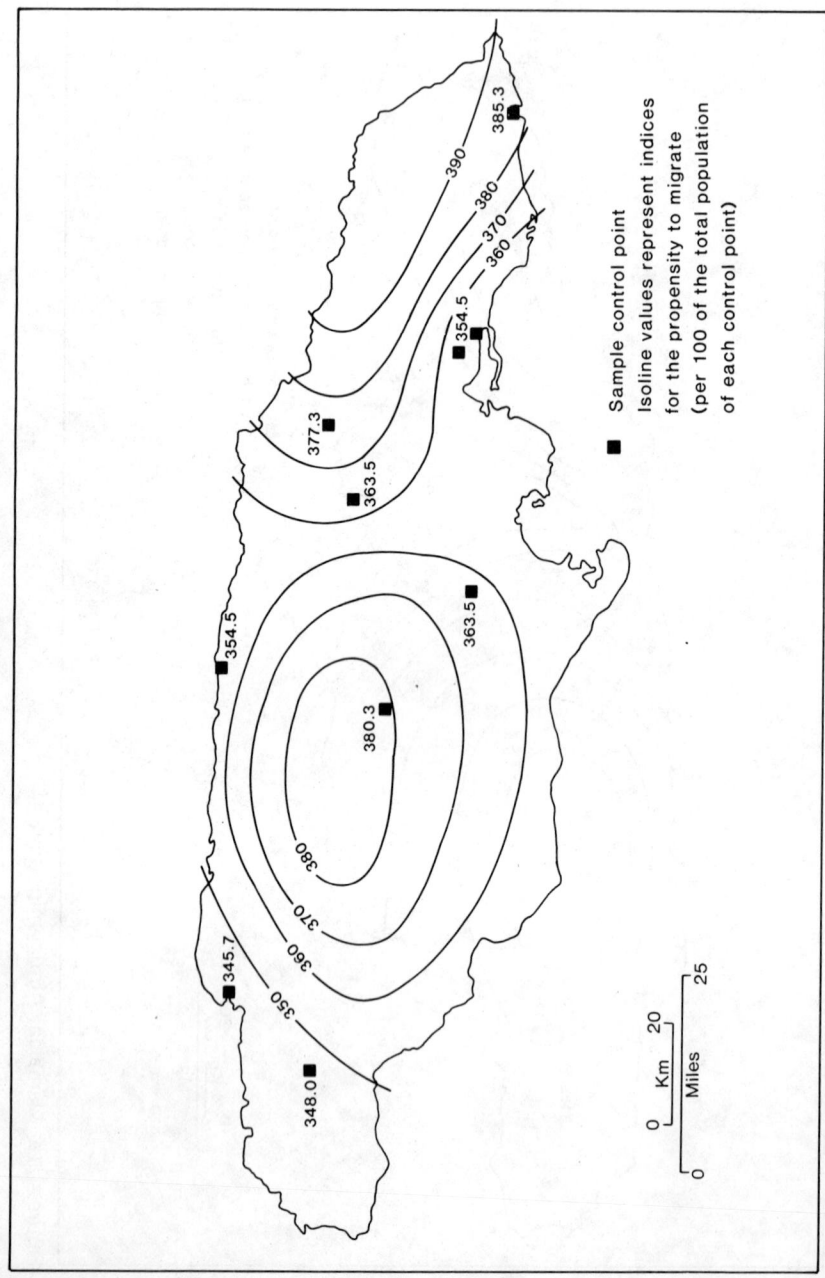

Figure 4.1b Jamaica: Propensity for migration

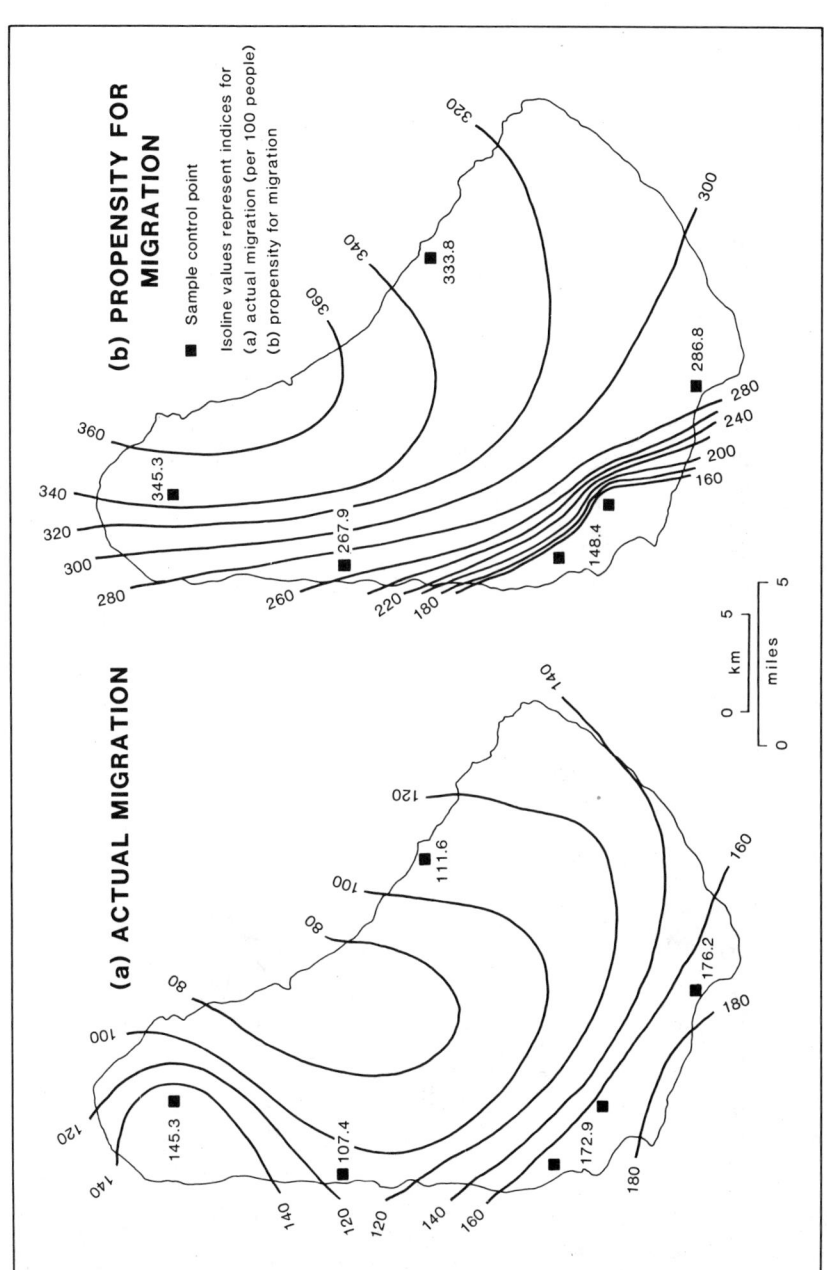

Figure 4.2 Barbados: a) Actual migration   b) Propensity for migration

104 Explanation in Caribbean migration

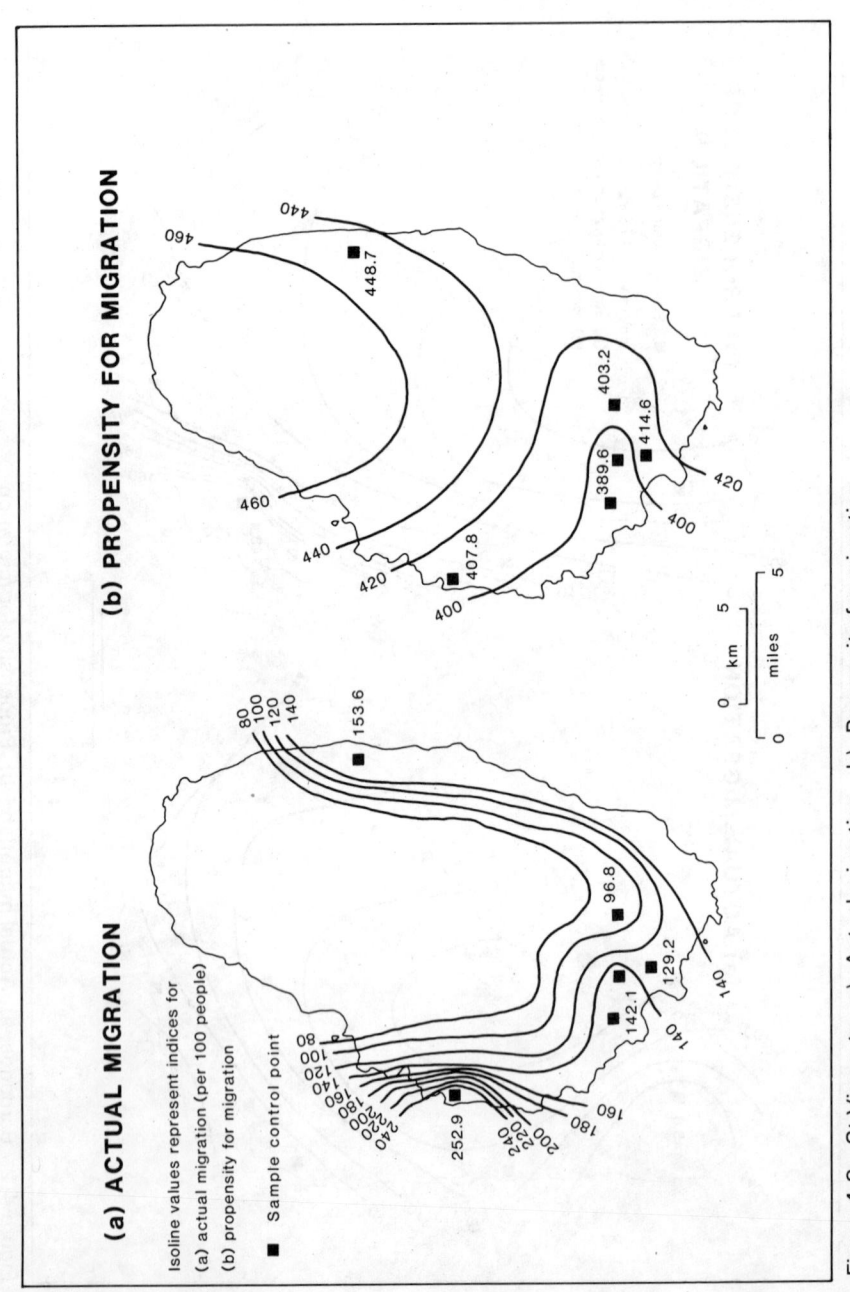

Figure 4.3 St Vincent: a) Actual migration b) Propensity for migration

at the other pole, namely having an exceptionally low index for desire to emigrate.

No simple pattern emerged whereby places of similar economic structure had similar emigration patterns. There was some correspondence between the pattern for rural areas and also urban areas, but this was not consistently the case. Both the relative location of places within the islands with respect to the capitals as well as their economic background could be important in this regard.

If location with respect to the capital was masking the effect of social characteristics and size of places, then the urban sample in Montego Bay was not likely to have an emigration pattern similar to that of small rural districts in Westmoreland. Likewise Barrouallie in St Vincent would not have the high emigration rate which it recorded by comparison with the urban sample in Murray district.

Within the islands, the largest gap between the indices for actual emigration and the propensity for emigration occurred in the rural areas, particularly those which were least accessible and where there was no diversification of the plantation or small-farming economies. Conversely, highly centralized places in each island had rates of actual departure which were commensurate with the indices for the propensity for emigration, thus the gap between them was small.

The areas of subsistence farming and plantations (both associated with low average incomes), were those areas which had high indices for the desire to emigrate but low actual departure rates. The second group of samples included the Christchurch area of Barbados, the low-income areas of Kingston and May Pen, the bauxite area of Ewarton, St Catherine, (that is, areas of easy access to, or actually in the capital). All recorded a similarly high desire to emigrate as found among the first group, but a commensurately high actual emigration rate and thus a lower gap between the two. Also in this group were Chapman's and Barrouallie, St Vincent. The third group comprised most parts of the island's capital, together with the St Ann district which was an area of high accessibility. This third group recorded emigration rates similar to those of the second, but with relatively lower desire to emigrate indices. Finally, the fourth group could be identified as having not only low desire to emigrate indices but also low actual departure rates. There was no obvious difference between the economic characteristics of the places which fell into this category and those in the third group described, suggesting that there is no simple explanation based on socio-economic factors.

Conclusion

Overall, a high migration propensity occurred in those places where actual emigration rates were low and, conversely, a low propensity for migration occurred in those places from which emigration had been high.

The closing of the gap between the propensity for migration and actual migration may be an integral part of what could be regarded as the maturing or stabilizing of the migration process. It was reasonable to assume that if the factors affecting out-migration were to change, they would bring about either a progression towards a more stable situation by having the effect of reducing the propensity for migration, or they would increase the discrepancy between actual migration and propensity, thus intensifying the conditions of instability. The configuration of the model suggested that the latter was the more likely to occur, reinforcing the view that the migration process was not tending towards the establishment of an equilibrium situation but rather, was increasing perceived and structural inequalities within each individual society and country.

The greatest differences lay between urban low-income groups and urban middle-income groups; but not all rural, low-income populations had the same level of migration propensity or migration rates from their households. There were distinct spatial patterns which combined the effects of location and income levels or class.

At the individual level migration behaviour showed no consistent relation to age, social status or occupation. Indeed, there was a marked absence of association between migration potential and any socio-economic or demographic characteristics, with the exception of gender as there was a slight tendency for increased migration propensity among women than among men. This exception apart, the differences in migration propensity were due to differences in the image which had no particular bearing on personal characteristics of a socio-economic or demographic nature.

The nature of the image reflected the temporal element in the sense that there was a time in the life of a person deemed to be appropriate for migrating even though the expectations of migration were tempered with the realization of possible limited success. Belief in the benefits to be derived from migration was also an important element of the image, and in relation to this, the evaluation of risk was minimized. The image further reflected the conditional element on which people based their expectations. Hence, it was believed that should migration take place, then certain objectives would be achieved and goals met. These applied to objectives of a material, educational, social and cultural nature.

Notes

1. A wide definition of the term household was current, reflecting a perception that even though some persons had been living abroad for several years with or without return visits, nevertheless, they were regarded as members of the household for an indefinite period of time. The point at which they ceased being seen as household members was based on qualitative changes in the relationship with the household, rather than with any specific time limit.
2. The number of members of households abroad was used to compute the out-migration rates to produce the number as a percentage of the total population in each sample.
3. Indices of migration propensity were computed from measures of migration orientation and the desire and intention to migrate for each population sample.

CHAPTER 5 | Evaluations of work, education and modernization in migration behaviour

Environments of themselves contain no objective meaning but are a function of the frame of reference and situation of the people who perceive them. Thus the impact of economic factors upon people's lives and decisions are more meaningful when translated into measures of employment potential and opportunities for work, especially as they are evaluated by the people who are themselves affected. The provision of educational facilities takes on special significance in terms of the way it fulfils the expectations of those affected. Likewise, the importance of a modernized infrastructure for migration behaviour must be evaluated in terms meaningful to the people whose lives are directly or indirectly influenced by it.

Opportunities for work

Economic disparities have been the basis for most interpretations of migration between places. This concept has invariably led to an oversimplification of the relationship between labour and capital and a deterministic explanation of the decision-making response. Assumptions concerning the nature of labour surplus have led to conclusions that it is a measure of the lack of employment possibilities and, in the rural context, landlessness.

Employment possibilities only present opportunities if they are perceived as such, and land is an asset only if it exists in such a form and is available for purposes deemed to be of value. Thus labour surplus in the Caribbean relates primarily to the perceptions of work and employment opportunities on the part of the workers themselves.

The characteristics of aspiration vary spatially chiefly on account of the distribution of social classes within each island, especially their urban concentration. But other factors, such as variations in reference groups, also affect the aspirations and thus the evaluations of people of the same social status living in different areas. For this reason, locally high employment rates, or high capital investment, rendering areas prosperous in terms of national productivity, are not surrogates for employment opportunities. This contributes to explanations of why areas of prosperity in the objective sense have not been the areas of low migration, nor areas of low national productivity the areas of high rates of migration or the strong desire to leave.

Perceptions of the work environment

In Jamaica, Barbados and St Vincent alike, the greatest discrepancies arose between the perceived desirability of industrial and service occupations over agricultural work. The high value placed on industrial work was reflected in the sense of deprivation of occupational opportunities felt about places without industry. However, the siting of industry in particular locations without the commensurate opportunities for work increased negative evaluations of the particular location by the people who lived there.

In areas of bauxite operations in Jamaica, for example, young men waited indefinitely for recruitment with the company, and the sense of work deprivation was greater in such areas than in those without bauxite. Even greater frustration was experienced due to the competition for jobs with people outside the areas and the fact that skilled workers were invariably recruited from other parts of the island.

Tourism provided a major focus of attraction in resort areas and, unlike bauxite, the opportunities for involvement were greater through the number of informal activities in which people could independently engage. Although employment in hotels, guest houses and clubs was sought after, self-employment within the broad framework of the tourist industry was also regarded as highly desirable. Operating taxis, making and/or selling souvenirs and craftwork, were among the occupations in which people found a livelihood. Like bauxite, however, tourism also attracted people into the industry who commuted from other locations. In the case of Ocho Rios, vendors travelled from as far away as Kingston on a weekly basis, and from places within a 25-mile radius on a daily basis, thus reducing the perceived opportunities of success for local inhabitants.

Negative attitudes and indifference shown towards agriculture were widespread throughout all rural areas, whether characterized by plantations, small-holdings or bauxite. In the bauxite area of Discovery Bay, for example, a few of the older people longed for land and regretted the destruction of fishing in the bay. Yet, despite these views, 61 per cent of the overall sample population were totally indifferent to the question of whether or not there was agricultural land available that they could buy or rent, nor were they personally concerned to engage in fishing as a livelihood.

A similar situation prevailed in Barbados. In the sugar plantation parish of St Lucy, 69 per cent of the population neither cared nor even thought about the question of cultivating land themselves. Besides, ownership of land made no difference to the pattern of household migration. Similarly, in the parish of St John more than two-thirds of the population were completely indifferent to the idea of land as a means of livelihood. While agriculture remained a semi-subsistence venture associated with low social status, it would be impossible to generate any real interest in it. Thus whether land was made available or not, migration opportunities would continue to be sought.

Perceived work opportunities

The perception of employment opportunities relates to the different aspects of 'opportunity'. From one perspective it refers to the perceived availability of suitable employment in the locality in the general sense. It also refers to satisfaction or dissatisfaction with individual employment opportunities believed to be available. From yet a third perspective, it relates to evaluation of the extent to which the individual's actual occupation approximated to his or her aspired occupation.

Caribbean people, especially in low-income groups, characteristically engage in more than one form of work. This pattern of multiple occupation provides a means of coping with poorly remunerated and seasonal or spasmodic work opportunities. By combining more than one type of work either simultaneously or in a repetitive sequence, subsistence and cash earning can be combined. Of importance also is the fact that menial work, as in agriculture or casual labour, can be combined with a higher status occupation such as a trade like carpentry or dressmaking. Invariably the higher status work brings in the lowest contribution by way of income or income-substitution through food production, but is valued because of its status. The image of work and the purpose for which it is intended determine the way in which opportunities for work are evaluated as a source of cash income, subsistence and status in the community.

The general availability of suitable employment in the local area
Evaluations of the general availability of suitable work in the locality could not be explained by either social or demographic differences in the population, though there was a tendency for greater dissatisfaction

among the more educated, the older age groups and those people who had considered migrating previously.

While social and demographic factors provided little explanation for variations in the evaluation of the availability of suitable work, there were definite locational differences in the evaluations which had to be explained.

The greatest dissatisfaction with the availability of suitable work in Jamaica occurred in the rural areas, chiefly in the St Ann bauxite area, the plantation zone (both in Westmoreland and St Thomas), and the hill farming district of St Mary. The only population experiencing a high level of satisfaction with work opportunities was the middle-class urban group in Harbour View. The contrast between this situation and that of the low-income, urban population of Grant's Pen in the evaluation of job availability in the same city was particularly striking. This demonstrated the important combination of both social and spatial factors in the overall pattern of evaluations.

The wide disparity between the perceived employment opportunities in different areas in Jamaica was in contrast with the more homogeneous situation in Barbados. Furthermore, not only were rural-urban differences slight, but the lower evaluation of work availability was to be found in Bridgetown rather than in the rural districts. This was to be explained by the fact that in rural areas there was perceived access to both local and urban work whereas people in the town, although aware of the difficulties of obtaining work, would not contemplate rural parishes in their perception of job opportunities.

The evaluation of local job availability strongly reflected the distribution of industries associated with those reference groups against which suitability of employment was judged. This reinforced the earlier observation that the availability of suitable jobs was related most to industrial employment in conjunction with a rejection of the employment potential in agriculture. At the same time, the considerable variation in the evaluation of employment opportunities found to exist in Jamaica, contrasted with the slighter difference occurring in Barbados and St Vincent. This was probably a reflection of the greater distances between urban and some rural areas in Jamaica. As a consequence of this, access to employment opportunities was seen far more on a local basis in Jamaica, and at the national scale, dominated by conditions in the capital town in the case of the smaller territories.

Personal satisfaction with local employment opportunities
This second element in the perception of employment opportunities was a measure of the extent of personal satisfaction with available employment opportunities.

A very low level of association between satisfaction with employment opportunities and social and demographic characteristics was evident, especially in Barbados and Jamaica. The exception to this was that men were much more dissatisfied with employment opportunities than were women in the Vincentian case. This tendency also occurred, though less so, among the Barbadian population.

With respect to migration experience, those who had previously been abroad tended to be those most dissatisfied in the case of St Vincent, to a lesser extent in the case of Barbados, and not at all in the case of Jamaica. Yet those holding a valid passport were, in all three islands, among those most dissatisfied with the work environment. This again reinforced the idea that perceptions of opportunities – in this case opportunities for work – were not closely associated with any specific social or demographic characteristics of the people themselves. Previous migration experience did influence people's evaluations of work opportunities, reflecting at least one major way in which migration occurring in the 'actual environment' became a factor affecting the 'perceived environment'.

Despite the low level of association with demographic characteristics, the spatial variation in the evaluation of work opportunities demonstrated an important variation along class lines, which was reflected spatially. Much greater satisfaction was expressed by the middle-class populations. Secondly, the very high level of dissatisfaction felt in rural areas was true for all three islands. Furthermore, within the rural areas, remoteness from the capital city or town also appeared important in affecting the satisfaction felt about the employment situation.

In most cases this consequence of remoteness existed in those areas which were in fact physically remote in terms of distance from the capital. This was the case for central Westmoreland in Jamaica, St Lucy in Barbados and Barrouallie in St Vincent. The populations of these areas all expressed low satisfaction levels with local employment facilities. At the same time, there were other areas, such as Belair in St Vincent and central St Mary in Jamaica, which, though not particularly distant from the capital towns, had a low degree of contact with the towns. They demonstrated the same tendencies towards high levels of dissatisfaction with local opportunities for work.

Actual and aspired occupations

The gap between the actual occupations individuals held and those to which they aspired was a measure of the frustration experienced in terms of available work (Table 5.1).

Differences in occupational frustration on the basis of social class were again exemplified in the contrast between the middle-class,

Table 5.1 Occupational frustration

	Very and fairly small gap between actual and aspired job	Intermediate or indifferent	Fairly and very large gap between actual and aspired job
JAMAICA			
Kingston Metropolitan Area			
Harbour View	86.7	5.3	8.0
Grant's Pen	42.6	14.7	42.7
Other urban			
Montego Bay	35.7	22.9	41.4
May Pen	50.0	12.2	37.8
Rural: bauxite			
North-west St Ann	26.0	14.2	59.8
Ewarton, St Catherine	40.5	9.5	50.0
Rural: plantation			
Central Westmoreland	42.7	28.0	29.3
Port Morant, St Thomas	52.0	12.0	36.0
Rural: small-farming			
Western St Mary	44.0	22.7	33.3
Central Manchester	64.5	3.9	31.6
BARBADOS			
Urban: Bridgetown			
Belmont, St Michael / Deacons, St Michael	41.7	16.0	42.3
Rural: tourism			
Oistins, Christchurch	42.7	25.0	32.3
Weston, St James	33.3	27.2	39.5
Rural: plantation			
St Martin's Bay, St John	42.9	14.2	42.9
Central St Lucy	36.0	14.7	49.3
ST VINCENT			
Urban: Kingstown			
Montrose	80.5	8.7	10.8
Murray Village	33.4	22.9	43.7
Rural: South			
Belair	45.2	25.8	29.0
Sion Hill/Arnos Vale	51.2	29.3	19.5
Rural: Windward and Leeward			
Chapman's (Windward)	39.0	36.6	24.4
Barrouallie (Leeward)	49.0	19.6	31.4

Figures represent percentages of the population in each sub-sample.

Harbour View residents and the experience of the rest of the Jamaican population; between the middle-class, Montrose population in St Vincent and the low-income urban group; similarly between part of the Belmont community in Barbados and that of the other urban areas. In all three middle-class populations, more than 80 per cent of each were in occupations to which the individuals aspired. For example, among 68 per cent of the Harbour View population and 63 per cent of that of Montrose, there was no real difference between the actual and aspired occupations.

In Jamaica the frequency of the occurrence of large gaps between actual and aspired occupations was not in the economically worse-off rural localities, but in the two bauxite areas of St Catherine and St Ann. Over 50 per cent of the population in each case experienced significant gaps between actual and aspired occupations. The next largest frequency of substantial differences between actual and aspired occupations existed in the urban areas (other than the Harbour View middle-class area as already mentioned). In Montego Bay and the Grant's Pen district of Kingston, over 40 per cent of the population fell into this category and in May Pen this was true of almost 38 per cent.

The pattern of 'occupational frustration' in both Barbados and St Vincent presented an interesting comparison with that of Jamaica. In particular, the urban reference groups were more important to local evaluations of employment in the small islands than was the case in Jamaica. The importance of the capital town, as well as the tourism of the south, were strongly reflected in Barbados and St Vincent. The residents of the parishes of St Lucy and St John, Barbados, had the highest rates of dissatisfaction with present employment, whereas in Christchurch and St James these rates were lower. The urban reference groups were more important to local evaluations of employment in the small islands than was the case in Jamaica.

This relationship of rural evaluation and urban proximity – whether in a real or perceived sense – was also evident in St Vincent. There, functional distances were considerably greater than in Barbados despite the similarity in size. The mountainous terrain and generally lower rural incomes available for transport in this island accounted for the low degree of overall contact with the capital. The Barrouallie population interacted with Kingstown to a greater extent than was the case with the residents of Chapman's village who travelled more to nearby Georgetown. However, it was very significant that the highest frequencies of employment frustration were found in both Bridgetown and Kingstown themselves, and also in Kingston, Jamaica (the middle-class population excepted). This suggested that, as in the bauxite areas in Jamaica mentioned above, the prevalence of reference groups with the greatest ambtion – thus the occurrence of over-optimistic expectations – created the greatest incidence of disenchantment with actual employment opportunities. As a consequence, the highest rates of occupational frustration existed among the lower-income groups of the capital towns and cities.

With the exception of the Harbour View, central Manchester and Ewarton populations, in which only a small minority had no clear idea as to the type of occupations they preferred, there was a considerable element of indifference. In the St Mary and Westmoreland rural areas, and in the Montego Bay urban area, more than 20 per cent of the population felt this way. What these comparative figures showed above all, was that in the more isolated rural areas there was a greater proportion of the population with no definite occupational aspirations. Elsewhere throughout the island more people had clear goals.

In Barbados and St Vincent the indifference rates were generally higher than in Jamaica, even among people in the towns. Nevertheless, the greatest gaps between actual and aspired occupations still occurred among the most accessible populations of Barbados and St Vincent; the largest gaps occurred in the lower-class urban areas and in the least accessible rural zones.

The gap between actual and aspired occupations presented a pattern which was essentially similar to that of the perceived availability of suitable jobs. First, the expected difference between the middle-class and lower-class experience was considerable. Second, the distribution of important occupational reference groups – such as in industry and the services – was the most significant factor in determining the distribution of attractive employment facilities. It also played an important part in the pattern of occupational frustration measured in terms of the gap between actual and aspired occupations.

Occupational frustration appeared to be the most sensitive indicator of the level of satisfaction which people felt about the work environment of their locality. Views on this aspect of the work environment were particularly informative because it demonstrated the comparisons between the actual and desired occupations in different areas. The indices for occupational frustration were shown to vary not so much with the objective work opportunities based on the location of bauxite, productive agricultural land and the like. Instead, the pattern of work evaluation reflected a combination of variations in class aspirations with regards to work, and variations in the perceptions of different types of environments at different locations as providing satisfactory work opportunities.

Perception of the opportunities for work and migration propensities

The close relationship between the ends for which work was perceived and the ends for which migration was seen, permitted migration to function as an alternative means of achieving, thus compensating for the inability to attain those results in the home area or country. This helped to explain the importance of *suitable* work in the evaluation of local environments and levels of satisfaction of the populations within those environments. But the evaluation of employment opportunities was not a major factor in explaining migration behaviour. There were only a very few cases where the propensity to migrate was even partly accounted for by the evaluation of occupational opportunities in the locality. Where the work environment played any role in migration decisions at all, it was in relation to the frustration caused by the gap between actual and aspired occupation. But even in these cases, implications for the propensity to migrate were minimal.

Although the greatest gaps between people's aspired and actual occupations occurred among the urban, low-income groups, there was a qualitative element in the image of work which gave a negative weighting to agriculture, which in turn produced the deepest frustrations with the work environment in agricultural areas. This greatly influenced the role which the evaluation of work opportunities had in migration behaviour. Consequently, the effect of frustration with work opportunities in the propensity for migration varied from one type of locality to another.

In general, the impact of low evaluations of employment opportunities upon the migration potential was greatest among communities in those rural areas where agriculture was the only major available means of work. In Jamaica this was true of the small-farming population of central St Mary and areas at the plantation-peasant interface of Westmoreland and St Thomas; in St Vincent of the remote peasant communities of Barrouallie and Chapman's; in Barbados of the rural areas in St Lucy and St John, and also in St James – at the interface of the sugar plantation area and the tourist developments of the coast. Thus, where there was no local alternative to agriculture the frustration with available occupations was greatest and the effect which this had upon the propensity to migrate was commensurately high. In addition to the small-farming and plantation communities, considerable occupational frustration also occurred among the low-income urban groups.

In the plantation zone of southern St Thomas in Jamaica, for example, those persons in the community experiencing high levels of occupational frustration were almost three times as likely to migrate as those for whom there was little difference between actual and aspired occupation. In the agricultural area of central Westmoreland and St Mary they were one and a half times as likely to migrate.

In the low-income area of Grant's Pen in Kingston, Jamaica, the populations with the large gap between actual and aspired occupations exceeded those with little or no employment frustration by more than one and a half times, in accounting for the propensity to migrate. Similarly, in St Vincent, in rural Chapman's and Barrouallie as well as the low-income district of Murray in the capital Kingstown, there was approximately a one and a half times difference in the extent to which frustration in employment accounted for the level in the propensity to migrate. The same may be noted for central St James in Barbados. On the other hand, Montego Bay, May Pen, Ewarton in St Catherine and the middle-class Harbour View area of Kingston, in Jamaica, as well as Belair and the Montrose middle-class population of Kingstown in St Vincent, showed that the difference between the additional contribution which these districts made (proportionate to the size of their populations) to the total propensity to migrate was negligible. It did not appear that in the more accessible or urbanized areas people who were dissatisfied with their actual work, by comparison with the work to which they aspired, contributed more to the potential for migration in their district than did people who were less frustrated with their employment opportunities.

It may have been that there were thresholds below which the levels of occupational frustration resulted in apathy which prevented the development of even the aspirations which might otherwise have stimulated the migration potential. Conversely, above a certain level of satisfaction, it could be that boredom with local opportunities might have resulted in an increase in the desire to migrate to seek more challenging situations. Whatever the connection between employment frustration and migration potential, the relationship was not simple. Increased frustration with work did not lead directly to a progressive increase in migration potential. This reinforced the argument that the low evaluations of the work or economic environment did not necessarily increase the desire to migrate, but more importantly, the levels of previous migration conditioned the references which affected evaluations of the work environment.

Though the image of work and its benefits in many respects coincided with the image of migration, a poor evaluation of work opportunities did not in any simple or direct way induce migration.

The evaluation of education

The functional relationship between education and occupation is a universal feature of modern society. Literacy is primarily evaluated in terms of the types of employment it permits, and in Caribbean society as in many others, literacy is seen as a way of escaping from the land, not a means of becoming a better farmer; school leaving certificates are perceived as the principal opening to high status occupations. Therefore, to claim that widespread regard was accorded education in the Caribbean would be to state the obvious – namely, that all people would like to acquire the instrument for obtaining well-paid, respected positions.

For large sectors of the Caribbean working class, education was regarded more as one of the good fortunes of life than as an achievement to be sought after and worked for. This is not surprising given the unequal availability, both in quantity and quality, to different sectors of the society. Because of this, even in those areas where school provisions existed, attitudes were dominated by the belief that educational achievement lay in the possession of exceptional ability, finance and special contacts. With improved educational opportunities in the Caribbean since the 1960s some changes in attitude had taken place, but there was no strong sense that more educational provisions would provide the solution.

Explanations for this situation can be found in the reduced commercial value of a primary education and even that of secondary school leaving qualifications due to the increased number of school places and widening school attendance in most of the islands during recent decades. As a result, few school leavers attained any meaningful standard in relation to the jobs they expected. The devalued currency of primary and even secondary education, meant that the greater availability of education was not seen by the majority to bear fruit on a wide enough scale to satisfy aspirations. Instead, the greater access to education has had the opposite effect, that of increasing levels of expectation and, at the same time, enhancing opportunities for obtaining visas and overcoming the practical obstacles to migration.

The evaluation of educational opportunities

It was only reasonable to assume that if education were an important aspect of the psyche and motivation of a community, the lack of schools in any area would create a sense of relative deprivation. Conversely, one would expect that the residents of areas well endowed with schools would feel appropriately satisfied with their higher than average advantage in the island society. This was not the situation. Instead, there was widespread resignation to the circumstances surrounding the unequal educational opportunities in different parts of the islands, rather than strong feelings of either a positive or negative nature. Whatever variation there was in the evaluation of educational facilities, this could be accounted for by the much stronger views held by women than by men, and by those with previous experience of migration. It was also the case that individuals in possession of a valid passport were among those with the poorest evaluations of the educational facilities.

The spatial pattern of the evaluation of educational facilities was also paradoxical. Rural populations reported greater levels of satisfaction with educational facilities than did people in the towns, yet rural areas were less well provided with schools than were the urban areas.

More than half of the middle-class Harbour View population of Kingston, Jamaica, were very, or fairly, satisfied with their educational opportunities, a third of the lower-class Grant's Pen group, also in Kingston, and well over a third in May Pen. Significant was the fact that the urban population of Montego Bay, as in the case of occupation evaluation, was again an exception to the overall urban pattern and more closely approximated the situation in the rural areas. By contrast, the Ewarton population in St Catherine, easily accessible to Kingston, had only 60 per cent dissatisfied with the educational facilities. In all other rural areas the dissatisfaction was high among at least 75 per cent of the population.

In Barbados there was little spatial differentiation in response to the evaluation of local educational facilities. This was partly a function of the small size of the island as it was common practice to travel across the island to attend secondary schools in Bridgetown. Indeed, the majority of people had thought very little about the provision of educational facilities, feeling confident that they were available and accessible, especially as private secondary schools of various standing were numerous and most made no educational demands for admission. What people believed to be the case largely explained their positive evaluations of educational opportunities without much conviction about their personal position in relation to them.

In St Vincent, the situation was different again, with the evaluation of available educational opportunities occupying a very low profile in people's perception of their life chances. Therefore, it was not surprising that the role of educational facilities in migration potential was minimal (Table 5.2).

Evaluations of educational opportunities available in the various localities could not be explained by the actual educational provisions.

Table 5.2 Evaluations of local educational opportunities

	Very and fairly highly evaluated	Intermediate or non-commital	Fairly and very poorly evaluated
JAMAICA			
Kingston Metropolitan Area			
Harbour View	53.4	12.0	34.6
Grant's Pen	37.4	44.0	18.6
Other urban			
Montego Bay	23.6	11.7	64.7
May Pen	31.1	48.6	20.3
Rural: bauxite			
North-west St Ann	11.6	13.0	75.4
Ewarton, St Catherine	28.4	12.2	59.4
Rural: plantation			
Central Westmoreland	12.0	13.4	74.6
Port Morant, St Thomas	15.2	68.3	16.5
Rural: small-farming			
Western St Mary	10.7	2.6	86.7
Central Manchester	29.0	9.2	61.8

Note: The measurements for Barbados and St Vincent have not been tabulated on account of the negligible spatial differences in the evaluation of educational facilities in Barbados and the general indifference to their availability in St Vincent.

This reinforced the argument that evaluations of opportunities were associated with an image which bore little relationship to specific characteristics of the objective situation and more to past experience and the articulation of expectations and goals.

The evaluation of educational opportunities and migration

Education, as indicated previously, was seen by the majority in the Caribbean as a way of increasing the chances of migrating, while for others migration was viewed as a means of improving the opportunities for education. Both education and migration were acknowledged by most people as a means of facilitating upward social mobility. Therefore, there was an unmistakable and dual relationship between these two processes, but that did not mean that there was necessarily a simple causal relationship between them. Not only was the correlation between the two variables low, but also slightly negative, signifying a weak, inverse relationship between them. In other words, instead of the desire to migrate tending to be consistently or progressively higher the greater the dissatisfaction with educational opportunities, the reverse situation tended to occur. This meant that those more satisfied with educational provisions were among those showing a higher propensity to migrate.

The exact nature of the relationship between the perceived opportunities for education and migration behaviour was difficult to ascertain. But one important point to emerge was that the propensity to migrate was not significantly associated with either the real or perceived opportunities for education in the locality.

As with work, so with education, the knowledge of good prospects overseas became an attraction to persons with a high propensity for migration. But for neither work nor education could one conclude that the local facilities as they existed or were seen to exist, had a similar overall effect upon the entire population, or even upon any single community. Explanations of Caribbean migration behaviour cannot rely solely, or even in major part, on either the real or even the perceived employment and educational opportunities.

Evaluations of the modernization of the local area

As the urban societies in the Caribbean tried to keep up with the metropolises of the North Atlantic, so the rural populations measured their prestige and level of advancement against their urban centres.

In all Caribbean territories levels of modernization were reflected in the perceived gradient of attractiveness of different parts of the country. At one end of the continuum areas of least attraction were those which had been little affected by the modernization processes. At the other extreme were the urban centres, particularly the primate cities, with the greatest concentrations of modern buildings and services. The internal migration history of the larger Caribbean islands since World War II reflects this (Adams, 1969; Tekse, 1967). Therefore levels of modernization were well worth inclusion in any consideration of migration behaviour and, so far, little is known about the relationship between them.

Employment and educational facilities apart, people evaluated the level of modernization of their locality in terms of the efficiency of transport and the existence of tarmacadam surfaces on roads, a supply of shopping and entertainment facilities and the provision of utilities such as electricity and piped water. The extent to which people believed their area to be equipped with these services, amenities and utilities, was important in determining their evaluation of the local environment.

The variation in this aspect of people's evaluations of their locality could be explained in part by their age, sex, educational background and occupation (Table 5.3). In St Vincent and Barbados there was also a strong relationship between evaluation of amenities and previous migration background, with a tendency towards lesser tolerance of local amenities among those who had already been abroad. For example, the greatest dissatisfaction over transport facilities in Jamaica was felt by the populations in, or accessible to, urban areas and districts relatively well served by public buses. While this expressed the greater need of the urban population for public transport facilities, at the same time, it also expressed the higher level of expectation on the part of urban dwellers. What the response did not reflect was a simple measure of the provision of this particular facility.

In contrast to the urban areas in Jamaica, in the rural areas of that island as also in St Vincent, where transport facilities in most cases were very poorly provided, people characteristically showed little concern about the inadequacies of the service. The only complaints were in the rising fares. In Barbados, where public bus services were relatively well provided and reliable, the overall satisfaction levels were not markedly higher than those found in Jamaica and St Vincent. Moreover, in the northern and eastern areas of Barbados, people felt more aggrieved about the deficiencies of their local bus services than was the case in northern St Vincent, where there was no regular bus at all.

Remarkably high levels of satisfaction with amenities other than transport were expressed by people everywhere. However, in most places there were also relatively large proportions of the population who were either simply resigned to the situation, whatever it was, or otherwise had few or no ideas about the whole matter of amenities and services.

The ways in which the modernization of the infrastructure varied spatially reflected the way in which it was evaluated relative to expectations. These expectations varied, at least in part, with the differing scales of reference, rather than with an objective measure of the provision of amenities. A modernized infrastructure was valued as much for the sense of status which it brought to a community as for the improvement in individual living conditions. Electricity, for example, was seen to bring status to the rural lower-class family whose house was supplied. But also, the existence of electricity in the local district affected the esteem with which people held the area because of the generally enhanced status associated with the provision of this utility. In any event, many a rural working-class household was unable to afford electricity even where it was available. Nevertheless, the brighter

Table 5.3 The evaluation of the local environment in terms of the perceived level of modernization

	TRANSPORT			AMENITIES		
	Very and fairly satisfied	Intermediate or non-commital	Very and fairly dissatisfied	Very and fairly satisfied	Intermediate or non-commital	Very and fairly dissatisfied
JAMAICA						
Kingston Metropolitan Area						
Harbour View	22.7	26.9	50.4	56.0	28.0	16.0
Grant's Pen	2.6	21.4	76.0	58.7	32.0	9.3
Other urban						
Montego Bay	44.3	37.1	18.6	77.2	14.3	8.5
May Pen	68.9	6.7	24.4	75.7	18.9	5.4
Rural: bauxite						
North-west St Ann	31.2	45.5	23.3	48.8	35.4	15.8
Ewarton, St Catherine	69.0	17.5	13.5	75.7	17.5	6.8
Rural: plantation						
Central Westmoreland	32.0	34.7	33.3	72.0	18.7	9.3
Port Morant, St Thomas	44.0	41.3	14.7	65.4	25.3	9.3
Rural: small-farming						
Western St Mary	40.0	32.0	28.0	46.3	37.0	16.7
Central Manchester	36.8	38.2	25.0	64.5	23.7	11.8
BARBADOS						
Urban: Bridgetown						
Belmont, St Michael Deacons, St Michael	44.5	31.9	23.6	56.9	29.4	13.7
Rural: tourism						
Oistins, Christchurch	72.0	13.3	14.7	26.8	18.2	55.0
Weston, St James	54.3	27.2	18.5	41.7	19.0	39.3
Rural: plantation						
St Martin's Bay, St John	22.1	36.4	41.5	22.8	16.2	61.0
Central St Lucy	22.7	42.6	34.7	48.7	17.0	34.3
ST VINCENT						
Urban: Kingstown						
Montrose	17.4	41.3	41.3	73.7	7.1	19.2
Murray Village	18.8	60.4	20.8	68.3	19.5	12.2
Rural: South						
Belair	12.9	38.7	48.4	32.3	41.9	25.8
Sion Hill/Arnos Vale	46.4	39.0	14.6	65.7	15.8	18.5
Rural: Windward and Leeward						
Chapman's (Windward)	29.3	39.0	31.7	78.0	19.5	2.5
Barrouallie (Leeward)	17.7	31.3	51.0	80.9	10.6	8.5

TRANSPORT = Evaluation of transport facilities servicing the local area.
AMENITIES = Evaluation of amenities in the local area.
Figures represent percentages of the population of each sub-sample.

appearance of the district was highly valued as people did not like to feel that their district was a backwater or that it was unpopular with outsiders.

The evaluation of a modernized infrastructure and migration

The relationship between migration behaviour and level of modernization was determined as much by the prestige value of modernization as by the actual convenience provided by modern amenities. As noted in the case of electricity, for example, a supply to the district was regarded as being of equal or greater importance than its supply to any particular household. The way in which people perceived their district or country in relation to other places, in terms of modernization (in other words, the status element of the image) appeared to be of considerable importance in determining the image of their home locality.

Conclusion

Lower-income groups expected to improve their conditions by relating more closely to the middle class and adopting not only their institutions, but also their material culture and lifestyle. The locality was evaluated in terms of the opportunities for achieving this objective.

Each locality was assessed primarily in terms of its ability to provide non-agricultural work, as well as its endowment with the symbols of modernization such as electricity and paved roads. In urban areas the need for housing took precedence in places where utilities were already provided. Of little significance in perceptions of localities were educational facilities.

The variation in the perception of amenities, like that of work and education, was more closely associated with references against which people measured these facilities rather than the objective characteristics of the facility itself. This reinforced the point that evaluations of the environment were associated with an image which bore little relationship to specific characteristics of the individual and more to past experience and the articulation of expectations and goals. These references, themselves both cause and consequence of the images people held of themselves and their goals, varied spatially as well as socially.

Certainly, migration behaviour would not significantly change in response to any particular improvements in the infrastructure. Change in the image would only occur if there were fundamental changes in the reference or base line against which opportunities were evaluated and their life chances assessed. This would depend upon changes in belief and the fundamental value system, not in superficial environmental changes such as infrastructural improvements. The spatial variation in references or in the nature of the image were significant. Furthermore, in that they were more closely related to accessibility than to any variation in the socio-economic characteristics of localities, the role of accessibility in migration behaviour had to be examined more closely.

Notes

1 To overcome the ambiguities of multiple occupations, the occupation taken to be the 'actual occupation' was the one in which the individual spent most of his or her work time. This was usually unambiguous, for even where two jobs occupied an equal or equivalent amount of time, there was never any conflict in terms of the category of work into which either would be classed.

The occupations to which people aspired were also placed into defined categories using the same classification. The differences, if there were any, between the category of the actual and aspired occupations were recorded and a measure allocated according to the extent of the difference between them. This measure of the gap, which was to some extent a measure of occupational frustration, was calculated for each individual and summed for each sub-sample of the population.

CHAPTER 6

Accessibility and information in migration behaviour

Accessibility has a physical as well as a social dimension; when combined, they influence interaction at various levels. Any group which is remote from the rest of society – spatially or socially – receives less information than those groups which are central and accessible. At the same time, places which are integral to the life of a country in a social, economic or political sense, are always the places in which the infrastructure and communication channels are well developed. The converse is true of those areas of less importance to the focus of national development. Thus, the information received is an indicator of the physical and social location of the individual, household, community or society within the national and international system. For these reasons the diffusion of information in a society, and the information received by any sector of that society, is a valuable indicator of accessibility in physical and social space.

Accessibility and information

The sphere of contact established historically and maintained by Caribbean countries through political and economic links determines the overall framework of their international accessibility and information fields. Colonial and former colonial territories in the Caribbean are, in many cases, in closer contact with their metropolises than with any other parts of the world or even with other neighbouring Caribbean territories.

Each Caribbean territory may be conceptualized as having a unique field of interaction. This may be defined by what amounts to a sphere of contact with elastic parameters which expand and contract in select global directions at different periods of time. This is largely the result of the nature and direction of the communication channels derived from colonial, neo-colonial, and other types of international relations. In turn, these determine the location of earlier migrations from Caribbean countries. These countries influence information more directly at the personal level.

Personal information fields reflect not only the location of the country within the international framework, but the location of the individual and community within their national space. The personal information fields create the detailed configurations of the national information fields. The less access individuals have to knowledge, either through the formal education channels or other means, the more reliant they are for their information upon personal networks. Personal contacts and, therefore, personal information fields are sometimes very specific.

Since the 1950s many Jamaicans had emigrated seasonally to the Bahamas. The information generated by those persons who resided in, or had visited the Bahamas, primarily flowed directly to those districts and communities from which the emigrants originated. As a result, more was known about the Bahamas among the population of remote parts of Westmoreland than among the urban dwellers in other parts of the island. The wide occurrence of migration to the Bahamas from Jamaica led to the return flow of sufficient information that throughout the island, notwithstanding location, most people were at least aware of the existence of the place if not also knowing something about its opportunities for work.

This contrasted with the situation in St Vincent where there were few (and then only the relatively well-informed) who had ever even heard of the Bahamas. Nevertheless, whereas Vincentians received a considerable amount of information generated by their compatriots in the British Virgin Islands, which, in physical terms, were as distant from St Vincent as they were from Jamaica, most Jamaicans had never heard of any of the British Virgin Islands.

The location and the age of the emigrant communities affected the amount of news travelling back to specific Caribbean countries. At any particular time each Caribbean country had its own spatial field within which access to information was greatest. Within these spatial fields, communities varied in their level of accessibility to information flows. The more accessible tended to receive more information and more quickly than the less accessible. As a result, in the more accessible communities changes in perceptions and in the images held occurred much more readily than in the most remote.

Information in migration behaviour

Information itself provides input for the migration process in various ways. It conditions the cognitions and attitudes which help create mental images as well as providing directives about the procedures and opportunities relating to specific migration activity.

Information is largely responsible for the types of mental images which people have of themselves and society, of their local area, their country and the rest of the world. These images condition attitudes relating to migration itself and to the perceived opportunities available in the home environment as well as in other parts of the world. For these reasons it is undoubtedly of great importance to the migration process.

In terms of the specifics of migration, people have to be informed about the legislative constraints and procedures involved and the means of dealing with these. Also important is information on work, education, housing and other practical issues relating to the destination. In addition information is needed on the acquisition of the birth certificate, photograph, passport, visa, shipping or airline ticket and other requirements for travel about which prospective emigrants have to know. Such information, which to the sophisticated is assimilated effortlessly and usually subconsciously over a long period, often has to be hurriedly acquired by the uninformed just at the moment it is needed. In some cases, job-finding agencies provide the specific information which facilitates the final move to a precise destination abroad. In this way, information assists in bringing about the actual move when the potential for migration already exists.

Personal space is not circumscribed solely by the individual's immediate surroundings, nor do people acquire all their knowledge by staying in one place. Mobility enhances the amount and variety of information which people acquire. Whether through frequent short stays for purposes of business, recreation or social visits, for longer sojourns or actual residential moves, accessibility is increased and information is acquired — intentionally or otherwise — about the space in which travel takes place and from the people encountered.

These means of communication, both at the group and individual scale, are important for the part they each play in controlling the overall environment of information, and subsequently their role in migration. Moreover, do the patterns of these 'expanded environments' vary according to the location of people: do people in some places travel farther and more frequently than those in others? It is likely that people in the largest, most accessible centres experience a greater number of residential moves than people in the smallest, most remote places. Do these factors affect migration behaviour, and if they do, what is the nature of their influence? The mechanisms whereby such an environment develops is through formal channels, including educational systems and the mass media, and through informal personal networks of friends and relatives and their own spatial mobility and activity. The nature of information fields thus demonstrates, in summary, the extent of interaction of countries as well as communities and individuals within the wider international and national environment.

Education

The education systems of the Caribbean cannot be quantified or isolated in terms of their influence as agents in the acquisition of information. Nevertheless, there is no question that in combination with other agents for the transmission of knowledge, formal schooling plays an important part in perpetuating those aspirations and attitudes which are incorporated into overall ideologies and behaviour, and not least, those which relate directly or indirectly to migration. Notions of great wealth and high standards of efficiency in Europe and North America have been well established through the educational process. Meanwhile, the Caribbean traditionally has been denigrated in popular perceptions, except in regard to its scenery and climate. This view has been modified in recent years and has been compensated for by the attachment generated through the sense of it being home, but a general lack of confidence in local standards and opportunities for achieving still prevails.

Mass communications

Of all forms of mass communication, the radio has the most widespread influence in the transmission of information in the Caribbean. Transistor radios were widely used throughout the region. In Jamaica and Barbados over 90 per cent of the households had at least one member in possession of a radio; in St Vincent this was true for about 78 per cent of the households. Those households without a radio were, understandably, in the poorest rural areas.

Though the radio contributed to the formation of mental images about Caribbean society as of many other societies, it provided no depth of information. On average for the three islands, 25 per cent of households had a radio which was played for most of the day, every day. News and other broadcasts of an informative nature, as well as the more frequent music programmes, were heard almost continually, but with little attention paid to them. As a consequence, the radio in such households was not very effective as a means of transmitting information.

Television viewing has increased dramatically, especially in urban areas. New stereotypes about places have been induced and former ones reinforced by television as well as cinema programmes. Even the advertisements played a critical role in governing impressions held about places outside the immediate environment of the viewer. Usually these impressions conjured up the image of a world which, for most 'other people in other places', was characterized by glamour and prosperity and, overall, was a world of considerable appeal.

Newspapers were read by an average of 21 per cent of the populations. Newspaper circulation was lowest among the rural populations, but even in urban areas coverage was not extensive. On account of the generally higher levels of literacy and education of the middle classes, these were the groups most influenced by the newspapers.

For the most part the media in the Caribbean provided a wash of information which passed across the entire population, but with considerable variation in its effect. As a consequence, the pattern of its influence could not be easily discerned. Urban communities were generally more knowledgeable than their rural counterparts and it took longer for information to reach the less accessible groups. Thus it took longer for the views and attitudes of the least accessible to alter and for their images to change.

Within the broad framework of the physical accessibility of places and the communities which occupied them, at the most detailed level, information was primarily determined by education. Neither low education levels nor inaccessibility played much part in determining information receipt, when the items of information were particularly meaningful and of interest to people. For example, where matters were specific to migration or conditions and opportunities abroad, there was a conscious effort made to keep informed. Whatever the influence of the mass media in the dissemination of information at times of massive migration flows, which attracted specific interest, the most effective on-going means of information diffusion was through the personal networks comprising relatives and friends already abroad.

Personal networks

Personal contacts provided an informal network of direct and indirect flows of information and other forms of feedback through remittances of various kinds. These interactions provided the individual with information and also the assistance in making the actual move. The 'chain migration' of persons from a single community to a particular destination overseas is a common feature of migration patterns.

Only a very small minority of persons in the Caribbean were not in contact with migrants already abroad. In the case of Jamaica,

6.7 per cent of the sample population had no contacts abroad, whereas in St Vincent it was a mere 2.7 per cent, and in the case of Barbados, an even smaller proportion, 2 per cent. The great majority of people had between one and five contacts among migrants, and some kept in touch with up to ten or more. The overall level of personal interaction and therefore of information flow between Caribbean societies and places abroad was substantial throughout, and in some islands – such as Barbados and St Vincent – it was overwhelmingly so. Furthermore, it was significant that the lower level of contact maintained with persons abroad by Jamaicans than by Barbadians and Vincentians was consistent with other aspects of the pattern of migration behaviour.

The nature of the contact maintained ranged from regular correspondence to very occasional communication or receipt of news. The frequency in the receipt of letters varied both between and within the three islands and in a pattern which did not seem to be random. The differences between islands showed the higher level of communication with people abroad maintained by the Barbadians, to a lesser extent by the Vincentians and less again by the Jamaicans (Table 6.1).

The main differences in the pattern of correspondence within the islands were along lines of social class and of accessibility of the place in which people lived. The highest levels of correspondence were maintained by the middle-income populations, for example of Harbour View in Jamaica, Montrose in St Vincent and Belmont in Bridgetown, Barbados. In Harbour View more than two-thirds of the population corresponded regularly or fairly regularly with persons overseas. Nowhere else in the island did this apply to as much as half of the population.

Centres close to the capital towns, whatever their economic characteristics, came next in level of correspondence maintained with migrants abroad. These included the Jamaican towns of May Pen and the plantation centre of Port Morant in the parish of St Thomas.

Much lower levels of correspondence with migrants occurred in the rural districts of central Westmoreland, Manchester and St Mary in Jamaica, Barrouallie and Chapman's in St Vincent and St Lucy and St John in Barbados. This confirmed that the populations least accessible in a locational sense were those with the least contact with people abroad. However, it was also very significant that in all the islands the low-income groups of the capital towns maintained the least contact with persons overseas.

The effect of the physical centrality of urban districts such as Murray Village and Sion Hill in St Vincent was counterbalanced in this respect by their peripheral position in a social sense. In Barbados the population of Christchurch, which in many other respects demonstrated a high

132 Explanation in Caribbean migration

Table 6.1: Frequency of the receipt of letters from persons abroad[1]

	0+1	2	3+4	C
JAMAICA				
Harbour View, K.M.A.	6.7	25.3	68.0	274.4
Grant's Pen, K.M.A.	45.3	29.3	25.4	135.8
Montego Bay	40.0	35.7	24.3	132.8
May Pen	25.4	29.8	44.8	198.6
North-west St Ann	31.2	32.4	36.4	188.5
Ewarton, St Catherine	35.2	31.0	33.8	158.2
Central Westmoreland	56.0	24.0	20.0	90.7
Pt Morant, St Thomas	38.6	22.7	38.7	178.8
Western St Mary	60.0	16.0	24.0	98.6
Central Manchester	36.8	39.5	23.7	281.9
MEAN	37.52	28.57	33.91	173.83
BARBADOS				
St Michael				
(Belmont and Deacons)	26.4	31.2	42.4	217.6
Oistins, Christchurch	11.8	38.2	50.0	246.9
Weston, St James	30.8	34.5	34.7	185.0
Martin's Bay, St John	32.4	31.2	36.4	191.0
Central St Lucy	26.7	38.6	34.7	202.8
MEAN	25.62	34.74	39.64	208.6
ST VINCENT				
Montrose, Kingstown	43.4	15.3	41.3	202.1
Murray, Kingstown	35.4	33.3	31.3	204.7
Belair	38.7	35.5	25.8	142.3
Sion Hill/Arnos Vale	57.5	25.0	17.5	95.0
Chapman's	58.5	14.7	26.8	102.3
Barrouallie	25.4	39.2	35.4	222.6
MEAN	43.15	27.17	29.68	161.5

1 Categories 0 and 1 are combined (never and rarely received letters); category 2 is listed separately (received letters occasionally); categories 3 and 4 are combined (received letters fairly, and very frequently). Figures represent the percentage in each category of the total populations of the sub-samples. C refers to the total index of correspondence frequency.

degree of accessibility, maintained a greater level of contact with people overseas than was the case for any other population group in that island. In St Vincent it was the population of Barrouallie, which in relation to external contact, as in other contexts already discussed, was very much more accessible in social terms than its size and physical location would suggest.

Despite the paucity of news items of any apparent consequence conveyed by letters, nevertheless, they provided a major set of criteria upon which impressions and images were based or, more often, confirmed. Personal networks had the further effect of providing information about the practicalities of migrating as well as the possibility of providing financial assistance.

Personal spatial mobility

In the Eastern Caribbean regular travel fields invariably extended to neighbouring islands, and throughout the region overseas visits, whether seasonal or infrequent, reflected the accessibility of the population. Their accessibility significantly affected their information levels.

Accessibility is as much a function of location as it is of mobility. Individuals who move around are more accessible than those who do not – wherever they happen to live. However, those who reside in remote areas are the least spatially mobile in any case. That is, people in some types of areas or locations tend to be predominantly 'space sitters' and thus information receivers, while people in other kinds of places are more 'space movers' and thus information searchers.

Regular travel out from the home locality and the arrival of new residents from other areas, all contribute to the enhancement of the overall contact maintained with people and places elsewhere and the accessibility of inhabitants to information. Three types of mobility are used to examine this: travel within the home island, previous residential moves and travel abroad.

Frequency of travel within the home area

Variations in patterns of internal movement occurred both between islands and within them. Comparing islands, the frequency of trips which people made on a regular, short-term basis were greatest in the smaller Caribbean territories, especially in those where bus routes were extensive.

Much of the regular mobility of Caribbean people was associated with trips from rural areas to markets in towns. The market place still remained not only a principal place for retail transactions but also a centre for the exchange of news. In Jamaica, where the relative distances were greatest, people's regular mobility was considerably less than in the smaller islands of Barbados and St Vincent. Only 10.1 per cent went infrequently or not at all to the capital, 14 per cent of the Vincentian population, and as many as 47 per cent of the Jamaican. While the relatively low level of interaction with the capital in the Jamaican case was significant, a large proportion of those who rarely travelled to Kingston did go regularly or fairly regularly to other centres closer to their place of residence. Because the cost of overcoming those distances was greater in Jamaica, the combined implications of poverty and remoteness were of considerable importance to people's levels of accessibility in that island.

In most rural areas of Barbados, for example, at least 40 per cent of the population made regular trips to the capital Bridgetown. In St Vincent the figure was similar, with the exception of the population of Belair of which over 80 per cent went to the capital, Kingstown, on a regular weekly basis. In Jamaica, on the other hand, even in districts fairly close to Kingston, visits were relatively few. St Catherine, May Pen and St Thomas which, as already shown, were among the most accessible parts of the island, did not have more than 18 per cent of the population making regular visits to the capital (Table 6.2).

Low-income urban populations recorded the lowest mobility indices in each of the islands. This was true of the Sion Hill district of St Vincent, which, though located outside the official limits of Kingstown was, nevertheless, a physical and social extension of the town. Outside the urban areas the highest mobility indices were found in communities close to, but not actually in the towns. In Jamaica the populations sampled in St Thomas, Ewarton in St Catherine and May Pen, fell into this category, as did the population of Christchurch in Barbados.

The within-island variations clearly demonstrated the same pattern of differentials as indicated by the foregoing analysis of patterns of overseas contact. Not only were the rural-urban discrepancies again evident, but the influence of the transport route and of points of intervening opportunities influenced internal mobility. As a consequence, all these factors contributed to the pattern of accessibility of the population.

While the major routes leading to the capital towns and cities had a compensatory effect upon distance, the existence of a town closer than the capital to any particular community offered a form of intervening opportunity. Such centres, therefore, functioned as 'barriers' in terms of contact and accessibility with the capital and with other centres in the country. In Barbados, Speightstown created a barrier effect with regard to mobility between the northern parish and

Table 6.2: Summary mobility indices

	T	R	A	M
JAMAICA				
Harbour View	136.0	234.7	247.6	618.3
Grant's Pen	100.9	108.1	3.1	212.1
Montego Bay	78.8	95.7	22.8	197.3
May Pen	215.0	131.6	50.5	397.1
North-west St Ann	144.2	122.2	52.0	318.4
Ewarton, St Catherine	209.0	127.5	38.2	374.7
Central Westmoreland	58.7	114.7	34.5	207.9
Pt Morant, St Thomas	221.4	186.1	49.3	456.8
Western St Mary	194.6	126.6	44.0	365.2
Central Manchester	149.6	80.0	10.4	240.0
MEAN	150.82	132.72	55.24	338.78
BARBADOS				
St Michael				
(Belmont and Deacons)	148.5	91.8	188.2	428.5
Oistins, Christchurch	294.3	47.3	108.9	450.5
Weston, St James	293.8	31.2	40.3	365.3
Martin's Bay, St John	300.3	− 7.7	61.1	353.7
Central St Lucy	195.8	− 15.8	68.9	248.9
MEAN	246.54	29.36	93.48	369.38
ST VINCENT				
Montrose, Kingstown	84.0	120.8	171.7	376.5
Murray, Kingstown	94.9	37.5	106.6	239.0
Belair	370.9	135.3	148.7	654.9
Sion Hill/Arnos Vale	273.0	− 44.0	85.4	314.4
Chapman's	188.5	72.7	111.5	372.7
Barrouallie	287.8	31.7	183.4	502.9
MEAN	216.52	35.4	134.55	410.1

Abbreviations used for column headings above are as follows:
T = frequency of Trips;
R = previous Residential moves;
A = visits to countries Abroad;
M = total Mobility (T + R + A).

Bridgetown. The population of central St Lucy recorded the lowest index for internal mobility for Barbados.

Similarly in St Vincent, Georgetown on the Windward coast absorbed much of the traffic which would otherwise have gone direct to Kingstown. The population of Chapman's district, north of Georgetown, recorded the lowest mobility index in the island.

The same situation pertained in Montego Bay in the west of Jamaica; it created an interruption to the interaction of the western parishes with Kingston. The Montego Bay population had a much lower pattern of interaction with the capital than did other urban populations. People who lived in the western parishes of the island made even fewer visits to Kingston or to any other areas east of Montego Bay. The Westmoreland sample population, which was both west of Montego Bay and also remote and rural, experienced the lowest level throughout Jamaica of interaction with Kingston, with a mere 4 per cent visiting the city regularly or fairly regularly.

The opposite situation – that is the absence of any intervening opportunities – was demonstrated by the high degree of contact existing between Barrouallie on the Leeward side of St Vincent and the capital Kingstown; the same was true for St John and Bridgetown in Barbados and between St Thomas and Kingston in Jamaica. As a consequence, the contact with the capital was greater in those parts of the island which were not only relatively close to the capital but also in locations on direct transport routes with the capital without any major centres intervening.

The frequency of travel within islands was shown to vary from place to place, forming a definite, recognizable pattern. Furthermore, there was confirmation of what one would expect, namely the much greater internal mobility in the smaller islands, especially Barbados where distances were reduced by the provision of better transport facilities. St Vincent, by contrast, though of comparable physical size, had greater 'real' distances separating its population centres because of the poorer transport facilities.

Previous residential moves

In the larger island of Jamaica, regular mobility was less than in the smaller islands where distances were shorter and intervening centres providing commercial and other services were fewer. By that same token, in Jamaica, associated with the relatively greater distances, the number of times people moved their place of residence was greater than in the smaller islands. As a consequence, people's interaction space was extended by having lived in more than one place in their lifetime, thus increasing the level of their personal contacts with people and places elsewhere.

Comparing Jamaica, Barbados and St Vincent in the context of residential moves, the greater mobility occurred in Jamaica, with only a quarter of the population having always lived in the same district or area. In Barbados and St Vincent, by contrast, there was much less residential movement. The greater ease of access in Barbados was reflected in the lowest record of internal residential mobility. Furthermore, in Jamaica, the majority had made a number of residential moves, whereas this was not the case for Barbados and St Vincent (Table 6.2).

Districts into which little in-migration had taken place tended to be not only the more static socially, but also the least accessible physically. In-migration increased the contact of the district with other places from which the migrants came and where, usually, they maintained links. At the same time, residential moves took place most to those districts which were already more accessible. In-migration, as in the case of regular mobility, was both cause and effect of accessibility.

The distribution of indices measuring 'previous residential moves' for Jamaica, Barbados and St Vincent demonstrated the high level of in-migration to the major towns. The populations of Harbour View in Kingston, Bridgetown, St Michael, and Montrose in Kingstown, all recorded high indices. In contrast were the lower-class populations of the capitals. In these cases the moves to the present urban place of residence were not preceded by as many moves as in the case of the middle-class populations.

There were high indices for 'previous residential moves' also recorded for centres other than the major towns. Belair in southern St Vincent and Port Morant in St Thomas, Jamaica, were two examples of this. In both there were high levels of accessibility and relatively close physical proximity to the capitals, which would explain their higher than average in-migration. By contrast, the very small number of previous residential moves experienced by the Sion Hill population in St Vincent was a further reflection of its social distance from the capital already observed. The close similarity between the pattern of previous residential moves and that of regular internal mobility, added weight to the hypothesis that mobility patterns, thus space searching and the acquisition of greater amounts of information, varied in a definite, recognizable pattern from place to place. On the other hand, the lack of movement of the Barbadians and Vincentians within the islands was counterbalanced by their previous travel and residence abroad.

Visits abroad

In St Vincent almost half of the adult population had been abroad during their lifetime, though most had travelled only to neighbouring

Barbados for cutting sugar cane. In Barbados the figure was lower (at 27.6 per cent), and in Jamaica lower still (at 13.69 per cent).

Overseas visits widened the sphere of contact of the individual and on their return to their home country affected the composition and amount of information to which the community was exposed. Seasonal labour accounted for much of the overseas travel, while in other cases it accounted for time periods of a week to several years. In St Vincent, for instance, many persons had lived for several years in Aruba, and approximately 4 per cent of the sample had been born there.

The very high rate of emigration and other overseas visits made by Vincentians was typical of the pattern in all the small islands of the eastern Caribbean and was in marked contrast to the situation for Jamaicans in the 1970s. Even by the mid-1980s, after the increase in contract work in North America and the movement of informal commercial importers (ICIs) to destinations in and around the Caribbean, the percentage of the sample population which had been abroad was 16.85, still low by comparison with the nearly 50 per cent of the Vincentian population who had travelled.

The variation within islands in the pattern of overseas visits replicated the patterns for other forms of personal mobility (Table 6.2). There was a marked social differential in the behaviour of the middle-class sample populations as compared to the predominantly lower-income working class populations. The middle-income populations of Harbour View in Kingston, Jamaica, Belmont in Bridgetown, Barbados, and Montrose in Kingstown, St Vincent, were the groups who had the highest record of overseas visits in the case of each island. The converse was true for the low-income urban groups, among whom overseas mobility levels were significantly low.

Thus income was closely associated with overseas travel, but so also was location. People in more remote rural areas travelled very much less than those from places which lay astride the major routes linking up with the capital towns. The number of overseas visits which had occurred among the population of the remote Westmoreland plantation area in Jamaica was the lowest for the island, contrasting with the pattern for the plantation area in St Thomas, located along the main route to Kingston. Likewise, in St Vincent, people in Belair, a centre close to town, had experienced a much higher level of overseas mobility than those in remote Chapman's village. In Barbados, the same difference occurred between Christchurch in the south and relatively remote St Lucy in the north.

Information as indicator of location in physical and social space

Information surfaces

Knowledge of the economic conditions in countries overseas was minimal, even when it concerned those countries about which there was most information. For many people there was a blanket perception of all foreign countries as simply being far more prosperous than any Caribbean territory. Other people referred to the North American and European nations as being 'rich', thus they could be relied upon for the availability of well-paid employment. Even within the Caribbean, preferences for some countries over others were rarely accompanied by much factual knowledge about their economies and potential for employment.

The only negative ideas about the overseas job market pertained to the situation in Britain. Reports had passed back to the islands on a substantial scale referring to redundancies among industrial workers and related difficulties in obtaining new jobs. Furthermore, as already indicated, the fact that relatively fewer people returned for vacation from Britain than from either Canada or the United States led to the deduction that migrants in Britain were less prosperous. So little was known about the economic circumstances of the African countries that even those who could differentiate between countries of the continent knew virtually nothing about specific conditions.

Social characteristics in the five places were dominated by stereotypes based on the items of news transmitted by the mass media and personal correspondence. For example, social tensions with racial connotations in Britain were well reported. There were very few persons, and then only among the middle class, who believed there to be even the slightest suspicion of racial or other social tensions in the United States. This was a reflection of the fact that lower-class Caribbean migrants in the United States competed for jobs and housing with the local black, rather than the white population, if they had to compete at all. The occasions for migrant-host conflict along racial lines were few, and where they did exist, they received no attention in the context of migration. Knowledge of social conditions in Africa was, with very few exceptions, vague and based on stereotypes rather than on specific information.

The regulations for entry into different countries were among the principal points of information known to most people. This was chiefly concerning entry to Britain, Canada and the United States. There was also widespread knowledge about entry to the Bahamas from Jamaica and to Barbados from St Vincent. Almost no information was known pertaining to entry conditions for African countries, although there was a general feeling among many West Indians that there were no restrictions on entry. One would have expected information about the economic and social conditions to be basic, if not essential, to any contemplation of moving to countries overseas. However, the details about economic and social circumstances were largely unknown.

Most information was known about the climate of places discussed and second was knowledge about the relative distances of these countries from the Caribbean. Even on these two matters there were numerous gaps in people's knowledge. Climatic conditions, as already noted, were among the principal points frequently mentioned in letters from friends and relatives overseas. With reference to distance, assessments were usually made on the basis of the cost of going to various places, as well as on evidence from those who had already emigrated of the frequency of their return visits. Return visits were taken as indirect measures of distance, on the assumption that the frequency of visits related to the ability of the emigrants to afford holidays or a permanent return to the home country.

The information about economic and social conditions of overseas countries was vague in the extreme. In all cases, there was a difference in the patterns generated by the middle-class population from those of the rest of the population. Irrespective of class, the spatial patterns which emerged were considerably consistent in their relation to the major communication routes and distance from the capital towns. Since information was a sensitive indicator of the combined social and spatial aspects of location, the information surfaces were particularly significant.

Accessibility and migration

Little is understood, or has ever been examined, concerning the variations in accessibility, its spatial configurations and the factors which conditioned that variation. Even less is understood about the role which various aspects of interaction through personal networks and mobility play in migration behaviour.

External contact through personal networks

The chain effect of migration, with the practice of new migrants following previous ones to the same destinations, is evidence that during any specific migration phase friends and relatives play an important part in determining the direction of subsequent moves.

While personal networks influence the direction and timing of movement, their impact upon the process of migrant selectivity is not consistent, nor is the impact it has upon information levels at all clear. In many cases in Jamaica, Barbados and St Vincent where there was contact with relatives abroad, there was a reduced potential for the migration of the dependant who remained at home. In some cases, certain family members had opted to remain, or had been obliged to remain in the family home while other members migrated. There were other cases where the migration of children or older people had actually been stimulated by the fact that their immediate family was permanently resident overseas.

In summary, the network of friends and relatives overseas had no consistent effect upon the level of information received or even upon the subsequent migration behaviour of those in the household or family. Nor was there any significant difference in migration propensity for those households with, and those without, members already abroad.

The more difficult question to address was whether personal networks actually affected the information of individuals and households significantly and in a way which would influence migration behaviour. This situation was examined in terms of the levels and nature of the communication actually maintained through those personal networks.

The receipt of letters from friends and relatives overseas reflected the extent to which people maintained contact with, and received feedback from, people abroad. The influence of such feedback should depend on whether it was favourable or unfavourable. The migrants' minimization of unfavourable aspects of the life abroad, as well as their maximization of the benefits, have been mentioned before. As a consequence of this situation, most communication had a predominantly positive impact on the formulation of images about overseas countries. It is interesting that in households with a high level of overseas contact the migration propensity was not commensurately high. This supported the previous observation of the negligible or inverse effect of friends and relatives abroad upon the subsequent migration of members of the same household.

Personal spatial mobility

Those persons who moved around most within their home country were not those with the highest potential for migration. Indeed, in the smaller Caribbean countries especially, mobility in terms of the residential move to or near the capital, may have compensated for the lack of migration opportunities, thus tending to reduce, rather than increase the migration propensity. Yet previous residential moves were associated with a tendency towards a higher migration propensity.

Furthermore, the places to which a large number of people had made previous residential moves were also the places from which higher rates of actual migration had occurred. In Barbados the background of previous residential moves and thus the stage of each place in such a hierarchy, accounted for about 38 per cent of the variation in the migration rates. In St Vincent the relationship between these two variables was considerably weaker, with the index for previous residential moves accounting for only 18 per cent of the variation in migration rates. The larger island of Jamaica demonstrated a still more remote connection between previous residential mobility and propensity to migrate. Only 14 per cent of the variation in the migration rates was accounted for by the fact that the individual had made previous residential moves.

Information levels

The level of information receipt related to variations in the actual migration rate and migration propensity in divergent ways. In Jamaica and Barbados there was a strong positive association between information and actual migration rates. In St Vincent the association was positive but not as strong, probably because much of the migration rate was accounted for by departures to neighbouring islands, which did not necessitate high levels of information.

Whereas high levels of information were associated with high migration rates, inverse relationships occurred between information and the potential for migration. That is, high levels of information were associated with a low potential for migration and in the places where information levels were lowest, namely in the least accessible districts, the desire to migrate was at its highest. The distance factor was particularly important. To be inaccessible in Jamaica was more significant than to be inaccessible in the smaller islands. The stronger set of relationships in the Barbados sample reflected the sharper differences previously shown to occur between the pattern for actual emigration rates and that for migration propensity.

Conclusion

The impact of accessibility in relation to the capital town or city reflected regular, distinct and interpretable spatial patterns. In Jamaica one could distinguish the compensatory effect of the route from the north of the island through St Catherine to Kingston, from the west through Clarendon and from the east through St Thomas. The areas aligned to these routes were associated with a high degree of mobility and overseas contact and also by high levels of information receipt. A similar pattern occurred in St Vincent, where the Leeward route from Barrouallie acted as a major artery connecting the settlement to the capital Kingstown. In Barbados, the route north from Bridgetown through St James, northeast to St John and east along the south coast to Christchurch, all demonstrated the characteristics of relative accessibility – namely high levels of space-searching activity, overseas contact and, consequently, information receipt. By contrast, areas which, in relation to the capital towns, lay beyond a secondary town, illustrated the influence of the barrier effect of that town upon their degree of accessibility. Westmoreland and Montego Bay in the case of Jamaica, St Lucy in Barbados and Chapman's in St Vincent, could be distinguished by their relative inaccessibility and their population's lower than average levels of information.

Distance, in combination with low income produced the greatest barriers to accessibility. As the information field of the population at each place was influenced by accessibility, it meant that their location in physical space was as important in governing their levels of information as was their location in social space.

CHAPTER 7 | Integration and mental images

Both local and more distant places take on meaning according to the knowledge that people have of them. For the immediate environment which people inhabit, their personal experience is a vital factor in the way they perceive it. With respect to more distant places, images are established on the basis of information received about them, whatever the degree of accuracy of that information. Thus the interaction with external environments influences the images which are generated in the minds of people and, therefore, the decisions they make. The external world is comprised of countries which form high or low points in relation to the home country and which, moreover, form clear or vague impressions in their minds.

To Caribbean people the home island was not viewed as being necessarily the high point in the comparison between countries. Thus the image which conditioned Caribbean perceptions of other countries in relation to their own country, and other parts of the country in relation to their own district, had a relational component and a component of clarity or vagueness which varied from one part of the region to another. A second observation concerned the vague perceptions held of previous migration destinations. For example, although there were still persons who remembered the migration to, and former popularity of Costa Rica, it was generally no longer a part of the Jamaican's mental image. New information also altered the image. It was the most accessible sectors of the population who were the first to experience changes in the image.

Evaluation of foreign countries

The way in which countries abroad were evaluated in relation to the home island illustrated not simply the perception of the world outside but the position of 'self' within a global frame of reference. The Jamaicans placed Jamaica itself third, after the United States and Canada, in their order of residential preference. There was a large gap between the scores totalled for these three places and that for the Bahamas, which was placed fourth, followed by Britain fifth. The Bahamas and Britain, unlike the United States and Canada, were regarded generally as less desirable than Jamaica as places in which to live, but the relatively high rank order they were designated reflected the positive perceptions held about them. Next in the rank of preferences came the larger territories in the Caribbean region, Trinidad, Guyana, Barbados and Panama, followed by Western Europe which was tenth in the priority order. Lastly, were the smaller Caribbean islands such as Grenada, St Vincent and Antigua, placed along with Africa and followed by Costa Rica, the US Virgin Islands and Martinique.

The element of clarity in the image of the outside world differed within islands as also between islands. These variations reflected, almost precisely, the variation in the accessibility of the populations between and within islands and thus in their receipt of information. In the perceptions of overseas countries the position of Britain – a recent migration destination – was noticeably low. Britain's greatly diminished position in the mental images of Caribbean people was not a result of dimmed memory, as in the case of Costa Rica. Instead, it was based on the information which had been received since the 1960s. Britain was placed eighth in the rank order of preferences by the rural populations in the Jamaican parishes of St Thomas and Manchester. From both districts a large number of migrants had gone to Britain in the 1950s and 1960s. In the St Ann district Britain was placed ninth, along with Grenada, East Africa and West Africa. In May Pen it came twelfth, after the group of small Caribbean islands including Grenada, St Vincent and Antigua, but before East and West Africa. It was only in St Mary and Westmoreland – the most remote areas sampled – that Britain was placed as high as fourth and fifth respectively. This undoubtedly reflected a time-space lag in the changes which had taken place in the image of places overseas, with the most remote communities still holding views long since replaced by new impressions among more accessible groups.

Finally, the low rating given to the Eastern Caribbean territories was reflective of attitudes generally articulated by Jamaicans towards the rest of the Caribbean. Caribbean territories assumed a low profile in the image of the world outside Jamaica.

Barbadians and Vincentians shared many of the viewponts of the Jamaicans in terms of their perceptions of the outside world. Unlike the Jamaicans, however, the Barbadians placed their own country first in most cases. Canada was ranked second after Barbados itself, and the United States was a close third. Britain was fourth in the preference order, though there was a large gap in the total scores between those for

Britain and those for the United States and Canada. The only other major points of departure between the pattern expressed by the Jamaicans and that by the Barbadians, concerned the view of the Caribbean itself. Whereas Martinique was placed last by the Jamaican sample population, in the case of the Barbadians it was placed in the middle, along with Jamaica, Trinidad and Guyana. The islands closest to Barbados, and from which migrants have frequently come, namely St Vincent, St Lucia and Grenada, were the lowest in the Barbadian's evaluations, along with East and West Africa.

A large proportion of the Vincentians were very limited in their knowledge and awareness of places abroad. A simple relational image existed with St Vincent seen in relation to a world comprised in any relevant way, of the United States, Canada, Britain and a few Caribbean countries, chiefly those in the southern part of the region. This indicated above all the lower place occupied by St Vincent in the hierarchy of information diffusion from outside the region. The image of the Vincentian's outside world was (except for the most educated), highly selective and circumscribed by a very limited horizon.

For the Vincentians, Canada and the United States competed for first place in the order of preferences. In the overall pattern, however, Canada was marginally ahead of the United States. In one sample district, that of Barrouallie, Britain was ranked first. This reflected the large number of emigrants from that area who had gone to Britain and the positively biased information which was transmitted back to St Vincent. In general, for the total island population, Britain was placed third or fourth, with St Vincent itself alternating positions with it; and below these came Barbados. Africa was consistently lowest in the perceptions of the limited world view articulated by the Vincentians.

Time is also an important factor in that the image of the outside world changes over time not only in shape and form, but also in terms of its clarity. Generally, the focus has altered with the emergence of new prospective migration locations since the destinations of Caribbean emigrants have been the origins of most external information selectively transmitted to the individual islands.

The relational component of the image reflected the positive way in which Barbadians regarded their own island within a global frame of reference, which contrasted with the situation in Jamaica and in St Vincent. (This is entirely consistent with the lower propensity for migration occurring among the Barbadian populations than was the case for Jamaicans and Vincentians discussed earlier.) In general terms, the United States and Canada had a high profile in the images of all Caribbean peoples; other places in the Caribbean itself had a low profile. This was especially true in the evaluation of the

Jamaicans with whom interaction with other parts of the region was minimal.

Evaluations of internal island environments

The perceptions which people had of places within their own island were based principally on pragmatic factors, chiefly the cost of living and services in different areas, their accessibility, physical attributes, agricultural productivity, employment potential and reputations of the local people. In addition to these considerations a number of aesthetic and esoteric elements helped to constitute spatial views. In Jamaica the image of the salubrious, highland areas, notably Mandeville and upper St Andrew, appealed to some people, and the believed prosperity of the tourist zones of Montego Bay and coastal St Ann were an attraction to others. The 'fruitfulness', (high agricultural productivity) of certain places such as St Mary and Manchester were regarded as desirable features, while 'too much rain' in St Mary and Portland and 'too little rain' in Westmoreland and St Elizabeth summed up the characteristics perceived as epitomizing these parishes.

The peacefulness and lack of congestion found in the countryside by comparison with the town were, to Barbadians and Jamaicans alike, among the more important considerations in evaluating local environments. In Barbados the presence or absence of the sea was also claimed to be important, especially by those who lived near to the coast. This view was in part accounted for by the presence of tourist developments in some coastal zones which were undeveloped except for small-scale fishing (chiefly for subsistence). The Martin's Bay residents of St John, Barbados, lamented the lack of coastal facilities which would popularise their stretch of coast, as they compared their locality with the perceived higher status of the Bathsheba area farther north, to which most visitors went.

The believed or actual popularity of an area to outsiders considerably enhanced local images of that place. Residents in these areas, whatever their social class, quoted tourist impressions, usually in relation to climatic and scenic qualities, when describing their local environment. The outsiders' judgement in this situation, as in many other circumstances, was acknowledged to be the authority in determining the relative rating of particular types of environments.

Despite the impact of the outsider's rating and the commercial potential, evaluations also reflected a genuine emotional attachment to the type of environment to which people were accustomed or regarded as home. Nevertheless, people felt defensive about the fact that they lived in little known, rural areas, regarded as backwaters. This probably explained why the same persons, in justifying their rural residence, lauded the attributes of rural areas, but then went on to rank rural parishes low in their order of preference as places in which to live. In addition, emotional ties and traditional attachment to specific environments were much less significant when migration was being considered. Neither the rural quiet nor love of the sea, for example, were reflected in the pattern of preferences, except in combination with other environmental attributes.

The sense of attachment to certain types of local environments found among Jamaicans and Barbadians, was no less evident among Vincentians. The Leeward and Windward sides of their island were perceived as contrasting widely in terms of residential desirability. The preference of one over the other was hardly determined by the intrinsic features of either, or even by their comparative economic potential. The preference was determined to an even greater extent by an inherent sense of belonging to one or other region.

Local attachments were compromised in some cases where the reputation of an area was undisputed. In this category, the south was regarded as an area of undeniable residential desirability by people of both Windward and Leeward sides of St Vincent. This assessment was based largely upon the accessibility of all parts of the south to the capital, Kingstown, and thus upon its greater potential for employment. The desirability of the south was also due partly to its concentration of tourism and the knowledge that it was popular to those Vincentians who had the greatest freedom of residential choice – the middle and upper classes. Again, this was a view which reflected the combination of the outsider's rating and the commercial value of places. In both Barbados and St Vincent, the south coast, east of the capital, had become areas of both tourist development and high cost housing for the island's upper middle-class population. To such places favourable evaluations were consistently attributed.

By contrast, negative views of northern St Vincent were both cause and consequence of that region's physical inaccessibility and its social isolation. The Rabacca dry river valley was a line of demarcation north of which Vincentians, (other than those from the north itself), had only the vaguest notion. The poverty of the north was well known and as the traditional stronghold of the Caribs, this area was not entirely without its legacy. But the most important single factor upon which the negative stereotype of the region depended, was its proximity to the active volcano Souffrière. The relative lack of contact with, and information about, the north nurtured an overwhelming sense of mistrust of that area.

The pattern of preferences

A dome of high preference existed around the home area, which was a characteristic of preference patterns found elsewhere. For example, this situation was found by Gould and White (1974) to be typical of the areas they studied in the United States and Western Europe, and also reflected in other studies of Barbados and St Lucia (Potter, 1985). This is consistent with the observation already indicated that clarity in the image influences preferences. That is, the better known places are perceived in a more positive light than places little known.

The 'view' of Barbados from four different places in the island exemplified the major characteristics of these patterns. Considerable loyalty was shown towards the home locality whether or not there was a genuine preference for it. At the same time, comparisons were readily made with other areas and most people did not simply accept the conditions or reputations of their home area without continual reference to other places.

In the majority of cases, the home area was ranked first in the order of preferences for places within each island. In the Jamaican sample the areas on the periphery of the sugar plantations in Westmoreland were the only ones not placed first in the order of preference by its own inhabitants. In St Vincent the population of Barrouallie did not favour their local area over the south, and Barrouallie itself was ranked second by its residents. In Barbados the same was true for plantation areas in the parishes of St Lucy and St John, whose residents ranked their own areas second, and even in Bridgetown, St Michael, people conceded that Christchurch was preferable as a parish in which to live.

As in the international context, so in the national framework, the focal points or points of greater clarity in the image were those around which people concentrated their impressions. For example, some of the parish associations were made solely with the main town of the parish. The image of St James in Jamaica was determined almost entirely by the characteristics of Montego Bay and most people outside that parish were hardly aware of rural areas of St James. Similarly, the image of Speightstown in Barbados largely determined the position of St Peter in the order of preferences; the same was true of the capital Bridgetown which was taken to be virtually synonymous with St Michael. Rural or coastal characteristics determined perceptions of some other parishes. St Lucy in Barbados and St Mary in Jamaica were predominantly rural and seen in those terms, but the coastal development of Christchurch in Barbados dominated the image of that parish despite its large inland area (Figures 7.1a, b and c).

150 *Explanation in Caribbean migration*

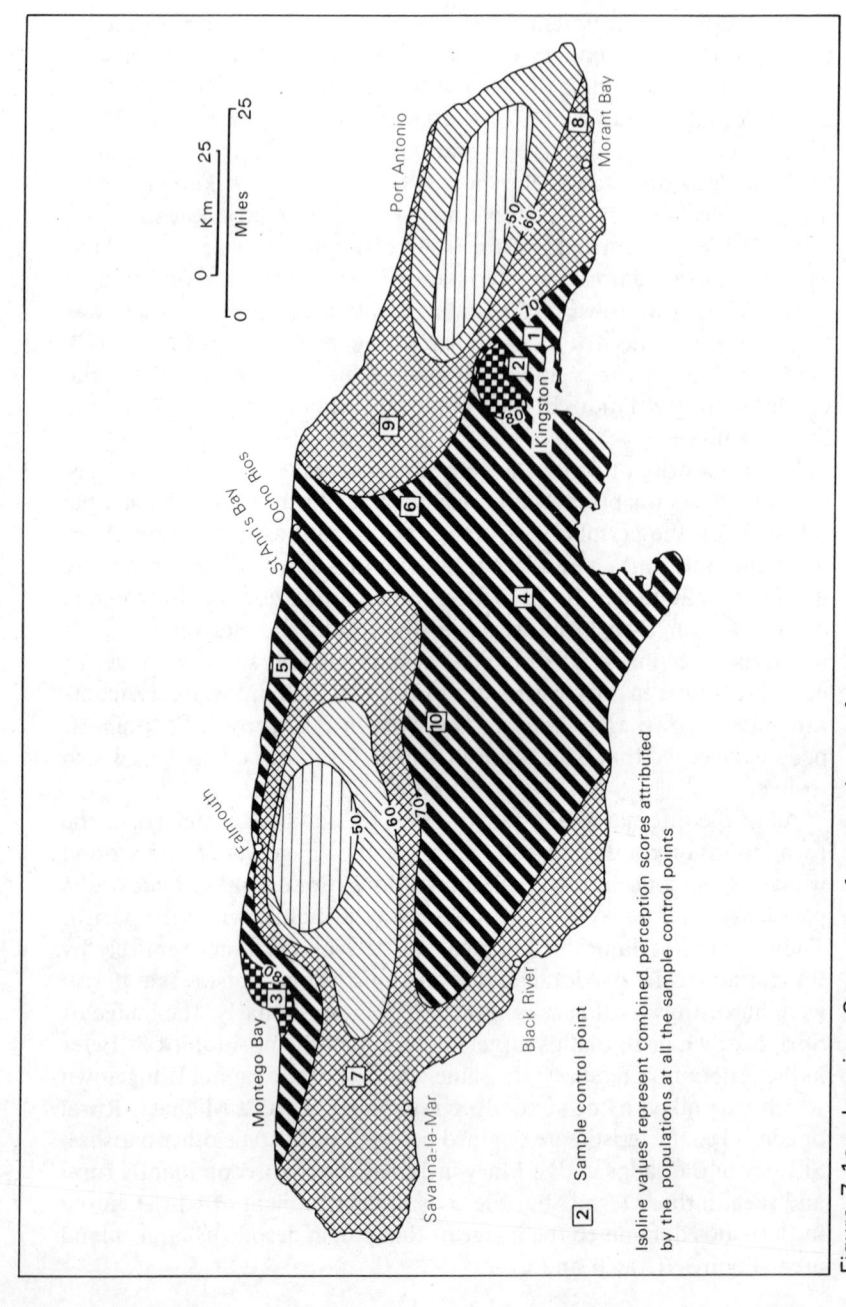

Figure 7.1a Jamaica: Summary of perception surfaces

Isoline values represent combined perception scores attributed by the populations at all the sample control points

☐2 Sample control point

Figures 7.1b and c Summary of perception surfaces for Barbados and St Vincent

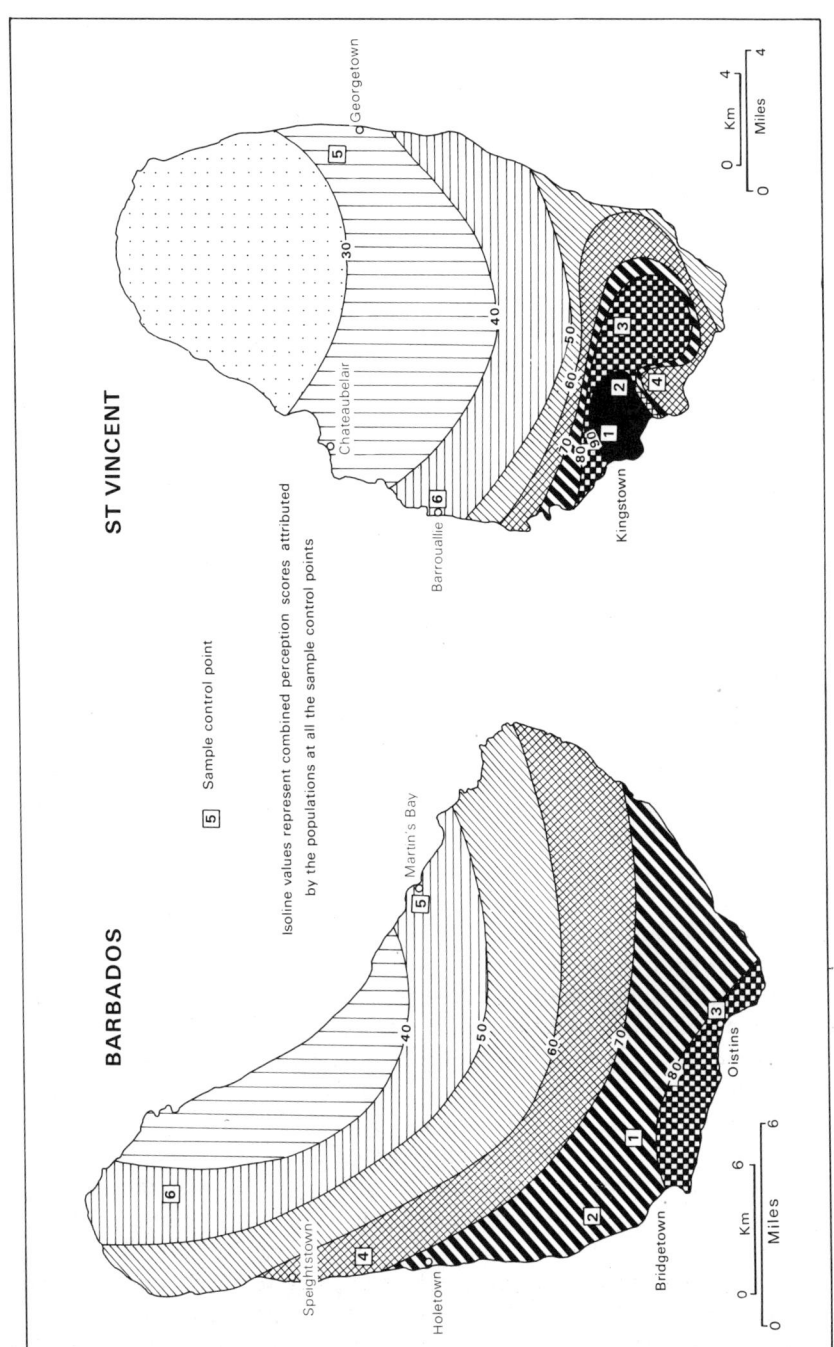

A gradient from high to low desirability tended to occur in each island outwards from the core area. In Jamaica, for example, the eastward bias towards Kingston was clear. This gradient of increased desirability was often expressed by people in the context of their disliking areas which were 'down' or 'back', referring to areas westwards from the Kingston-St Catherine core. These expressions incorporated definite connotations of backwardness and low evaluation. But elements of change in perceptions were evident. Kingston itself was not preferred in the way that it had been up to the 1960s, principally because of the reputation for violence with which it had become associated. Yet, the change in the image was again only partial, for despite the information about violence, the attraction of the Kingston area was in general still very marked. Montego Bay was a point of secondary attraction in that island, with its influence most strongly felt by residents in the western parishes, notably Westmoreland, Hanover and St James itself (the parish in which Montego Bay is located).

Likewise, in Barbados a definite spatial bias demonstrated the diminishing preference for places roughly along a south-north axis from Bridgetown. A secondary trend of diminishing preference ran north-eastwards from the capital. In St Vincent the bias of spatial preferences also ran roughly south to north away from Kingstown and the south. The tiny Grenadine islands south of Kingstown formed another area of low perceived desirability. In both Barbados and St Vincent the north was colloquially referred to as 'down' and the south as 'up', reflecting the qualitative difference ascribed to them by island residents.

The image further reflected not only clarity but clarity combined with a strong element of status. The major, and probably intuitive, attraction towards the core of each island was a phenomenon by no means unique to the Caribbean. The south-east of Britain and the north-east of the United States of America exerted the same type of power over the images held by people in those countries (Gould and White, 1974). Nevertheless, despite the consciously acknowledged drawbacks of living in the major cities of south-east Britain and the north-east United States, people were subconsciously attracted towards such centres of high population concentration. No less in the Caribbean, and probably even more so on account of the small size of the countries, places of increasing distance from the core areas had a proportionately decreasing power upon mental images. In turn, this was reflected in the spatially expressed pattern of desirability for different types of environments and places within each country.

The views of Caribbean people pertaining to their home country demonstrated the influence of two sometimes conflicting forces. First there was a strong sense of attachment felt towards the areas which individuals regarded as 'home', reflecting an emotional element to the image. Second, there was a sense of alienation felt towards places which were regarded as being of low status, principally places which were remote *vis-à-vis* the core or other major centres of the islands. This was the case whether or not the places happened to be the 'home' area. Socio-economic factors alone did not usually dominate images. However, in so far as they reflected a certain type of economy or level of development, socio-economic factors did enter into considerations about the prestige and desirability of places.

In summary, at least three factors either consciously or subconsciously influenced the evaluations made by individuals of different parts of their home islands. One was the location of the place, principally in terms of its accessibility to the capital or other major town. The second were the known or believed attributes of the place itself, especially with respect to practical issues and the status ascribed through levels of modernization or recognition by outsiders. Third were aesthetic considerations, the emotional attachment felt towards familiar environments and the sense of home.

Perception of place and migration behaviour

The highest migration rates occurred in those areas which were most preferred by the island's inhabitants. That is to say that in the Caribbean, the peaks and troughs of locational preference did not coincide with areas of low and high migration respectively. This seemed paradoxical and contrary to what might appear to have been a logical means of prediction – namely that the areas perceived as being the least desirable would indicate those areas from which the greatest migration rates were likely to take place. Conversely, it has been commonly assumed that areas of high migration were those in greatest need of attention and development, and government policies have at times reflected this belief, focusing upon the improvement of the infrastructure in an attempt to reduce out-migration (for example, the Integrated Rural Development Programme (IRDP), Ministry of Agriculture, Jamaica, initiated in 1977).

The reverse situation was closer to the reality. Places which were the epitome of backwardness, such as the Callaloo Gutter area of central Westmoreland, Jamaica, situated on the remotest and poorest margins of sugar estate land, recorded a markedly low migration rate. In contrast, the popular, residentially desirable areas of urban St Andrew, St Catherine and Manchester had a history of relatively high migration. The Barbadian experience was similar. The rate of actual migration varied from high, in St Michael and Christchurch, to much lower in the case of the parish of St John and St Lucy. Yet St Michael and Christchurch were greatly preferred over St John and St Lucy by the majority of Barbadians. Likewise, Belair and Sion Hill in southern St Vincent had low migration rates while Barrouallie on the Leeward Coast had a relatively high rate.

This study has tended to confirm the fact that migration was not associated with negative conditions, or even perceived negative conditions, in a simple causal relationship. The areas evaluated in a positive way were those areas which had experienced the highest levels of out-migration. The areas evaluated negatively had lower migration rates, but at the same time experienced a higher degree of migration propensity.

Port Morant in St Thomas recorded the highest index for the propensity to migrate in Jamaica, while in the order of preferences that area was ranked last (followed by Trelawny and Hanover). In Barbados the propensity to migrate indices recorded for St John and St Lucy were the highest for the island, while the perception of these places was the lowest. In St Vincent the same was true for the Chapman's and Sion Hill areas, where again there appeared to be an inverse association between the two trends.

The close association between the perception of places and rates of out-migration implied that those factors which were important in determining perceptions and preferences — namely the area's accessibility, level of modernization and prestige and other environmental attributes — were relevant to the behaviour associated with migration as well.

Thus the most positive perceptions were associated with the most accessible areas, and they were also related to those places where most information was received. It could readily be concluded that information increased the opportunities for active migration. Not so obvious was why the populations in the most remote and negatively evaluated areas with least information recorded not only the lowest migration rates but the highest levels of propensity for migration.

The importance of reference groups and the relational aspect of the image was already evident in the fact that evaluations were determined more by the extent to which people believed they were receiving a fair share of the national advantages in work, education and modernization than by the extent to which a facility did or did not exist. This role of the relational aspect of the image applied to people's perceptions of themselves and the place where they lived. It reflected also a relational perspective in the way people evaluated themselves in the national system in terms of their overall share in the opportunities and the status of their locality in relation to what they believed to be the case in their country as a whole.

Location, integration in society and migration

If one accepts that the way people see themselves, and especially the way group feelings are affected, reflects their perceptions of their surroundings (in a total sense – physical, cultural and social), then one could regard such environmental perceptions as indicators not only of isolation or interaction, but also of alienation or integration.

The connection between the physical and social aspects of people's locations and their socio-psychological position within the society was an important one. In general, the most physically remote areas were also those whose communities were the least accessible and integrated into the national life. But there was no simple rural-urban differential, nor was the spatial factor the only or necessarily the most important aspect of inaccessibility and isolation. For most of Kingstown, St Vincent and Bridgetown, Barbados, the sense of isolation of rural communities and a sense of alienation among lower-class urban people everywhere reflected poor integration in the mainstream of national life. Social distance and physical distance interacted and compensated the one for the other and the net social space was therefore a reflection of both the social and spatial aspects of location.

This relationship between people and places reinforced the idea that there is no sharp distinction between the objective or actual environment, and the perceived or meaningful environment (Brookfield, 1969; Brown, 1972; Moore, 1976). It has been observed in a number of quite different situations, that people at a place were important in giving that place the characteristics it exhibited and were believed by people to possess (Gerson, 1976; Buttimer, 1972).

The characteristics of both people and the places they inhabit are responsible for the nature of the mental images generated by those same people. There can be no sharp differentiation, therefore, between the integration of a place in a country and the integration of its inhabitants in the society.

Spatial bias in level of integration[1]

The spatial bias in the integration of communities in the national system reflected once again some of the trends seen in the pattern of migration rates and the potential for migration. The spatial biases reflected a high evaluation of the home district in relation to the rest of Jamaica held by the population in close proximity to, but not actually part of, the capital, Kingston. The populations of Montego Bay, like those of Bridgetown, Barbados and Kingstown, St Vincent, maintained higher evaluations of the towns in which they lived. This suggested that there was a threshold of size of town or city above which perceptions by the residents themselves, though not necessarily of other people, declined. The tempo or pace of large centres together with congestion and the matter of space and spaciousness were the basis of the perceived desirability or undesirability of the towns. There was some uncertainty over whether the undesirability or lack of space experienced in the towns outweighed the desirability of their centrality in the country as a whole.

For Jamaicans, levels of integration in the national system diminished both eastwards and westwards from the triangle of high local evaluation found in the parish of St Catherine and partly also in St Andrew. The westward decline in the integration of communities was more gradual than that towards the east and there was, in particular, a marked extension of the zone of high levels of personal integration along the major westward route through Clarendon and into Manchester. Beyond the town of Mandeville in the parish of Manchester there was a more rapid decline in the scores recorded. A corridor of relatively high integration levels also followed the route northwards from the St Catherine triangle, centred on the industrialized zone and following the major routes northwards to the St Ann coast.

By contrast, the population in the plantation area of Westmoreland emerged as the group with the lowest sense of integration. Second after the Westmoreland marginal plantation communities was the group in the plantation area of St Thomas; this was despite the considerable accessibility of this area. Even the small-farming communities in upland St Mary and central Manchester had higher evaluations of themselves in the context of opportunities nationally.

The poor sense of integration into the national life experienced by marginal plantation communities was especially important in the light of the role that accessibility played in the evaluation of place. It was apparent that the plantation context was the strongest single negative element in people's image of themselves in relation to national opportunities. Since accessibility mitigated the effect of social alienation, the combined effect of location in terms of place as well as in terms of actual and perceived social position in the national space were paramount in conditioning the images which people held of themselves, their oppportunities and their place in the national system.

Integration in society and migration

Migration behaviour was more closely related to the integration of people and places into the country and institutions of the country than it was to any specific characteristics or deficiencies of the environment in itself. The influence of the sense of integration in migration behaviour was strongest in Barbados, somewhat less in St Vincent and least of all in Jamaica. This was entirely consistent with the fact that the sense of alienation in a small society, where it cannot be attributed to physical inaccessibility, had a deeper impact upon people's image of themselves and their chances in society. In Jamaica, the lack of integration was to some extent expected, or at least accounted for by physical remoteness and inadequate infrastructure. This returned the argument to the role of the references against which people evaluated themselves and their positions in society. In an island such as Barbados, small and with a good infrastructure, of relatively high living standards and standards of welfare, the expectations or frame of reference in the light of which people saw themselves produced a more acute sense of deprivation than in places where opportunities and standards were expected to be lower.

Conclusions

Personal and corporate experience and the way people saw themselves in relation to the wider society, its institutions, opportunities and life chances greatly affected their views of places both far and near. These perceptions reflected the relational aspect of the image and the element of clarity which influenced perceptions and preferences for places. The difference between the individual's perception of the home area and that of the island as a whole reflected (at least partially) the relative way in which that place, community and individual was involved in the national life and perceived life chances of the respective islands.

Physical isolation and/or social alienation both tended to bring about an increase in the migration propensity. But this did not always bring with it the opportunities, chiefly those of a practical nature, for actually leaving the home island. On the contrary, the most accessible places had the highest rates of actual migration. In some cases, as in central St Lucy, Barbados and Barrouallie, St Vincent, the populations experienced both high migration rates and strong propensities for migration, despite their physical isolation from the core areas of Bridgetown and Kingstown, respectively. In both cases there was a curious combination of a sense of isolation, yet at the same time, considerable interaction with the capital.

How people perceived themselves in relation to national institutions was of major importance in determining their migration propensity as well as the likelihood of their making the actual move. Furthermore, where people were located within the wider national system and its priorities had a profound effect upon their image.

The world and total environmental experience of Caribbean people incorporated other countries outside the homeland. The perception of that world and the hope engendered by it, were key elements in Caribbean migration behaviour. However transient the meaning or symbolism of the world outside might have been, it was inseparable from the image which people held of the home country, the future and the goals to which they aspired.

The mental images of Jamaicans, Barbadians and Vincentians were powerful reflectors of the differences between places which were meaningful to them. They combined those aspects of the total environmental experience which showed the importance of their location in both social and physical space. They sensitively filtered meaning from the information, experience and expectations of places. In summation, the mental images mirrored the Caribbean countries themselves and the other countries with which they interacted in terms of their social significance to Caribbean people. These geographies of socio-spatial significance pointed to the factors most appropriate in interpretations of behavioural patterns, including those pertaining to migration.

Notes

1   The size of the gap between the perceptions of the home district and all other areas in the island was used as a crude indication of the levels at which each population viewed its own area and environment in relation to the country as a whole. Where a population had a high corporate perception of its own location relative to the rest of the island, then the gap between the score for that area and the average score for all other areas in the island was large. Conversely, where a population indicated a low perception of their own locality by comparison with the average score for other parts of the island, then the gap between the two scores was commensurately small.

Conclusion

The migration of one generation of Caribbean people becomes part of the image of the next. For migration, as part of the material or real environment, is interpreted as a component of the cultural environment and therefore becomes part of the image. The migrants – those still abroad and those who have returned to the Caribbean – are never completely displaced from their home society nor lost from the system (Thomas-Hope, 1988). They themselves and their migration are part of the reality for a time but remain part of the myth forever.

Explanation of migration as total displacement conceptualized from the perspective of a paradigm based primarily or solely on materialistic forces, fails to understand the variability of migration and the meaning of the environment, in a total sense, to different societal groups. Former colonization and continued neo-colonial linkages provide the background for the movement of personnel of all types, including labour, from Caribbean countries. But even the structural explanation is only relevant if the image is consistent with migrating and translates migration opportunities into meaning, however variable the nature of that meaning may be to different sectors of Caribbean society.

The system of values (from which meaning of the environment is derived) is determined by the cultural framework of the society. But culture itself, like the values which emanate from it, is also influenced by the structural aspects of the total environmental system, which in turn affects the relational dimension of the images held. Thus the emphasis on values such as materialism in some societies or groups within societies reflects more the absence or unequal distribution of material goods than it does any difference in the innate nature of the society or group itself.

The perceived economic poverty of the materially poor is definitely no more significant in the context of migration than the perceived cultural sterility of those who are culturally bored, the perceived career vacuum of the ambitious, the lack of status of the socially immobile, or the political frustration of the powerless. Thus the worker migrates to work, the artist to receive recognition in a wider cultural milieu, the scientist to engage in activities at the centre of technological and intellectual innovation. These factors become part of the value system against which people evaluate migration on the one hand and their microenvironment or life-space on the other.

Migration and the perpetuation of disequilibrium

There is no process toward equilibrium. On the contrary, migration in the Caribbean context is a process which perpetuates itself. The more people go, the more there are who want to go. The impact of migration is felt in subsequent years in the image. If a simple functional explanation was appropriate, the vindication of such an approach would be evident in the existence of a trend towards equilibrium and a policy to stem migration would be clear. Unfortunately, sometimes policy in the Caribbean has assumed such an explanation chiefly because it has been misguided by the notion of a push-pull explanation based on conventional wisdom of classic economic theory. Improvements in infrastructure and modernization of rural facilities may be applauded for the greater equality of services which they provide and the increased accessibility which they afford. But they do not, nor are they likely to reduce outward migration; quite the reverse.

It was not the least accessible, the least informed or the poorest who went. The process led to high potential among these groups but not to the highest movement of them. Work contributed, like education and modernization, to enhanced accessibility and increased migration when the opportunities presented themselves.

Frustration with employment opportunities of the home locale had a definite bearing upon the propensity for migration in the case of Jamaica, Barbados and St Vincent. Differentials in opportunities were primarily determined by the social reference groups whereby the 'actual' opportunities were measured. The spatial dimension of this pattern reflected the ways in which different parts of the islands variously fulfilled their demands and expectations. As a causal relationship, the position was not straightforward. People migrated in order to work, as well as worked in order to migrate.

Educational opportunities were evaluated according to a similar set of principles. To some, migration was a means of acquiring an education, to others, migration was the main reason for it. Their strongest association was in their common role. Migration, like work and education, was seen to promote the achievement of goals.

Even varying levels of modernization were only meaningful in terms of the reference bar which measured their prestige primarily, and their usefulness secondarily. They assumed significance in the migration process through their contribution to the value attributed to the status and perceived status of places. The symbols of modernization combined in this respect with those of employment and educational opportunities to produce variations in local levels of development. These all played their part in moulding the total perception of places.

Friends and relatives overseas were inconsistent in their impact upon migration behaviour. There was a tendency for the desire to migrate to be lessened when remittances were received from family members abroad. In other cases, the subsequent departure of the migrant's dependants was taken as a matter of course.

Accessibility facilitated the transmission of information through education, the mass media, personal networks of contact and personal mobility. Accessibility influenced the interaction of people and places within their own island, and of their island within the wider world. Environments were expanded or restricted depending largely upon the socio-spatial location of people in the systems of information diffusion.

Accessibility was not solely a function of place of residence. Accessibility was constantly enhanced and environments expanded through personal mobility. In some cases mobility was regular, entailed only short distances and repeated the same paths. In other cases, travel patterns incorporated long distances. Overseas countries might have been included in such travel fields and a sojourn of days or years involved. Even the travel patterns and previous migration histories of Caribbean people were not determined simply by chance. The distribution of 'space sitters' and 'space searchers' was profoundly affected by their combined social and spatial distance from the core of their country. There were spatial variations even in the extent to which, and the direction in which, regular patterns of mobility occurred.

The importance of location in environmental experience and environmental meaning was a constantly recurring theme. The location of a place, coupled with the symbolic meaning of its inherent attributes, governed the views which were held about it. The element of isolation or centrality, levels of development or underdevelopment, prestige or unpopularity, denoted desirability or undesirability. Evaluations of these characteristics sometimes conflicted with the sense of belonging to particular places and types of landscapes. Thus the tempo of city life both at home and abroad simultaneously magnetised and repelled rural dwellers. Attachment to the sea coast or to the mountains conflicted with the resentment felt of the poor livelihood with which they were associated. The industrialized world presented an imagined utopia for those whose agricultural toil and rural lifestyle had degenerated into a status of the lowest order.

But migration was induced as much by positive as by negative factors. Negative evaluations of the local environment and isolation were associated with a high propensity for migration. Actual migration, however, demanded accessibility to information as a prerequisite. Was the overt behaviour, or the actual move, a result of the build-up of frustration among remote sections of the population in poorly developed areas? Or was it the result of the positive ambitions of the more accessible, well-informed, educated and employed? If the negative factors of alienation were alone important, those groups in the most developed, accessible areas should not have migrated most, but in fact, they did.

Integration and accessibility were associated with high migration rates, while remoteness and marginality were associated with low actual migration. Perception of place was important in explaining much of the inverse relationship between the propensity for migration and actual migration.

The propensity for migration was the key to the overall behavioural process, even though the actual move overseas represented the overt aspect of the behaviour. The overt behaviour would not exist without the propensity. If the propensity for migration was significant, so too were the factors which governed it – namely the perception of the environment as a total experience and of one's position within it.

The association of negative evaluations and high migration potential on the one hand, and positive evaluations and high actual migration on the other, were not as contradictory as they might have appeared at first. The selectivity of the migration process tended to pick out those who were not the least educated, poorest or least integrated. Even among lower-class families, where the passage money was collectively accumulated, it was not invested in the migration of the least ambitious or least able member of the family. Caribbean migration, therefore, was a selection of the fittest.

This was a most serious problem in so far as loss of skills from the islands was concerned, but not all migrants had skills. In the case of prolonged migration phases, free from restrictive official legislation, the effects of selectivity were greatly reduced and the constraints of location lessened, as was found at the time of the major movements to Panama, Costa Rica, Cuba and Britain.

Both negative and positive factors were part of the environmental experience, and for Caribbean people they were both oriented towards migration. Frustration and aspiration were usually two sides of the same coin.

The push-pull hypothesis – a blunt and simplistic analytical tool, explaining migration from a functional perspective, explains migration as a response or reaction to events or circumstances. It does not recognize migration as being part of a process which incorporates both negative and positive elements of the environment, translating them into meaning. The meaning of the environmental circumstances is relevant not just for one particular time but in an ongoing way, as part of the culture and consciousness of the society.

Structure and migration behaviour

Global, national and local factors interact to form the environmental framework within which people make decisions to move across international boundaries. It is true that in migration even the options involved in moving are conditioned by factors over which the individual and even the state has no direct control. Legislation provides the mechanisms of control to movement, and this conditions the volume of legally permitted flow. In turn, legislation is a reflection of the economic need and the socio-political mood of society, especially in the destination countries. Whether liberal or highly selective, these regulations determine, by direct and indirect methods, the types of migrants who enter that country at a particular time, their occupations and skills, nationality, race and demographic characteristics. These factors provide explanation for the *pattern* of migration, they do not explain the *process*.

Historical-structural factors reflected in the unequal development of countries influences the images held by all people – not just migrants. It determines the images of migration, its benefits and problems, held by policymakers both in the Caribbean and in the countries of traditional or potential migrant entry. This contributes to the nature of political decisions and therefore the migration controls or superstructure of the system.

The ways in which the environment comprised of international, national and local circumstances affect the migration process are determined by the position or location of the society in the international framework, and the location of the various sectors of society, classes, communities and individuals in relation to the national system. Where these social units are located with respect to the system of production and the distribution of profits, their position in relation to the power of the state, or in relation to the status of the society and the network of economic, political and social relations, influences both directly and indirectly the implications of the historical-structural framework.

The location of household units and individuals with respect to those structures determines the vantage point from which they consciously and subconsciously experience and perceive their life chances. This is translated into the mental image, and on the basis of the image, decisions are made and behaviour is influenced. The behaviour is rarely individualistic or anomalous for perceptions of the environment cogently reflect evaluations imposed by society at large. 'There is no doubt', commented Moore (1976: 141), 'that communication and coming to have shared impressions of the world influences how each one of us structures our own individual world.'

To a greater or lesser extent, people are constantly interacting with each other within their shared environment. In small island societies this phenomenon is particularly pronounced. As Clarke has remarked: 'Caribbean societies are rarely impersonal. Social distance is mitigated by spatial proximity' (Clarke, 1976: 10). All sectors of Caribbean society, whether socially or spatially differentiated, see their environment partly through their own life experience and partly through the eyes of the rest of society. The image, whether consciously or subconsciously, embraces those elements of the past, present and future which are meaningful to the individual. It incorporates the structural conditions and within these the spatial implications and the social symbolism of the total environment.

Whatever the difficulties in evaluating the composition and formation of the image and its role in migration, it is the abstraction which brings us closest to understanding the generation of the potential energy or propensity for different types of migration behaviour.

The image in Caribbean migration

Migration reflects the combination of a myriad of personal images shared by others of the same social group. But the image is always the property of the individual. The individual's image reflects the meaning of that person's micro-environment and the nature of the person's psychological life-space. This is determined to some extent by the actual occurrences, characteristics and information of the environment and, even more, by the location of the individual within the total social, physical and temporal space of the system of which he or she is a part.

The image which is held is integral to decision-making and thus to generating the propensity for migration. It does not determine the transfer of potential to active energy nor the precise characteristics of the actual migration behaviour. Practical factors comprised of the economic, social and political constraints and selectivity of the final stages of the process, control the volume and pattern of actual movement, the overt migration behaviour.

The interaction of the image, the behaviour which occurs and the transmission of information from environment to individual, generates the dynamic of the migration process. Because the image itself changes so slowly and reluctantly, the same migration pattern is sustained for long periods of time provided the facilitating control mechanisms also prevail. As the practical circumstances alter and the actual migration trajectories change, migration volume is affected, duration and frequency and displacement opportunities are altered, and so the overall pattern is transformed. The new and evolving migration pattern then provides new information which goes towards the alteration in the image and the potential for perpetuating the system.

It is only if the image of migration itself, its value and purpose should change that any fundamental transformations in the process would occur. This is unlikely to happen unless the structural factors which condition the environment, and the value systems whereby those environments are evaluated, are significantly altered.

In the absence of fundamental change in the structural framework there will be no change in the image. Where the value system remains fundamentally unaltered, the feedback from the real world will continue to produce messages which reinforce the existing image of the environment, one's position within that environment and the value of migration. Thus migration remains a self-perpetuating process with its own dynamic, the forces of which are part of the wider influences upon the society as a whole.

Explanation must combine the macroanalytical approach of the global system of which each Caribbean country is a part, as well as the microanalytical approach to understand the issue from the perspective of the decision-maker. This is necessary in order to come to terms with, and appreciate, the role of historical-structural factors in the formation of the personal image and thus the collection of personal images which sustain the propensity for migration.

Despite the strongly connected roots of Caribbean migration with the internationalization of capital, and though migration is propelled by the continuing dynamic of international capital, at the same time, it has evolved in such a way that it has generated its own dynamic with its own element of freedom. The essential freedom is in the decision-making component of the process. But even decision-making is itself partly a reflection of latent consciousness, derived from the structural constraints articulated in a variety of material and non-material ways; these include the tensions derived from internal class relations and external political relations. All these determine the environment of reality within which each individual and group occupies a particular location in a multi-dimensional space comprised of social systems, physical attributes and the relativity of time.

The image of the migration alters once abroad, for the new experience, opportunities and goals become part of the real and perceived environment of the individual. But that reality is only partly transmitted to those still in the Caribbean, nor are these experiences as bleak in the image as they are in reality. This is partly because the value of migration remains paramount in the minds of the migrant and partly because the position of self in relation to those experiences is tempered by the fact that they are migration experiences. They are regarded as part of the expectations of migration, not the ultimate goal for which migration was intended. Thus hardship in migration gives rise to a sense of heroism in the image portrayed. The successes are valued even more on account of the difficulties undergone.

The image of migration is not totally positive in the nature of the sojourn abroad and the migrant, like Brathwaite's *New World Mariners*, does not always find the 'magic keys' to open 'gold endragoned doors'.

> But now the claws are iron: mouldy
> dredges do not care what we discover here:
> the Mississippi mud is sticky:
>
> men die there
> and bouquets of stench lie
> all night long along the river bank.
>
> In London, Undergrounds are cold.
> The train rolls in from darkness
> with our fears
> and leaves a lonely soft metallic clanking
> in our ears.
> In New York
>
> nights are hot
> in Harlem, Brooklyn,
> along Long Island Sound
>
> This city is so vast
> its ears have ceased to know
> a simple human sound
>
> Police cars wail
> like babies
> an ambulance erupts

> like breaking glass
> an elevator sighs
> like Jews in Europe's gasses
>
> then slides us swiftly
> down the ropes to hell.
>
> (Brathwaite, 1967: 52-3)

It is known that conditions will be difficult; it is part of the image of migration. There is a time to migrate and a time to return. The migrant abroad is sustained by nostalgia of the homeland and the return component of the migration image.

> Where is the bell
>
> that used to warn us,
> playing cricket on the beach,
> that it was mid-day: sun too hot
>
> for heads. And evening's
> angelus of fish soup,
> prayers, bed?
>
> (Brathwaite, 1967: 53).

Migration is not just a response to presumed negative conditions in the Caribbean and positive conditions elsewhere, but behaviour which is part of a wider reality. That reality is contained in the image, for the image reflects both the corporate and personal evaluation of the actual environment and also the latent consciousness which influences value and ascribes meaning to social relationships, places and events. This dimension of reality cannot be explored when conceptualized within paradigms of migration in which analysis is premised on the assumption that the only relevant aspects of reality are negative and objective or external to the decision-makers. It is only by understanding the factors conditioning the image of the decision-makers in the process that the relationship between the actual and the perceived environment, as well as the paradoxes of migration, can be understood.

APPENDIX

Stratification used in the selection of a representative sample population

Jamaica
The Kingston Metropolitan Area: The official KMA limits and all Census Enumeration Districts (EDs) contiguous with it. This included all of the Parish of Kingston and the urban and peri-urban areas of the Parish of St Andrew.
The urban stratum: Centres classified by size and function, with a minimum population of 4,500 and a 75 threshold index of services (computed from Planning Department statistics).
The bauxite zone: The EDs influenced by bauxite operations (1974-84) calculated in terms of radii around each bauxite plant proportionate to the size of the employing capacity of each.
The plantation stratum: Areas influenced by sugar plantations calculated in terms of plantation size given as tonnes of sugar produced. Coconut and banana estate areas were also included.
The zone of mixed farming: EDs dominated by farming and not included in the other strata. Most farm units were less than 5 acres, many less than 1 acre.

Barbados
Bridgetown: The area officially specified by the Census plus all other EDs in the Parish of St Michael.
The tourist area: All EDs in the coastal area of St James and Christchurch.
The sugar plantation zone: EDs dominated by sugar, which comprised all those not falling into the Bridgetown and tourist strata.

St Vincent
Kingstown: The official Census delineation of 'Kingstown and suburbs'.
The south: The area east of Kingstown, extending from the coast northwards to Mesopotamia.
The north: All areas not included in Kingstown and the south as specified. This comprised the constituencies of Colonaire, Georgetown and Sandy Bay on the east or Windward side, and Layou, Barrouallie and Chateaubelair on the west or Leeward side.

References

Adams, Nassau A. (1969) 'Internal Migration in Jamaica: An Economic Analysis.' *Social and Economic Studies.* **18**: 137-51.

Anderson, Patricia Y. (1985) 'Migration and development in Jamaica.' In Pastor, R. A., *Migration and Development in the Caribbean: The Unexplored Connection,* Boulder, Westview Press, 117-34.

– (1988) 'Manpower losses and employment, adequacy among skilled workers in Jamaica 1976-85.' In Pessar, Patricia (ed.) *When Borders Don't Divide: Labor Migration and Refugee Movements in the Americas,* New York, Center for Migration Studies.

Austin, Diane J. (1984) *Urban Life in Kingston, Jamaica: The Culture and Class Ideology of Two Neighborhoods,* New York, Gordon Breach Science Publishers.

Baksh, Ishmael J. (1984) 'Factors influencing occupational expectations of secondary school students in Trinidad and Tobago.' *Social and Economic Studies,* **33** (3):1-29.

Basch, Linda (1987) 'The politics of Caribbeanization.' In Sutton, C.R. and Chaney, E.M. (eds) *Caribbean Life in New York City: Sociocultural Dimensions,* New York, Center for Migration Studies.

Basch, L., Wiltshire-Brodber, R. and W. (1987) *Caribbean Regional and International Migration: Transnational Dimensions,* Ottawa, International Development Research Centre, Canada, (mimeo).

Beckford, George, (1972) *Persistent Poverty: Underdevelopment in Plantation Economies of the Third World,* Oxford University Press.

– (ed.) (1987) 'Impact of Bauxite-Alumina on Rural Jamaica.' (Special Number) *Social and Economic Studies,* **36** (1).

Besson, Jean, (1984) 'Family land and Caribbean society: toward an enthnography of Afro-Caribbean peasantries.' In Thomas-Hope, Elizabeth M. (ed.) *Perspectives on Caribbean Regional Identity,* University of Liverpool, Centre for Latin American Studies, Monograph Series No. **11**, 57-83.

Besson, Jean and Momsen, Janet, (eds.) (1987) *Land and Development in the Caribbean,* London, Macmillan Caribbean.

Betley, Brian J. (1976) Stratification and Strategies: A Study of Adaptation and Mobility in a Vincentian Town, Unpublished Ph.D. thesis, University of California, Los Angeles.
Boulding, K.E. (1956) *The Image: Knowledge in Life and Society*, Ann Arbor, Univerity of Michigan Press.
Brathwaite, Edward Kamau, (1967) 'The Emigrants.' In *Rights of Passage,* Oxford University Press.
– (1986) *Roots: Essay,* Havana, Casas las Americas.
Brodber, Erna, (1975) *Yards in the City of Kingston,* Kingston, Jamaica, Institute of Social and Economic Research, Working Paper No.9.
Brookfield, H.C. (1969) 'On the environment as perceived.' In Board, C., Chorley, R.J., Haggett, P. and Stoddart, D.R. (eds) *Progress in Geography: International Reviews of Current Research,* (1) London, Edward Arnold, 53-80.
Brown, H. (1972) 'Perception and Meaning.' In Recher, N. (ed.) *Studies in the Philosophy of the Mind,* American Philosophical Quarterly Monograph Series, No. **6**:1-9.
Bryce-Laporte, Roy S. (1976) The United States' role in Caribbean migration: background to the problem.' In Bryce-Laporte, Roy S. and Mortimer, Delores M. (eds) *Caribbean Immigration to the United States,* Washington D.C., Research Institute on Immigration and Ethnic Studies, Smithsonian Institution, Occasional Papers No.1.
Buttimer, Anne, (1972) 'Social space and the planning of residential areas.' In Lowenthal, David (ed.) *Environment and Behavior,* **4** (3):282-87.
Carnegie, Charles, V. (1982) 'Strategic flexibility in the West Indies: a social psychology of Caribbean migration.' *Caribbean Review,* **11** (1):10-14.
Chaney, Elsa M. (1985) *Migration from the Caribbean Region: Determinants and Effects of Current Movements*, Hemispheric Migration Project, Washington D.C., Georgetown University, Center for Immigration Policy and Refugee Assistance and Intergovernmental Committee for Migration.
Chernick, Sidney E. (1978) *The Commonwealth Caribbean: The Integration Experience,* Baltimore and London, The Johns Hopkins University Press for the World Bank.
Clarke, C.G. (1966) 'Population pressure in Kingston, Jamaica: a study of unemployment and overcrowding.' *Transactions of the Institute of British Geographers,* **38**:165-87.
– (1975) *Kingston, Jamaica: Urban Growth and Social change, 1692-1962,* Berkeley, University of California Press.

- (1976) 'Insularity and identity in the Caribbean.' *Geography,* **61** (part 1).
Cohen, Robin, (1987) *The New Helots: Migrants in the International Division of Labour,* Aldershot, Hampshire, Gower Publishing Company.
Conway, D. (1980) 'Step-wise migration: toward a clarification of the mechanism.' *International Migration Research,* **14**:3-14.
- (1988) 'Conceptualizing contemporary patterns of Caribbean international mobility.' *Caribbean Geography,* **2** (3):145-163.
- (1989) 'Caribbean international mobility traditions.' *Boletin de Estudios Latinoamericanos y del Caribe,* **46**:17-47.
Conway D. and Brown, J. (1980) 'Intraurban relocation and structure: low income migrants in Latin America and the Caribbean.' *Latin American Research Review,* **15**:95-125.
Crane, Julia G. (1971) *Educated to Emigrate: The Social Organization of Saba,* Assen, Netherlands, Van Gorcum.
Cross, M. and Schwartzbaum, A.M. (1969) 'Social mobility and secondary school selection in Trinidad and Tobago.' *Social and Economic Studies,* **18** (2):189-207.
Cross, Malcolm, (1979) *Urbanization and Urban Growth in the Caribbean,* Cambridge University Press.
Dann, G. (1984) *The Quality of Life in Barbados,* London, Macmillan.
Davison, R.B. (1962) *West Indian Migrants,* London, Institute of Race Relations, Oxford University Press.
Dirks, Robert, (1972) 'Network groups and adaptation in an Afro-Caribbean community.' *Man,* **7** (4).
Dixon, Herberto, (1980) 'Emigration and Jamaican employment.' *Migration Today,* **8** (3):24-7.
Downs, R.M. (1970) 'Geographic space perception: past approaches and future prospects.' In Board, C. *et al.* (eds) *Progress in Geography,* (**2**) London, Edward Arnold: 65-108.
Downs, R.M. and Stea, D. (eds) (1973) *Image and Environment: Cognitive Mapping and Spatial Behavior,* Chicago, Aldine.
Europa, (1987) *South America, Central America and the Caribbean,* London, Europa Publications Ltd.
Fawcett, J.T. (ed.) (1985-86) *Migration Intentions and Behavior. Population and Environment,* **8** (1-2).
Foner, Nancy, (1973) *Status and Power in Rural Jamaica,* New York, Columbia University Teachers Press.
Frucht, Richard, (1967) 'A Caribbean social type: neither 'peasant' nor 'proletarian'.' *Social and Economic Studies,* **16**:296-300.
- (1968) Emigration, remittances and social change: aspects of the social field of Nevis, West Indies.' *Anthropologica,* **10**(2):193-208.

— (1972) 'Migration and the receipt of remittances.' In *Resource Development in the Caribbean,* Montreal, Centre for Developing-Area Studies: 275-314.

George, Eugenia, (1990) *The Making of a Transnational Community: Migration, Development and Cultural Change in the Dominican Republic,* New York, Columbia University Press.

Gerson, Elihu M. and Gerson, M. Sue, (1976) 'The social frameworks of place perspective.' In Moore, Gary T. and Golledge, Reginald G. (eds) *Environmental Knowing: Theories, Research and Methods,* Stroudsburg, Pennsylvania, Dowden, Hutchinson and Ross, 214-18.

Girling, R.K. (1974) 'The migration of human capital from the Third World: The implications and some data on the Jamaican case.' *Social and Economic Studies,* **23**(1):84-96.

Girvan, Norman, (1967) *The Caribbean Bauxite Industry,* Mona, Institute of Social and Economic Research, UWI.

— (1972) *Foreign Capital and Economic Underdevelopment in Jamaica,* Mona, Institute of Social and Economic Research, UWI.

Glass, Ruth, (1960) *Newcomers,* London, George Allen and Unwin and the Centre for Urban Studies.

Golledge, R.G. (1967) 'Conceptualizing the market decision process.' *Journal of Regional Science,* **7**(2):239-58.

Golledge, R.G., Brown, L.A. and Williamson, Frank, (1972) 'Behavioural Approaches in Geography: An Overview.' *The Australian Geographer,* **12**(1):59-79.

Goodey, B. (1973) *Perception of the Environment: An Introduction to the Literature,* Birmingham, Centre for Urban and Regional Studies, Occasional Paper No. 17, University of Birmingham.

— (1974) *Images of Place: Essays on Environmental Perception, Communications and Education,* Birmingham, Centre for Urban and Regional Studies, Occasional Paper No. 30, University of Birmingham.

Gould, P.R. (1965) 'Wheat on Kilimanjaro: The perception of choice within game and learning model frameworks.' *General Systems,* **10**:157-66.

— (1969) 'Problems of space preference, measures and relationships.' *Geographical Analysis,* **1**:31-44.

Gould, P.R. and White, R. (1974) *Mental Maps,* Harmondsworth, Penguin Books.

Gould, Peter and Lyew-Ayee, Anne, (1983) 'Jamaican Television: Images and Geographic Connections.' *Caribbean Geography,* **1**(1): 36-50.

Gmelch, G. (1980) 'Return migration.' In Siegal, B. (ed.) *Annual*

Review of Anthropology, Palo Alto, California, Annual Reviews, 9:135-59.
- (1987) 'Work, innovation and investment: the impact of return migrants in Barbados.' *Human Organization,* **46**:131-40.
Grasmuck, S. (1982) *The Impact of Emigration on National Development: Three sending Communities in the Dominican Republic,* New York Research Program in Inter-American Affairs, Occasional Paper No. 33.
- (1985) 'The consequences of Dominican urban out-migration for national development: The case of Santiago.' In Sanderson, Steven E. (ed.) *The Americas in the New Division of Labor,* New York, Holmes and Meier.
Guengant, Jean-Pierre, (1985) *Caribbean Population Dynamics: Emigration and Fertility Challenges,* Conference of Caribbean Parliamentarians on Population and Development, Barbados, June 14-15.
Hall, E.T. (1959) *The Silent Language,* New York, Doubleday.
- (1966) *The Hidden Dimension,* New York, Doubleday.
- (1968) 'Human needs and inhuman cities. In *The Fitness of Man's Environment, Smithsonian Annual* Vol. **2**, Washington, D.C., Smithsonian Institution, 162-72.
Harewood, J. (1983) 'White collar migrant labor: Some observations on the case of Trinidad and Tobago in the last two decades.' In Marks, A.F. and Vessuri, H.M.C. (eds) *White Collar Migrants in the Americas and the Caribbean,* Leiden, Royal Institute of Linguistics and Anthropology, 19-37.
Harvey, D. (1967) 'Behavioural postulates and the construction of theory in human geography.' Bristol, Department of Geography, Seminar Paper Series 6, University of Bristol.
Hendricks, Glen L. (1974) *The Dominican Diaspora: From the Dominican Republic to New York City: Villagers in Transition,* New York, Columbia University Teachers College Press.
Hill, Donald Raymond, (1977) 'The impact of migration on the metropolitan and folk society of Carriacou, Grenada.' New York, The American Museum, of Natural History vol.**54**, Part 2.
Hills, T.L. and Iton, S. (1983) 'A reassessment of the "traditional" in Caribbean small-scale agriculture.' *Caribbean Geography,* **1**:24-35.
History Task Force, (1979) *Labor Migration Under Capitalism: The Puerto Rican Experience,* New York, and London, Monthly Review Press.
Hoffman-Nowotny, H-J. (1981) 'A sociological approach toward a general theory of migration.' In Kritz, M., Keely, C., and Tomasi, S. (eds) *Global Trends in Migration: Theory and Research on Inter-*

national Population Movements, New York, Center for Migration Studies, 64-83.
Hope, Kemp R. (1983) 'Urban population growth in the Caribbean.' Cities, 1:167-74.
– (1986) Urbanization in the Commonwealth Caribbean, Boulder, Westview Press.
Hope, Trevor J. (1985) 'The impact of immigration on Caribbean development.' In Pastor, Robert A. (ed.) Migration and Development in the Caribbean: The Unexplored Connection, Boulder, Westview Press, 237-54.
Jamaica, (1978, 1986, 1990) Economic and Social Survey, Kingston, National Planning Agency.
Kearney, M. (1986) 'From the invisible hand to the visible feet: Anthropological studies of migration and devlopment.' In Siegal, B. (ed.) Annual Review of Anthropology, Palo Alto, California, Annual Reviews, 15:331-61.
Koot, Wim (1974) 'Peach and the mono-causal explanation.' Caribbean Studies, 14(2):145-58.
– (1981) 'Socio-economic development and emigration in the Netherlands Antilles.' In Craig, Susan (ed.) Contemporary Caribbean: A Sociological Reader, Maracas, Trinidad, The College Press, vol.1, 129-42.
Kritz, Mary M. (1981) 'International migration patterns in the Caribbean Basin: an overview.' In Kritz, Mary, Keely, Charles B., and Tomasi, Silvano. (eds) Global Trends in Migration: Theory and Research in International Population Movements, New York, Center for Migration Studies, 208-33.
Lewis, G. (1982) Human Migration: A Geographic Perspective, London, Croom Helm.
Lowenthal, David, (1961a) 'Geography, experience and imagination: Towards a geographical epistomology.' Annals of the Association of American Geographers, 51(3):241-60.
– (1961b) 'Caribbean views of Caribbean land.' Canadian Geographer, 5(2):1-9.
– (ed.) (1967) Environmental Perception and Behavior, Chicago, Aldine Press.
– (1972) West Indian Societies, Oxford University Press.
Lowenthal, David and Comitas, Lambros, (1962) 'Emigration and depopulation: some neglected aspects of population geography.' Geographical Review, 52 (2):195-210.
Mabogunje, A.L. (1970) 'Systems approach to a theory of rural-urban migration.' Geographical Analysis, 2:1-18.
Maingot, A. (1985) 'Political implications of migration in a socio-cultural

area.' In Pastor, Robert A. (ed.) *Migration and Development in the Caribbean: The Unexplored Connection,* Boulder, Westview, 63-90.

Manners, Robert, (1965) 'Remittances and the unit of analysis in anthropological research.' *Southwestern Journal of Anthropology,* 21(3):179-95.

Marshall, Dawn I. (1982a) 'Towards an understanding of Caribbean migration.' In Kritz, Mary (ed.) *US Immigration and Refugee Policy: Global and Domestic Issues,* Lexington, D.C. Heath.

– (1982b) 'Migration as an agent of change in Caribbean island ecosystems.' *International Social Science Journal,* 34(3):451-67.

– (1984) 'Vincentian contract labour migration to Barbados: the satisfaction of mutual needs?' *Social and Economic Studies,* 33:63-92.

– (1985) 'International migration as circulation: Haitian movement to the Bahamas.' In Prothero, R. and Chapman, M. (eds.) *Circulation in Third World Countries,* London, Routledge and Kegan Paul, 226-40.

McCoy, T.L. and Wood, C.H. (1982) 'Caribbean Workers in the Florida Sugar Cane Industry,' Gainesville, Florida, Occasional Paper No.2, Centre for Latin American Studies, University of Florida.

McElroy, J.I. and de Albuquerque, K. (1988) 'Migration transition in small northern and eastern Caribbean states.' *International Migration Review,* 22:30-58.

McHugh, K.E. (1984) 'Explaining Migration Intentions and Destination Selection.' *The Professional Geographer,* 36(3):315-25.

McLean-Petras, Elizabeth, (1978) 'The role of national boundaries in a cross-national labor market.' Paper presented at the meeting of the American Sociological Association, San Francisco.

– (1981a) 'Black Labor and White Capital: the formation of Jamaica as a Global Labor Reserve, 1830-1930, Unpublished Ph.D. thesis, Binghamton, State University of New York.

– (1981b) 'The global labor market in the modern world economy.' In Kritz, Mary, Keeley, Charles B. and Tomasi, Silvano (eds) *Global Trends in Migration: Theory and Research on International Population Movements,* New York, Center for Migration Studies, 44-63.

Midgett, Douglas K. (1975) 'West Indian ethnicity in Britain.' In Safa, Helen I. and Du Toit, B. (eds) *Migration and Development: Implication for Ethnic Identity and Political Conflict,* The Hague, Mouton.

Mintz, Sidney W. (1961) 'The question of Caribbean peasantries: a comment.' *Caribbean Studies,* 1(3):31-34.

– (1971) 'The Caribbean as a socio-cultural area.' In Horowitz, Michael M. (ed.) *People and Cultures of the Caribbean: An Anthropological Reader,* New York, Natural History Press.

– (1974) *Caribbean Transformations,* Chicago, Aldine.

- (1983) 'Reflection on Caribbean peasantries.' *Nieuwe West-Indische Gids,* **57**(1/2):1-17.
Mintz, S.W. and Price, S. (eds) (1985) *Caribbean Contours,* Baltimore, Johns Hopkins University Press.
Moore, Gary T. (1976) 'Theory and research on the development of environmental knowing.' In Moore, G.T. and Golledge, R.G. (eds) *Environmental Knowing: Theory, Research and Methods,* Stroudsburg, Pennsylvania, Dowden, Hutchinson and Ross.
Nanton, Philip, (1983) 'The changing pattern of state control in St Vincent and the Grenadines.' In Ambursley, Fitzroy and Cohen, Robin (eds) *Crisis in the Caribbean,* London, Heinemann, 223-46.
Olwig, Karen Fog Pedersen, (1977) 'Households, exchange and social reproduction: the development of a Caribbean society.' Unpublished Ph.D. thesis, University of Minnesota.
- (1987) 'Children's attitudes to the island, community: the aftermath of out-migration on Nevis.' In Besson J. and Momsen, J. (eds) *Land and Development in the Caribbean,* London, Macmillan Caribbean, 153-70.
Palmer, Ransford W. (1974) 'A decade of West Indian Migration to the United States, 1962-1972: An economic analysis.' *Social and Economic Studies,* **23**(4):571-87.
- (1983) 'Emigration and the economic decline of Jamaica.' In Marks, Arnaud F. and Vessuri, Hebe M.C. (eds) *White Collar Migrants in the Americas and the Caribbean,* Leiden, Royal Institute of Linguistics and Anthropology, 59-72.
Pastor, Robert A. (1985) 'Introduction: the policy challenge.' In Pastor, Robert A. (ed.) *Migration and Development in the Caribbean: The Unexplored Connection,* Boulder, Westview Press, 1-22.
Patterson, Orlando, (1978) 'Migration in Caribbean societies: socio-economic and symbolic resources.' In McNeil, William H. and Adams, Ruth (eds) *Human Migration: Patterns and Policies,* Bloomington, Indiana University Press, 106-45.
Peach, C.G.K. (1968) *West Indian Migration to Britain: A Social Geography,* London, Institute of Race Relations, Oxford University Press.
Pessar, Patricia, (1982a) *Kinship relations of production in the emigration process: the case of Dominican emigration to the United States,* New York, Center for Latin American and Caribbean Studies, New York University, Occasional Paper No.22.
- (1982b) 'The role of households in international migration and the case of US-bound migration from the Dominican Republic.' *International Migration Review,* **16**(2):342-64.
Philpott, Stuart B. (1973) *West Indian Migration: The Montserrat*

Case, London, Athlone Press, London School of Economics Monographs of Social Anthropology.
Population Policy Coordinating Committee, (1982) *A Statement of National Population Policy*, Kingston, Jamaica, Ministry of Health.
Potter, Robert B. (1983) 'Congruence between space preferences and socio-economic structure in Barbados, West Indies.' *Geoforum*, **14**:249-65.
— (1984) 'Mental maps and spatial variations in residential desirability: a Barbados case study.' *Caribbean Geography*, **1**:186-97.
— (1985) *Urbanization and Planning in the 3rd World: Spatial Perceptions and Public Participation*, London, Croom Helm.
— (1986) 'Spatial inequalities in Barbados, West Indies.' *Transactions of the Institute of British Geographers*, new series **11**:183-98.
Potter, Robert B. and Unwin, Tim, (eds) (1989) *The Geography of Urban-Rural Interaction in Developing Countries*, London, Routledge.
Prothero, R.M. and Chapman, M. (eds) (1985) *Circulation in Third World Countries*, London, Routledge and Kegan Paul.
Richardson, Bonham C. (1980) 'Freedom and migration in the Leeward Caribbean, 1838-48.' *Journal of Historical Geography*, **6**(4):391-408.
— (1983) *Caribbean Migrants: Environment and Social Survival on St Kitts and Nevis*, Knoxville, The University of Tennessee Press.
Roberts, George W. (1955) 'Emigration from the island of Barbados.' *Social and Economic Studies*, **4**(3):245-88.
— (ed.) (1974) *Recent Population Movements in Jamaica*, Paris, CICRED.
Roberts, George and Mills, Don, (1958) 'Study of External Migration Affecting Jamaica, 1953-1955.' *Social and Economic Studies, Supplement*, vol.**7** (2).
Roseman, C.C. (1971) 'Migration as a temporal and spatial process.' *Annals of the Association of American Geographers*, **61**:589-98.
Rostow, W.W. (1960) *The Stages of Economic Growth: A Noncommunist manifesto*, Cambridge University Press.
Rubenstein, Hymie, (1982) 'Return migration to the English-speaking Caribbean: review and commentary.' In Stinner, William F., de Albuquerque, Klaus and Bryce-Laporte, Roy S. (eds) *Return Migration and Remittances: Developing a Caribbean Perspective*, Washington D.C., Research Institute for Immigration and Ethnic Studies, Smithsonian Institution, Occasional Papers No. 3, 3-34.
— (1983) 'Remittances and rural underdevelopment in the English-speaking Caribbean.' *Human Organization*, **42**(4):295-306.
Salt, John, (1986) 'International migration: a spatial theoretical approach.' In Pacione, M. (ed.) *Population Geography: Progress*

and *Prospect,* London, Croom Helm, 166-93.
Sassen-Koob, Saskia, (1981) 'Exporting capital and importing labor; the role of women.' In Mortimer, Delores and Bryce-Laporte, Roy S. (eds) *Female Immigrants to the United States: Caribbean, Latin America and African Experiences,* Washington D.C., Research Institute for Immigration and Ethnic Studies, Smithsonian Institution, Occasional Papers, No. 2, 203-34.
Segal, Aaron, (1975) *Population Policies in the Caribbean,* Lexington, Massachussetts, Lexington Books.
Senior, Clarence and Manley, Douglas, (1955) *A Report on Jamaican Migration to Great Britain,* Kingston, Jamaica, Government Printing Office.
Simmons, Alan B. (1982) *Migration and rural development: conceptual approaches, research finding and policy issues,* Social Sciences Division, International Development and Research Centre, Ottawa, Canada, (mimeo).
Simon, H.A. (1957) *Models of Man: Social and Rational,* New York, John Wiley.
Skeldon, Ronald, (1990) *Population Mobility in Developing Countries: A Reinterpretation,* London, Belhaven Press.
Smith, M.G. (1984) *Culture, Race and Class in the Commonwealth Caribbean,* Department of Extra-Mural Studies, University of the West Indies.
Spinelli, Joseph, (1973) 'Land Use and Population in St Vincent, 1763-1960,' unpublished Ph.D. thesis, University of Florida.
Standing, Guy, (1981) *Unemployment and Female Labour: A Study of Labour Supply in Kingston, Jamaica,* London, Macmillan.
Stone, C. (1986) *Power in the Caribbean Basin: A Comparative Study of Political Economy,* Philadelphia, Institute for the Study of Human Issues.
Taylor, Edward, (1976) 'The social adjustment of returned migrants to Jamaica.' In Henry, Frances (ed.) *Ethnicity in the Americas,* The Hague and Paris, Mouton, 213-29.
Tekse, Kalman, (1967) *Internal Migration in Jamaica,* Kingston, Jamaica, Department of Statistics.
Thomas-Hope, Elizabeth M. (1977) 'West Indian Migration: The Role of Environmental and Perceptual Differentials.' Unpublished D. Phil. thesis, University of Oxford.
— (1978) 'The establishment of a migration tradition: British West Indian movements to the Hispanic Caribbean in the century after Emancipation.' In Clarke, Colin G. (ed.) *Caribbean Social Relations,* Liverpool, Centre for Latin American Studies, Monograph Series, No. 8, 66-81.

- (1980) 'Hopes and Realities in the West Indian Migration to Britain.' *Oral History: Journal of the Oral History Society,* **8**(1):35-42.
- (1981) 'Regional systems and the population component: the search for development strategy in the Caribbean.' In Mabogunje, A.L. and Misra, P.R. (eds) *Regional Development Alternatives: International Perspectives,* Singapore, Marzuen Asia for UNCRED, 277-99.
- (1982) 'Identity and adaptation of migrants from the English-speaking Caribbean in Britain and North America.' In Verma, G.K. and Bagley, C. (eds) *Self-Concept, Achievement and Multi-Cultural Education,* London, Macmillan, 227-39.
- (1983) ' "Off the Island": Population mobility among the Caribbean middle class.' In Marks, A.F. and Vessuri, H.M.C. (eds) *White Collar Migrants in the Americas and the Caribbean,* Leiden, Royal Institute of Linguistics and Anthropology, 39-59.
- (ed.) (1984) *Perspectives on Caribbean Regional Identity,* Liverpool, Centre for Latin American Studies, Monograph Series No. 11.
- (1985) 'Return migration and its implications for Caribbean development.' In Pastor, Robert A. (ed.) *Migration and Development in the Caribbean: The Unexplored Connection,* Boulder, Colorado, Westview Press, 157-77.
- (1986) 'Transients and settlers: varieties of Caribbean migrants and the socio-economic implications of their return.' *International Migration,* **24**(3):559-72.
- (1988) 'Caribbean skilled international migration and the transnational household.' *Geoforum,* **19**(4):423-32.
- (1990) 'Caribbean international movement in urbanization.' In Bui Dang Ha Doan (ed.) *Urbanization and Geographical Distribution of Population,* Paris, Committee for International Cooperation in National Research in Demography (CICRED), 76-91.

Thomas-Hope, Elizabeth M. and Nutter, R.D. (1988) 'Occupation and status in the ideology of Caribbean return migration.' In Appleyard, R.T. (ed.) *The Impact of International Migration on Third World Development,* Paris, OECD, 97-119.

Tidrick, Gene, (1966) 'Some aspects of Jamaica emigration to the United Kingdom 1953-62.' *Social and Economic Studies,* **15**(1):22-39.

Tidrick, K. (1971) 'Need for achievement, social class and intention to emigrate in Jamaican students.' *Social and Economic Studies,* **20**(1):52-60.

Todaro, M.P. (1976) *International Migration in Developing Countries,* Geneva, International Labour Organization.

Toney, J. (1985) *Emigration from St Vincent and the Grenadines: Contextual Background,* New York, Columbia University, (mimeo).

Tuan, Yi-Fu, (1975) 'Images and mental maps.' *Annals of the Association of American Geographers,* **65**:205-13.
Walmsley, D.J. (1982) 'Mass media and spatial awareness.' *Tijdschrift voor Economische en Sociale Geografie,* **73**:32-42.
Watson, Hilbourne A. (1982) 'Theoretical and methodological problems in Caribbean migration research: conditions and causality.' *Social and Economic Studies,* **31**(2): 165-206.
White, P.E. and Woods, R.I. (1980) 'The geographical impact of migration.' In White P.E. and Woods, R.I. (eds) *The Geographical Impact of Migration,* London, Longman, 42-56.
Wiltshire-Brodber, Rosina, (1986) *The Transnational Family*, St Augustine, Trinidad, Institute of International Relations, UWI, (mimeo).
Wiltshire-Brodber, R. and W. (1985) *Caribbean Regional Migration,* St Augustine, Trinidad, Institute of International Relations, UWI.
Wolpert, Julian, (1965) 'Behavioral aspects of the decision to migrate.' *Papers and Proceedings of the Regional Science Association,* **15**:159-72.
Wood, Charles H. (1982) 'Equilibrium and historical-structural perspectives on migration.' *International Migration Review,* **16**(2):298-319.
Zelinsky, W. (1971) 'The hypothesis of the mobility transition.' *Geographical Review,* **61**:219-49.
– (1983) 'The impasse in migration theory: a sketch map for potential escapees.' In Morrisson, P.A. (ed.) *Population Movements: Their Forms and Functions in Urbanization and Development,* Liege, Ordina Editions, 19-46.
Zolberg, A. (1981) 'International migrations in political perspective.' In Kritz, Mary, Keeley, Charles B. and Tomasi, Silvano (eds) *Global Trends in Migration: Theory and Research on International Population Movements,* New York, Center for Migration Studies, 3-27.

Index

(Page numbers in italics refer to illustrations)

accessibility: and migration, 11, 40, 71, 73, 99, 125, 126-43, 148, 154, 157, 160, 161, 162
actual migration, 10, 23, 93-7, *101, 103, 104*, 153-4, 162, 164, 167
and propensity for migration, 88-93, 94-5, 1-6
Africa: migration to, 5, 6-7, 145, 146
ALCAN Bauxite Company, 70-1
alienation: and migration, 155, 157, 162
amenities, local: and migration, 122-4
Arnos Vale, St Vincent, 75, 76, 95, 113, 123, 132, 135
Aruba, 8, 38, 59, 96
attitudes: and image, 28, 35
to migrants, 12

Bahamas: migration to, 127, 139, 145
Barbados, 13, 40-9, 63, 132, 145, 157
actual migration, *103*
amenities, 122, 123
demographic characteristics, 56-61
education, 119
employment in, 111
localities, 65, 73-4
location and size, 37-40
major routes, *69*, 99
mobility, 135, 137
occupational frustration, 113-15
perception surfaces, *151*
population, 39-40, 78-80
propensity, for migration, 94, 95-6, *103*
sample areas, *69*
social structure, 49-52
stratification of socio-economic zones, *67*
transport, 122, 123
view of, 149
Barouallie, St Vincent, 76, 96, 99, 105, 112-14 *passim*, 116-17, 123, 131-2, 135-6, 143, 146, 149, 154, 157
bauxite industry: in Jamaica, 42-3, 47, 59, 64, 70-1, 109, 111

behaviour, 8-11, 17, 127-30
and image, 34-5
Belair, St Vincent, 75, 95-6, 100, 112-13, 117, 123, 132, 135, 137-8, 154
belief: and image, 29, 30
and perception, 6
benefits of migration, 84-6, 106
Bridgetown, Barbados, 65, 73, 94, 95, 99, 100, 111, 113-14, 119, 123, 131-2, 135-8 *passim*, 143, 149, 155, 157
Britain: *see* United Kingdom

Canada: migration to, 13, 14, 60, 139, 144-6 *passim*
Central America: migration to, 18, 38
Chapman's Village, St Vincent, 77, 95, 96, 99, 105, 113-14, 116-17, 123, 131-2, 135-6, 138, 143, 154
Christchurch, Barbados, 73, 94-5, 105, 113-14, 123, 131-2, 134-5, 138, 149, 154
class, social: and migration, 2, 3-4, 12, 50, 84, 112
hierarchy, 49
spatial variation, 64
stratification, 50-1
conditional dimension: of image, 27-8
correspondence: with migrants, 131, 132
Costa Rica, 7, 96, 144, 162
Cuba, 8, 37, 59, 96, 162
culture: gains, and migration, 84
landscape, 64-5
and reality of image, 30
role of, in migration, 21, 159
and value scales, 33
Curaçao, 38, 59, 96

decision-making, 35, 98, 164, 167
demographic characterisitcs: *see under* population
Discovery Bay, Jamaica, 70, 95, 99, 109

181

Index

economic: change, and social stratification, 50-1
  factors, impact of, 108-25, 159
  performance, 40-9
education, 53-5, 79, 80, 108, 160
  and information, 129
  opportunities, 118-21
emotional dimension: of image, 28
employment: local, 110-12
  opportunities, 108, 116-17, 160
  perception of, 110-15, 116-17, 124
  see also occupations
environment: actual, 29-30, 35
  expanded, 128
  and image, 25, 35-6
  micro-, and migration, 63-83
  perceived, 10-11, 24, 25, 29
  reality of, 2, 163
  tensions in, 22
Europe: migration to, 5, 145
Ewarton, Jamaica, 70, 94-5, 99, 105, 113, 115, 117, 119-20, 123, 132, 134-5
external economic dependence, 41-5

family migration, 4
female-headed households: and migration, 4
'foreign': countries, evaluation of, 144-7
  image of, 6
functionalist approach: to migration behaviour, 16-18

gender, 4, 79
  and employment, 112
  and migration opportunities, 90, 106
  and socio-economic opportunities, 90, 106
Georgetown, St Vincent, 77, 114, 136
Grant's Pen, Jamaica, 65, 70, 94-6, 111, 113-14, 117, 119-20, 123, 132, 135

Harbour View, Jamaica, 65, 94-6, 111, 113-15, 117, 119-20, 123, 131-2, 135, 137-8
health care, 53-5
historical-structural approach, to migration behaviour, 18-19, 163-4
  and image, 130
home locality: loyalty to, 149, 155
household: members abroad, 93
  and migration, 14, 21, 64, 107

image, mental, of migration, 1, 5-6, 87, 158, 164-7
  components of, 26-9
  corporate, 32
  effect on behaviour, 34-5
  formation and change, 29-34
  individual, 32
  and information, 128
  and location, 11-12
  nature of, 25-6, 106, 125
  re-cycling of, 34
  and status, 152
  theory of, 22-4
  validity, 24
India: immigrants, 17
  migration to, 5
indices: migration, 98
individual migration, 4, 16, 25
industries, 64, 70, 109
information, 33, 35, 126-43, 144
  and accessibility, 126-7
  diffusion, 126
  flows, 7, 8
  levels, 142
  receipt and distribution, 29-30, 32
  surfaces, 139-40
integration: in society, and migration, 156-7, 162
  spatial bias in, 155-6
intention to migrate, 91-2
interaction, field of, 126, 164
internal economic disparities, 45-9
internal migration, 87, 147-8
international migration, 14, 86-7
isolation: and migration, 155, 157, 161

Jamaica, 13, 40-9, 63, 132
  actual migration, *101*
  amenities, 122, 123
  demographic characteristics, 56-61
  education opportunities, 119-20
  employment in, 111
  locality, representation of, 65-73
  location and size, 37-40
  loss of trained personnel, 17
  major routes, *68*, 99
  mobility, 135, 136-7
  occupational frustration, 113-15
  perception surfaces, *150*
  population, 39-40, 78-80
  propensity for migration, 94-5, *102*
  sample areas, *68*
  social structure, 49-52
  stratification of socio-economic zones, *66*
  transport, 122, 123
  welfare, 53-5

Index

Kingston, Jamaica, 47, 100, 105, 114, 117, 119-20, 123, 132, 134-6, 143 152, 155
Metropolitan Area (KMA), 65, 66, 70, 94-5, 99, 113, 120, 123
kinship networks, 4-5
Kingstown, St Vincent, 65, 75, 95-6, 99, 113-14, 121, 123, 132, 134-8 *passim*, 143, 155, 157
and employment, 148

labour: Caribbean as source of, 1
demands, and supply, 15-16, 17, 18
by metropolises, 12, 16
as economic commodity, 5
and employment, 58-9, 108
loss of skilled, 58, 61
land tenure, 5, 72, 109-10
legislation: and migration, 12, 33, 128, 163
life cycle: stage in, and migration, 33
location, 12, 37-40, 161, 163-4
and image, 11-12, 29-30, 35
preference, 153-4
and variations and propensity for migration, 93-8, 100

Manchester, Jamaica, 72, 94, 99, 100, 113, 120, 123, 131-2, 135, 145, 147, 153, 156
mass communications: and information, 129-30
May Pen, Jamaica, 70, 94, 95, 99, 105, 113-14, 117, 119-20, 123, 131-2, 134-5, 145
metropolitan linkages, 7
migrants: selectivity of, 60
migration: chain effect, 140
and demographic trends, 61
destinations, 5-8
and disequilibrium, 160-3
fields, 13, 38, 164
flows, 59, 61
and negative conditions, 154, 162, 167
potential, 54-5, 58
as preferred option, 89-90
propensity to, 48, 162, 164
and perception of, 84-107
short-term, 14
structural framework, 8
variability, 159
see also return migration; seasonal migration
mobility, 128, 136-7
modernization: evaluation of, 121-4, 154, 160-1

Montego Bay, Jamaica, 47, 70, 94-5, 97, 99, 100, 105, 113-15 *passim*, 117, 119-20, 123, 132, 135-6, 143, 147, 149, 152, 155

national factors, in migration, 14
need: to migrate, 1, 18

obligations: in kinship networks, 4
occupational frustration, 112-15, 125
occupations, 79, 80
actual, 112-15, 125
aspired, 112-15
Ocho Rios, Jamaica, 47, 109
out-migration: from Jamaica, 47
overseas visits, 137-8, 161

Panama, 7, 38, 59, 96, 145, 162
passport, valid: possession, and migration, 90, 91
per capita income, 40-1
perceptions, of migration, 84-8
destinations, 6
and image, 15-36
of place, and migration behaviour, 153-4
of world, 158
personal: information fields, 127
networks, and information, 130-3, 140-1
spatial mobility, 133, 141-2
plantation: farming, 71, 105
and propensity for migration, 97
social structure, 49
political systems theory, of migration, 19-20
population, 39-40, 55, 56-61
age distribution, 78
dependency ratios, 57
and education, 79
inter-censal growth rates, 56
and occupation, 79
sex distribution, 78
trends, 56-7
Port Morant, Jamaica, 71-2, 94, 100, 113, 120, 123, 131-2, 135, 137, 154
potential migration, 10, 23, 106
poverty, indices of, 46
preferences: *see* residential
propensity, for migration, 1, 48
and actual migration, 88-93, 106
in Barbados, *103*
in Jamaica, *102*
and perception of, 84-107
in St Vincent, *104*
push-pull migration, 16, 160, 162

qualitative dimension: of image, 29

relational dimension: of image, 27, 144-58 *passim*
repatriates, 96
residential preference, 144-7, 149-53
return migration, 61, 167
risk: evaluation of, 106
  perception of, in migration, 87-8
routes, major, *68, 69*
  and pattern of migration behaviour, 98-100, 105, 134
rural areas: isolation, 155, 157
  and residential preference, 147-8
  and social stratification, 52

St Catherine, Jamaica, 105, 113, 123, 134, 153, 156
St James, Barbados, 73, 94, 100, 113-14, 116-17, 123, 132, 135, 143, 149
St John, Barbados, 74, 94, 100, 113-14, 116, 123, 131-2, 135-6, 143, 147, 149, 154
St Lucy, Barbados, 74, 94-6 *passim*, 100, 110, 112-14 *passim*, 116, 123, 131-2, 135-6, 138, 143, 149, 154, 157
St Mary, Jamaica, 72, 94, 99, 100, 111-13 *passim*, 115-17 *passim*, 120, 123, 131-2, 135, 145, 147, 149, 156
St Vincent, 13, 40-9, 63, 127, 132, 149
  actual migration, *104*
  amenities, 122, 123
  demographic characteristics, 56-61
  educational opportunities, 119
  localities, representation of, 65, 75-7
  location and size, 37-40
  major routes, *69*, 99
  mobility, 135, 137
  occupational frustration, 113-15
  perception surfaces, *151*
  population, 39-40, 78-80
  and propensity for migration, 94, 96, *104*
  sample areas, *69*
  seasonal migration, 59
  social structure, 49-52
  stratification of socio-economic zones, *67*
  transport, 122, 123
  welfare, 53-5
selectivity: of migrants, 9, 162

settlement patterns, 51, 64
Sion Hill, St Vincent, 95-7 *passim*, 100, 113, 123, 131-2, 134-5, 137, 154
size: of islands, 37-40
small-farming, Jamaica, 71-3 *passim*
social field, 21
social structure, 49-52
  stratification, 50-1
  spatial distribution, 51-2
societal systems approach: to migration, 20-2
society: and migration, 9, 35-6
socio-economic environment, 37
spatial: aspect, of image, 26-7
  disequilibrium, economic, 46-9
  fields, 20
subsistence farming, 105
sugar industry, 43, 63, 71, 74

temporal image, 26-7
tension, and migration, 21-3, 50-1
time: changes over, and migration, 146
tourist industry, 43-5, 48, 64, 73-4, 109
towns: and integration, 155-6
transport: and migration, 122-4
travel: frequency of, 133-6
Trinidad, 38, 96, 145

underdevelopment, 41, 61
unemployment rates, 58, 70, 80
United Kingdom: image of, 6, 85, 139
  migration to, 13, 16, 59, 60-1, 145, 162
United States: migration to, 13, 14, 59, 60, 139, 144-6 *passim*, 149
urban centres: accessibility to, 131, 142, 161
urbanization, 43, 46, 51, 64

value: of international migration, 86-7
value scales (system), 28, 32-4, 159-60, 164, 165, 167

welfare: and migration, 53-5
Westmoreland, Jamaica, 71-2, 94, 97, 99, 100, 105, 111-13, 115-17 *passim*, 120, 123, 127, 131-2, 135-6, 143, 145, 147, 149, 152, 156
work environment: perceptions of, 109-10

yards: household, 64, 70